What parents say about the Calmer, Easier, Happier Parenting approach:

"You have made me see things differently, understand emotions differently and respond differently – thank you."

"I learned how to help my children be more cooperative and more confident. A year later we are all still calmer and happier. My only regret is that I didn't go on the course earlier when my children were younger. It would have saved us all the struggle and stress we went through."

"There's less arguing now. And tantrums are a thing of the past – ours as well as the children's!"

"Thank you! I never really believed that my children would just follow the routines without arguing or complaining. But it's working!"

"Within weeks of putting into practice the new skills Noël taught us, our adopted daughter became a different child, sunny, cooperative, and much more flexible. And we became different parents, calmer and saner. It hasn't always been easy to stay positive, firm and consistent, but Calmer, Easier, Happier Parenting has supported us every step of the way."

"It's a transformed house. My son will always be a challenge, but we now have the skills and strength to cope with that."

"These parenting skills have totally changed our way of approaching things. My family

"Thank you! I never really believed that my children would just follow the routines without arguing or complaining. But it's working!"

"My teenage daughter really knew how to push my buttons. There was shouting every day, and not just from her! Now I've learned to stay calm and not to react in the old ways. I have a new toolbox of positive skills – and a new daughter!"

"These techniques really do work. The best reward of all is seeing my son's happiness and self-confidence return."

"I assumed that it would take weeks, but the 'Never Ask Twice Method' started working in one day!"

"I couldn't leave my children alone together. It always ended in tears. I'm so glad I learned new ways of handling them. They still bicker sometimes but much, much less than before."

"My son was very anxious after his father and I split up. He was all right during the day, but bedtimes were dreadful. I was amazed that the Calmer, Easier, Happier Parenting strategies I learned helped him, not only to feel better about the separation, but he was able to relax and sleep better as well."

"We used to do so much nagging and shouting. Now we have a bag of really useful tools which have helped us enormously with lots of everyday situations."

ABOUT THE AUTHOR

Noël Janis-Norton graduated from teacher-training college at New York University. Her career as a learning and behaviour specialist spans more than forty years. She has been a classroom teacher, a special needs teacher and advisor, a tutor specialising in learning strategies, a head teacher and a parenting educator.

Noël is the founder and director of the Calmer, Easier, Happier Parenting Centre in London, which works with families and leads courses for parents of toddlers through teens.

A regular speaker at professional conferences, Noël has also been featured on numerous television and radio programmes. In addition to lecturing widely in the UK and the US, she also trains teachers and parenting practitioners in her unique and highly effective methods. She is the spokesperson for National Family Week and the parenting expert for Macaroni Kid (a popular website for parents in the US).

Through her seminars, courses and talks for parents, and through her books, CDs and DVDs, she has helped transform the lives of tens of thousands of families.

Noël has two grown children, a foster daughter and six grandchildren.

CALMER
EASIER
HAPPIER
PARENTING

NOËL JANIS-NORTON

yellow
kite

First published in Great Britain in 2012 by Hodder & Stoughton

First published in paperback in 2016 by Yellow Kite Books

2

A CIP catalogue record for this title is available from the British Library

Paperback ISBN 978 1 444 72992 4
eBook ISBN 978 1 444 72991 7

Printed and bound by Clays Ltd, St Ives plc

Hodder & Stoughton policy is to use papers that are
natural, renewable and recyclable products and made
from wood grown in sustainable forests. The logging and
manufacturing processes are expected to conform to the
environmental regulations of the country of origin.

Yellow Kite Books
Hodder & Stoughton Ltd
Carmelite House
50 Victoria Embankment
London EC4Y 0DZ

www.yellowkitebooks.co.uk

This book is dedicated to all parents who are searching for a calmer, easier, happier life for their children and for themselves.

CONTENTS

Section Two – Transforming family flashpoints: Using the core strategies to improve behaviour all day long   279

ACKNOWLEDGEMENTS

My deepest gratitude goes to:

Laura Runnels Fleming, my dear friend and trusted coach, who helped structure and organise my ideas in order to make this book as accessible as possible.

Jill Janis, my sister, friend and colleague, for her wisdom and clear thinking, her valuable advice, her thoroughness and tireless attention to detail, her love of language, her artist's soul, her compassion and her sense of humour when I need it the most! Jill's profound understanding of family relationships has helped me, over the past forty years, to hone the principles of this programme. Without her, this book would not exist.

Clare Hulton, my agent, for believing in me and in this book.

Nicky Ross, my patient and persistent editor at Hodder & Stoughton; it is due to her foresight that this book is now a reality.

Gillian Edwards, to whom I owe a great debt for the extraordinary generosity, understanding and kindness she has showered on me over the last twenty years, and especially for holding my hand on the emotional journey of the past year, helping guide this book to fruition. As well as being my p.a., Gillian has been my all-hours typist, my problem-solver, my exactly-the-right-word-finder, cook, nursemaid and voice of reason – above and beyond the call of duty.

Naia Edwards for her commitment to helping me write this book and for her calm positivity throughout.

Isabel Irish, Michael Rose and Diana Callaway for the endless hours of typing and retyping.

My colleagues, past and present, at the Calmer, Easier, Happier Parenting Centre (in the UK and the US), for their insight, sensitivity and determination, and for sharing my vision of what family life can be:

Heleni Achilleos, Rosalie Ajzensztejn, Nancy Albanese, Suzanne Burdon, Miriam Chachamu, Amanda Deverich, Suzanne Ferera, Sherry Fink, Lou Fleming, Michael Foulkes, Isabel Irish, Bebe Jacobs, Annie Saunders, Luke Scott, Robin Shaw, Grazyna Somerville, Dorian Yeo, Sylvia Young, and the many others who have also contributed to this work, too numerous to mention.

My children, Jessica, Jordan and Chloe, for the constancy of their support and encouragement.

The many parents who shared their stories and experiences for this book, including Dan Goldthwait, Judith Whitaker, Kirsten Simonsgaard, Dr. Andrea Davis, Ph.D., Lynn Serwin, Megan Foker, Marnie Aulabaugh, Sue Feldmeth, Laura and Lou Fleming, Saeed Jaffer, Beth and Dan Bootzin, Romney O'Malley, Jamie Rosenblatt, Robyn Wisinski, Felicia Young, Kelly Laghaei, Peter Perez, Kim Okubo and Linda Sue Runnels.

And finally, special thanks to the tens of thousands of parents and professionals with whom I have had the privilege to work in the Calmer, Easier, Happier Parenting and Teaching programme. They have tried this new approach and reported back, 'It works!' Their courage and honesty continue to touch me and inspire me. I am deeply grateful for their passionate support of this programme.

INTRODUCTION

Many years ago I was a new and inexperienced teacher, fresh out of teachers' college at New York University. In my first post I noticed that in some classrooms the children were shouting out, finding excuses to get out of their seats, throwing paper aeroplanes across the room as soon as the teacher's back was turned and ignoring the teacher's repeated pleas for silence. But in other classrooms the pupils were sitting where they had been told; they were concentrating and learning – and smiling. Clearly they were enjoying school, and they were proud of what they were achieving.

I was in awe of the excellent teachers who were able to motivate and inspire. I could see that it was not a coincidence that these were also the teachers who were able to give an instruction and know that it would be carried out. Within my first few days in the classroom I became painfully aware that my four years of teacher-training had taught me almost nothing about how to manage a classroom. I had learned a lot about how to teach, but the unspoken assumption of my professors had been that all I had to do was turn up, and I would be greeted by a classroom full of quiet, motivated children gazing up at me raptly with sunshiny faces, eager to soak up everything I could teach them.

I had assumed, without having given it much thought, that I would enjoy teaching and that I would be good at it. But I saw immediately that I just wasn't equipped for reality. The pupils in this school did not automatically respect teachers. These children did not believe that it was their job to pay attention or do their best. So during my lunch hours in the staff room I listened carefully to the conversations of the seasoned veterans, hoping to learn the secrets of their success. I approached the teachers I admired and asked them how they managed to achieve such calm, focused classrooms.

One kindly teacher tried to reassure me, 'Don't worry, dear. In a few years you'll get the hang of it.' This did not reassure me because I was worried that unless I figured out how to bring order to my classroom, I wouldn't last a few years. One teacher, whom I frequently heard shouting at her unruly class, interrupted to give me this piece of advice, 'These children! They're animals! Don't expect too much from them, and you won't be disappointed.' I knew that couldn't be right because there were a handful of teachers at the school who had earned the respect of their pupils. These teachers expected a great deal from their pupils, and they were not disappointed.

One teacher tried to explain, 'You just have to show them you mean business.' This sounded promising, but it didn't tell me how. Another teacher told me, 'You have to show them you believe they can do good work.' This also sounded good, but once again, I didn't know how. And another teacher told me, 'You just have to let them know who's boss.' When I asked the all-important how, I was told, 'You just have to put your foot down.' I felt like asking, 'Which foot?'

I realised that these excellent teachers had been good at their job for so many years that they no longer had to think about how they got the results they got. They just didn't know how to put into words what they were doing that worked. So, sadly, they were not able to give me any useful advice.

That's when I began carefully observing those teachers and

taking detailed notes on what they did and how they did it, what they said and how they said it. From distilling and studying my notes I realised that it was not any intrinsic quality of a teacher that got the children to behave and want to learn, but certain techniques the teachers used. I figured I had nothing to lose so I started using these same techniques with my class, even though I was not confident that I could pull it off. I hoped that with time and practice I would eventually start getting some good results.

To my intense delight, the techniques started working within days. When I started doing what those effective teachers did, the kids quickly responded to me as if I were one of those senior teachers I admired so much. Within weeks, not years as that teacher in the staffroom had predicted, I started to feel confident that I could achieve what I set out to do.

I was amazed when other teachers started noticing. One teacher said, 'Has Frank B. been absent recently? I haven't had to tell him off in assembly for a while,' and another teacher replied, 'No, he hasn't been absent. He's just much quieter now. Noël's working her magic on him.' Soon I found that teachers were asking me, a rank beginner, for advice on how to handle the difficult kids!

Then the parents started asking me for advice. They could see that I was able to get their little tearaways to sit and listen and do their work in school, so surely I would know how to get them to do their homework or go to bed without a tantrum or do what they were told. I was flattered to be asked, but as I had no children at the time I felt I had no useful advice to give these parents. All I could think of to say was, 'This is what I'm doing in the classroom, and it's working. Why not try it at home?' Within days, parents came back to me saying, 'It works!'

That's when I realised that a lot of parenting is really teaching, and that anyone can learn the techniques to become a more skilled teacher, and consequently a more skilled parent. I learned that the behaviours and habits that annoy or trouble us in our children can be improved, and in many cases completely erased, once we start thinking about each problem as a teaching opportunity.

As I continued working with children, and then with parents and teachers, I learned more and more about how to help children become more cooperative, confident, motivated, self-reliant and considerate. My fascination with this subject led me to further study. And as a mother, step-parent and foster-parent (and now as a grandmother) I learned even more. Over the years I learned about the effects of temperament on behaviour, and how children with extreme temperaments can be helped to develop more balanced responses. I learned that many children with behaviour problems are suffering from subtle and often unrecognised learning difficulties, and that addressing the learning problems always improves behaviour and attitude. I learned that chronic stress undermines a parent's best efforts, and what can be done to reduce stress. Gradually I put together into one comprehensive package all the techniques, skills, strategies and principles that I could see worked. I call this method Calmer, Easier, Happier Parenting and Teaching.

Over time I went from advising parents at the school gates to giving seminars, courses and lectures. My next step was opening a centre for families. Then I put what I had learned into books and CDs and DVDs so that parents who did not live near London could benefit from these techniques. As the word spread, I started to fill the need by training Calmer, Easier, Happier Parenting practitioners who coach parents worldwide, in person or by telephone.

Parents always tell us that their biggest frustration is having to repeat instructions numerous times before their children listen and cooperate. As you read this book, you will see that the Calmer, Easier, Happier Parenting approach gives you a step-by-step method to solve this problem (and many other typical family problems). Using positive and respectful techniques, parents can guide children into the habit of cooperating the first time and without a fuss most of the time.

In this book you will find strategies that will transform many typical family issues – everything from homework and music practice and sibling rivalry to tidying up and bedtimes and mealtimes. These strategies teach children to see themselves as capable, considerate and worthy of appreciation. This method helps parents to feel more relaxed and more confident in their role as parents. And it makes family life significantly calmer, easier and happier.

In the forty years that I have been consulting with parents, I have never seen these techniques fail. It gives me great pleasure to share them with you now.

CORE STRATEGIES FOR CREATING A CALMER, EASIER, HAPPIER FAMILY LIFE

CHAPTER 1

WHAT MAKES MODERN PARENTING SO STRESSFUL, AND WHAT WE CAN DO ABOUT IT

Changing frustration to freedom

I used to regularly shout at my children around bedtime. And, like clockwork, as soon as they were finally asleep, I would slump onto the sofa, almost in tears, so frustrated and feeling bad about myself. It happened so many evenings. I would vow to be more patient and calm. What I didn't realise back then was that I didn't have a clue how to get them to do what I asked. So I was making a vow that I just couldn't keep.

Now I have the tools so my children do cooperate most of the time. Life is calmer, I'm not spending time bargaining, negotiating and shouting, and I actually have time to get some of the things done that I need to do!

Mother of three, aged 9, 7 and 4

When I'm talking to a room full of parents, laughter always erupts when I say to them, 'It would be a whole lot easier to be a parent if we didn't have kids. They slow you down. They get in the way. They make a fuss while you're trying to get something done.'

As parents, we can all identify with this. Our 'to-do list' is pages long. Yet when we cradled our newborn in our arms and looked lovingly into his eyes, we didn't think, 'I can't wait to hand you over to someone else so I can get on with all my tasks.' Of course we wanted to nurture and spend time with our child. We envisioned a life of calm and happy parenting.

But the reality is that many of us are juggling work, children's schedules, volunteer commitments, managing household chores, etc. We have an agenda, and we're constantly looking ahead to see what needs to get done. When our kids aren't listening or doing what we ask, it is incredibly frustrating. We find ourselves losing patience and feeling stressed because of all the hassle – the repeating, reminding, negotiating and shouting we have to do to get our kids to do all the things that need to be done each day!

Does this sound familiar? It may be that you've picked up this book because you are at your wits' end from dealing with whingeing, defiance, tantrums and disrespect or with mealtime, bedtime or homework battles. It may be that one of your children has a relatively more extreme temperament – more sensitive, more intense and more inflexible – and you are at a loss as to how to parent this child. It may be that the problems you are dealing with are quite mild, and you just want to learn positive and effective strategies to help you be the best parent you can be. Maybe your child has a diagnosed special need and you want to know how to bring out the best in him.

This book is for all of you. In this book I will give you specific strategies and skills to significantly improve cooperation and all the other habits that you want your child to develop. I will share with you ways to make the job of parenting calmer, easier and happier.

The unique challenges that modern parents face

Why is parenting more stressful today and what makes our to-do lists so long? Certainly being a parent in modern times presents new and different challenges from those our parents faced. Parents experience more stress today for a variety of reasons.

Most of us don't have extended family living nearby to support us. There is pressure on parents to fulfil an impossible number of roles, especially in families with two working parents – an ever-increasing percentage. With parents working longer and longer hours, tasks such as food shopping, cleaning and cooking are increasingly experienced as hurried and stressful.

Modern telecommunications have made it almost impossible for parents to completely switch off. Mobile phones and the internet have crept into every corner of our lives – our homes, our cars, our handbags, pockets and attached to our ears. On the one hand, technology makes our lives easier, and on the other hand, the communication and the pressure to respond are coming at us 24/7!

Another role that affects our stress level is that of 'family taxi driver'. The number of enriching activities kids have available to them today is staggering, and it starts in infancy! This is an enormous shift from our parents' generation. Everything begins earlier for kids today: football, ballet, music lessons and even yoga can all start by age three or younger! This presents opportunity, but also stress. We want to expose our children to lots of wonderful experiences, so we are enticed by all these enriching programmes. Then, as much as our child may enjoy the activity, we end up in the role of chauffeur. All this carting them back and forth in traffic to classes and matches plays havoc with our patience and raises our stress level. We find ourselves over-scheduled right alongside our children.

The perceived threat of 'stranger danger' has also drastically changed how children play and consequently our job description. In addition to our other roles, we've also become 'entertainment directors'. It used to be that when kids came home from school, they had a snack, and then they were out of the door. Parents had time to get things done while the children were out with the neighbourhood kids, exploring, playing hide-and-seek, climbing trees, etc. Kids didn't come home until supper. Homework either didn't exist or was so minimal that it wasn't even on parents' radar screens. Our parents didn't worry about sexual predators so kids had the freedom to explore. Now kids are playing at home more, pleading for more screen time, exercising less, wanting us to play with them or to drive them to play dates.

Given the challenges facing modern parents, it is no wonder that we feel so stressed and are driven to nagging, threatening, criticising and shouting to try to make sure everything gets done that needs to get done every day. It's unlikely that any of these stressors will be going away, so it's up to us to find ways to reduce family stress and to guide our children to become more cooperative so that parenting can be calmer, easier and happier.

Parenting: The job with no training

Parenting is the most important job there is. But it's a job for which no training is generally given beyond childbirth classes. How can it be that a job as diverse and demanding as raising children can come without training? This isn't a management job we can just quit when it's hard and our employees are annoying us! Parenting is a job we have to get up and go to every day without pay. Of course it's also a job that can be incredibly rewarding. And we find the job of parenting the most rewarding when we feel confident that the way we are parenting is positively impacting our children.

When we became parents, we were suddenly thrown into the role of educators. Most of us didn't go to school to become teachers, yet this is the job we perform every day with our children. In fact, teaching is our main job. I'm not talking about teaching academic subjects. I'm talking about teaching our children the habits, skills and values that we believe are important and right. But how do we effectively teach and train our children in the habits that are important to us?

How we learn to parent

So, since there's no job training for being a parent, how <u>do</u> we learn how to parent? Most of us probably parent the way we were parented. Louise, a mother who attended my seminars, shared how her mother dealt with sibling fighting. Louise said her mother's infamous threat was always, 'If you kids don't stop fighting, I'm going to knock your three heads together!' Louise and her siblings were always puzzled about the specifics of how their mother would actually accomplish such a task, which, thankfully, she never attempted. But what drove her mother to make this empty threat? Extreme annoyance with the sibling squabbles, probably. No doubt, Louise's mother had learned this threatening tactic from her own mother and, in the absence of any other parenting tools she knew of, she said it to her own children, regardless of whether it worked. If Louise had not learned the skills of Calmer, Easier, Happier Parenting, she would probably be using similarly ineffective threatening techniques with her own children today!

The training most parents seek

When you decided to have a baby, you probably prepared yourself for the pregnancy and birth in many ways. Maybe you took classes to prepare for childbirth and the challenges of newborn parenting. You probably read all about the baby's developmental stages. And if you had trouble getting your baby to sleep, you might have consulted books about how to get your child to sleep through the night. And that's where the training ends for most of us. So that takes you up to your child's first birthday. The training is over. You're on your own now for the next seventeen years, thanks very much!

The training parents really need

So eighteen months pass, and now you have a darling toddler – <u>most</u> of the time. You also happen to have a toddler who throws tantrums, tosses his food on the floor and fights you over getting into his car seat. *Help!* Your toddler becomes two-and-a-half and suddenly everything is 'No!' He won't stay on his chair to eat. You can't change his nappy without straddling him. He's started hitting the new baby. *Help!* Between the ages of three and five your strong-willed daughter becomes increasingly defiant, whingeing and resisting so much that you're ready to lose your mind. She dawdles endlessly about getting dressed so your mornings always feel rushed. Bedtime has become a nightly battle. *Help!* Between the ages of five and ten your son begins to tune you out, and you find yourself endlessly repeating and reminding. Your stress level grows. *Help!* And then come the teenage years. *Help!*

Lack of cooperation is very stressful!

Parents generally show up at my seminars desperate for more effective ways to reduce misbehaviour and to improve listening and cooperation. Parents realise that what they are doing isn't working, but they are not sure how to get their kids to do what they are told. The father in the following story had an especially challenging three-year-old, Katie.

Headstrong and defiant

Our first child, Thomas, had a sensitive temperament, but he was basically cooperative. Then we had Katie, and everything changed. By age two, she was headstrong and defiant, and my wife and I were pulling our hair out trying to figure out how to get her to do the things we needed her to do each day. She would resist by crying, throwing tantrums and biting.

At age three she became more physical. The final straw was when she was at the supermarket with my wife. Katie got frustrated because my wife made her put something back on a shelf that she wanted. Katie expressed her frustration by actually biting my wife on the bottom in the supermarket.

A few days later we had a friend visiting and she commented on a picture of Katie that she saw on the wall, mentioning how cute she was. I told her that there are only two times when Katie is cute. She's cute in pictures and she's cute when she's sleeping!

Father of two, aged 6 and 3

This is how a lack of cooperation can make us feel about these little human beings that we couldn't wait to bring into the world. Does it mean we love them less? No. But <u>liking</u> our children and wanting to be with them are equally important, and it's no fun spending time with an uncooperative child. The good news is that there are many simple and effective tools you can quickly learn that will help you develop cooperative children – at all ages. When you practise using these techniques, you can move from repeating and reminding and shouting to never having to ask twice, and you can achieve this miraculous transformation in a remarkably short period of time.

A tale of two boys

Let's look at two very different snapshots of what mornings were like for a five-year-old boy named Jimmy. The first scenario illustrates what can happen when a child isn't yet in the habit of doing what he's asked to do in the mornings. The second scenario shows what mornings can be like for this same boy after his parents have been putting the Calmer, Easier, Happier Parenting skills into practice. Of course, Jimmy's mother loves him very much in both the before and after versions and, of course, she's doing the best she can to try to get him into good habits. In the first scenario, she simply didn't realise that the way she was reacting was contributing to Jimmy's dawdling and to his uncooperative behaviour. Once this mother learned more effective strategies and started doing things differently, she saw that she could communicate in a way that makes Jimmy feel good and helps him want to do the right thing.

Uncooperative Jimmy's bad morning

'Jimmy! You're still in bed? It's time to get up – we're going to be late for school!'

Ten minutes later his mother goes back into his room. He has his socks on and nothing else. 'You've been up for ten minutes and you only have your socks on? What have you been doing all this time? You've got to hurry now, and don't forget to make your bed.'

Five minutes later his mother returns, and by now Jimmy's got his underwear on, but he's playing with some toy cars. Her frustration grows. 'You're playing with your cars? You know this is getting dressed time, not playing time.' 'But Mum, I never get to play!' Jimmy's mother starts helping to dress him because it's faster and she's worried about being late. She gives up on the idea of his bed getting made today.

Jimmy comes into the kitchen and sits down to eat his breakfast. He gets up from the table several times during breakfast to play with the dog, to find a toy and to tease his sister. 'Jimmy, sit down and eat. If you get up from the table one more time, breakfast is over.' Jimmy gets up again. 'Jimmy, I mean it.' Jimmy gets up again. 'OK, that's the last warning. If you get up again, I'll take away your TV time after school.'

Jimmy finishes his breakfast and leaves the table. 'Jimmy, you forgot to clear your dishes again! We talked about this yesterday.' Jimmy whinges and complains. 'Why do I have to? Polly doesn't have to.' 'Polly's too little. Act like a big boy and set an example for your sister. Don't argue with me.' He reluctantly comes back and clears his dishes, kicking his sister's chair along the way.

'Come on, we've got to hurry and clean your teeth.' Jimmy slowly walks to the bathroom and cleans his teeth for about ten seconds. 'OK, run and get your shoes on so we won't be late for school!' Jimmy slowly walks to where his shoes are. His mother ties his shoes for him, even though he knows how, and helps him into his jacket, even though he can do it himself, because they are running late.

They leave the house in a rush. Jimmy is silent in the car and his mother is feeling annoyed and stressed, as she does most mornings. When they get to school, she drops him off and says, 'Have a great day!'

Parents tell me that once their children are at school, the most stressful part of their day is over. They are exhausted by nine a.m.! For the first two hours of their day, they've been trying to get a seemingly immovable object to complete all the necessary morning tasks. But the children are ignoring instructions, dawdling and misbehaving. And when we try to get them to hurry up, they seem to go even slower.

We may become impatient and resort to nagging, repeating, threatening and shouting. Lack of cooperation brings out the worst in us. And even if we can see that our annoyed reactions aren't helping to achieve cooperation, often we don't know what else to do. In order for us to break this endless cycle of repeating and reminding, we have to do something different to get a different result. We have to communicate differently with our children so they are motivated to do what we ask.

Let's fast forward. Jimmy's parents have been using the Calmer, Easier, Happier Parenting strategies so now he does what he needs to do in the morning, most of it without even having to be reminded.

Cooperative Jimmy's good morning

Jimmy is awakened by an alarm that he himself set the night before. He gets out of bed, turns off the alarm, puts on the clothes that he laid out the night before and makes his bed. When his mother comes into his room, she gives Jimmy a hug and a big smile. Jimmy smiles and hugs her back. She notices what he's already accomplished and mentions it: 'Jimmy, you're remembering to do so many things in the mornings. You're getting up to your own alarm, you're getting dressed without anybody helping you, and today you made your bed without my reminding you! You're becoming very self-reliant.'

Jimmy comes downstairs and does his morning chores. At breakfast, Jimmy eats without getting up from the table, sings a silly song with his little sister, clears his bowl without being asked and puts it in the dishwasher. His mother notices this and comments that he's helping to keep the kitchen tidy. She also mentions that because he did all his chores without being reminded, he's on track to earn his computer time that evening after his homework is done.

His mother asks him to come to the bathroom for teeth cleaning, and he willingly cleans his teeth. He brushes his hair too quickly, missing a part at the back. 'There's one bit of your hair that looks like it still needs brushing.' He looks in the mirror, finds the part that's sticking up and brushes it. His mother says, 'You got that part to lie flat'.

He then goes and puts his shoes on and ties them himself. He's ready for school a bit early so he has some time to play with his cars. Mother and son are ready to leave the flat when she notices that he doesn't have his backpack. She doesn't get annoyed; she just gives him a little clue. 'Jimmy, there's still something to remember that you'll need for school.' Jimmy looks around and sees his backpack and runs back for it.

They leave early enough to get to school on time. They chat during the drive, and they arrive a bit early so he can play with his friends in the playground. They say goodbye and hug briefly. His mother gives him a big smile and says she's looking forward to seeing him after school.

Perhaps this second scenario sounds far too good to be true, but it is entirely achievable when parents are equipped with the right tools. Imagine how much calmer we could be in the mornings if we had this level of cooperation and self-reliance from our children! We could easily accomplish our morning tasks, we wouldn't feel annoyed or frustrated, and we would actually have time to enjoy our children. Thousands of families who practise the strategies have experienced this transformation.

How our behaviour affects our kids

Let's think about the cooperative Jimmy. He's getting positive attention from his parents for being self-reliant and coopera-tive. He's getting smiles and hugs instead of annoyance. He's hearing all about what he is doing right, instead of criticism about what he's not doing. He's developing confidence because he's doing so many things for himself. He's proud of himself. He is rewarded for his behaviour with extra playtime and relaxed, unstressed parents. He starts his school day feel-ing confident.

On the other hand, the uncooperative Jimmy is only hearing about what he's doing wrong from the moment he wakes up until he gets to school. Instead of smiles, he gets annoyed looks. He sees himself as someone who does things wrong and forgets everything because that's what he hears most days. Of course he starts to tune his parents out because it seems like all they ever do is nag and threaten. He stops looking his parents in the eye because it's no fun being told off. Because Jimmy is not being required to do what he is capable of doing, he is not getting the opportunity to grow in confidence. He resents his little sister because she gets to be the baby – where's the fun in being older? He feels like there's nothing he can do to please his parents. He starts his school day feeling deflated.

I've painted two scenarios that may seem extreme because I want to make a point. But for many families, the first scenario is not all that extreme! Many of us recognise our kids and ourselves as we read about the first Jimmy. Maybe we've nagged and shouted and done too much for our children. Maybe we've gone further and even smacked our kids out of frustration with the lack of cooperation. The two scenarios illustrate how our communication affects our children. We want cooperative, confident and self-reliant children, and when we're not getting that, we feel frustrated and angry.

I've included these before and after scenarios to help parents understand that what we say and do either helps our children achieve the habits we want or unintentionally robs our children of the opportunity to develop those habits. The well-behaved Jimmy wasn't born that cooperative and self-reliant. He developed those habits because his parents had learned how to motivate him to want to be cooperative and self-reliant. They had learned simple proactive strategies to help prevent most behaviour problems.

If you have a child who is older, perhaps eleven to thirteen, the type of uncooperative morning behaviour you are faced with may be different. Your teen or preteen might moan or talk disrespectfully, 'I'm too tired to get up – you're always having a go at me.' It's easy to get sucked into an argument about why she's tired and what she needs to do: 'Well, if you didn't stay up so late texting your friends, you wouldn't be so tired and grumpy. If you don't get up now, you'll make us all late. Don't be selfish.'

As understandable as that kind of reaction may be, arguing isn't how we want our child's day (or our day) to begin, and it won't motivate her to get into better habits. The proactive strategies I'll be sharing with you will. I know many thirteen-year-olds who get up to an alarm, make their bed, greet their parents with warmth and respect, practise their instrument before school and even do a few morning chores with no prompting from their parents. It is achievable.

Every family can make the transformation from a typically stressed household to a Calmer, Easier, Happier household. It's never too late, even if your children are already teenagers.

Who this book is for, and how to use it

Whether you are a parent, grandparent, teacher or a professional working with children and families, I've written this book for you. The strategies I'll be sharing will bring out the very best in children – and in you! Whether you want to know how to deal effectively with major misbehaviour or minor misbehaviour or anything in between, you'll find specific strategies in this book. These strategies are effective with all children, including children with more extreme temperaments or with diagnosed special needs.

My primary goal is for this to be a 'how to' book that you will refer to for a lifetime of parenting. The strategies I'll be sharing are so essential for improving cooperation and reducing family conflict and stress that once you start practising them, you'll never want to go back to the old ways! These are strategies you will use every single day with your children, all day long. All of the skills are positive, all are practical and the bottom line is – they work. I've never seen these strategies fail in the forty years I've been coaching families. I'll measure the success of this book by how dog-eared, bent, stained, highlighted and marked up it becomes. A book that's well used is the greatest compliment I could receive.

Although this book is primarily written for parents with children aged three to thirteen, all the strategies will work for teenagers as well. Your delivery may need to be altered slightly for your 'cool teen', and some of the issues will be different, of course. But the core strategies I'll be sharing in this book are essential to help bring out the best in teens too.

I have two strong recommendations. The first is that you read this with your partner, if you have one, and that you discuss the strategies together. The strategies will be much more effective if you are being consistent and both following them. My second recommendation is that you start at the beginning and read this book from beginning to end. Now I know that I have no control over how you read it, but I can beg! There's a very specific reason the book is organised the way it is. You'll have much more success, and see bigger improvements in your children's behaviour, if you read the chapters and practise the strategies in the order I've given them.

Of course it's natural to want to jump right to the chapters that talk about how to stop misbehaviour. Here's the problem. If you start with consequences and how to stop misbehaviour, it won't result in <u>less</u> misbehaviour. It may help you stop whatever is going wrong more quickly than you are able to now, but it will not do anything to prevent it from happening again. You'll be caught in a crisis-management cycle.

If your goal is to have less misbehaviour, start at the beginning. Chapter 2 will explain what Calmer, Easier, Happier Parenting is and why it is so effective. Then read the rest of Section One in order. Each chapter explains one core strategy in depth, giving many examples. You will also read real stories from real parents about how they overcame behavioural challenges by using that specific strategy.

At the end of each chapter, you have an Action Plan to help you put the new strategy into practice successfully. And, at that point, I recommend that you set the book down and practise that strategy for two weeks (but keep the book close by for reference!).

As you learn the next strategy, you'll be able to combine it with the previous one. Each chapter will expand upon the last, and the examples and case studies will not make sense without an understanding of the strategies that came before. These strategies all work together to create Calmer, Easier, Happier Parenting.

When you learn how to motivate your child to want to listen to you and cooperate, and when you learn a few simple strategies that prevent most misbehaviour from happening in the first place, you'll understand better the chapters which deal with misbehaviour.

The second section of the book will give you a road map for using all the Calmer, Easier, Happier Parenting strategies and skills to effectively tackle what we call the typical family flashpoints. These are the times of day and the issues that tend to be the most problematic. I encourage you to wait to read Section Two until after you've been practising the core strategies of Calmer, Easier, Happier Parenting. That way you will have the tools you'll need to improve the flashpoints that you find challenging.

Many parents return to our classes and our support materials again and again, so expect to keep referring to this book as you're learning these strategies! This book will become your new support network.

Thank you for seeking out this resource. I am passionate about helping parents put these skills and strategies into practice successfully. You can achieve Calmer, Easier, Happier Parenting, and with this book you've got the tools to do it.

CHAPTER 2

THE CALMER, EASIER, HAPPIER PARENTING PROMISE: YOU CAN TRANSFORM EVEN THE MOST FRUSTRATING ASPECTS OF PARENTING

I can make this promise to you: You will begin to see improvements in your child's behaviour within a few days (and for some families within even the first few hours) when you start using the Calmer, Easier, Happier Parenting strategies. Based on my experience of helping many thousands of families, I feel completely confident in making this promise to you. As you continue to practise these strategies – and I will be giving you a detailed plan for putting them into practice successfully – within two to four weeks you will see positive changes at home.

When parents are willing to learn and practise the highly effective strategies I'll be sharing with you, profound changes take place. Within weeks, family life becomes calmer, children are more cooperative, parents feel less frustrated and more in charge, siblings get on better with fewer disagreements. Family flashpoints, such as homework, chores, bed-times and mealtimes, all become less of a battleground.

These are achievable goals! The Calmer, Easier, Happier Parenting tools have been used by parents around the world to achieve exactly these results. Of course, there are variations in children's temperaments, so it may take longer with some children than with others. But you <u>will</u> get there!

The more you practise these parenting strategies, the more confident you'll become. And eventually using these skills will simply become a habit you don't even have to think about much. The skills will just come naturally.

What's different about Calmer, Easier, Happier Parenting?

With so many parenting books and websites available, you might be wondering what could possibly be different about this approach. Parents tell me that they are passionate about Calmer, Easier, Happier Parenting for two main reasons. The first is that this approach is practical and usable. I give you step-by-step techniques with clear examples so that you can get started right away and see results very quickly. The second reason is that these simple techniques work across all behaviour issues. You don't have to learn a new strategy for each behaviour challenge that pops up as your child enters a new stage. Once you've learned the core strategies, you'll have the tools to overcome typical and not-so-typical behavioural challenges. The Calmer, Easier, Happier Parenting programme brings together the most effective techniques in positive parenting and breaks them down into practical steps that are easy to understand and easy to use.

What frequently happens when we read parenting articles or books is that we come across a strategy that seems like a good idea so we decide to try it. We may have some success, but we tend to abandon the technique the moment we encounter resistance because the book or article didn't go far enough. It didn't teach us exactly how to put it into practice, and it didn't teach us how to troubleshoot when things got difficult. This book is different. Not only will I give you simple steps to put the strategies into practice, but I will also answer all the questions parents usually ask and give you additional tips to overcome obstacles. What you'll also find invaluable in each chapter are the real stories from parents explaining how they used the Calmer, Easier, Happier Parenting strategies to transform so many aspects of family life. In the forty years I have been working with children and families, I have never seen these techniques fail to improve family life.

A realistic approach

The first thing I always ask parents to notice about this programme is that the name of it <u>isn't</u> 'Calm, Easy, Happy Parenting'. Even with the best parenting tools in the world, life with our children will never be just plain calm, easy and happy. Our kids aren't robots or angels, nor do we want them to be. So I can't take away all of your problems or offer you bliss. What I can do is share strategies that can make parenting significantly calm<u>er</u>, easi<u>er</u> and happi<u>er</u>. It's all in the '<u>er</u>'.

There are two words I always use to describe the Calmer, Easier, Happier Parenting strategies: practical and effective. Practical means you can do them. Effective means they work.

These practical strategies will help children want to cooperate the first time you ask them to do something. And the strategies begin to work as soon as you start using them. If you have a child with an easy-going temperament, you are likely to see results immediately. If your child has a trickier temperament – more sensitive, intense, impulsive or strong-willed – you may see some improvement immediately, but significant results can take two to four weeks.

Some parents feel that two weeks is a short time, and others think it's a long time. The reality is that if you've been living with problematic behaviour for months, or maybe even years, two weeks is a relatively short time to practise strategies that will significantly improve family life. Please think of it this way: If you don't do anything different – if you don't try any of these strategies – in two to four weeks your life will be the same, and you'll still have the same challenges. Why not put your efforts into doing something that can make a difference? The more you practise these techniques, the better results you'll experience.

What frustrates parents the most

If your family life was calmer, easier and happier, how would things be different at home? Whenever I ask this question in a seminar, hands go shooting up, and the first answer is always the same:

> *I want my kids to listen the first time. I can't stand it when they talk back or just ignore me! I don't want to have to keep repeating myself and then finally shouting.*

When we feel forced to repeat instructions, our annoyance and irritation rises, until we finally reach the breaking point. Maybe the breaking point is after we have repeated ourselves three times; maybe it's ten times. Some parents say that their child 'doesn't listen', some say their child 'ignores' them or 'tunes them out'. Some parents tell me they frequently have to shout or get angry before their children will take them seriously. However we describe it, this lack of first-time cooperation from our children is maddening, making us feel compelled to scold, nag, shout, threaten or punish. Parents don't want to repeat themselves endlessly or to keep reminding their child to do what he's supposed to do. Parents want the child to do what they ask, and to do it the first time they ask. What parents want is cooperation. I'll be talking a lot about cooperation in this book, so let me explain how I define it.

Cooperation: Children do what they are asked to do the first time and without a fuss ninety percent of the time.

Imagine how much calmer and easier parenting would be if the first time you asked your daughter to put on her shoes, she did it? Or if you asked your son to put his lunchbox on the kitchen counter and he followed through? When some parents hear my definition of 'cooperation', they worry that ninety percent is too much, that this degree of cooperation would somehow squash their child's spirit. When children are learning to behave sensibly, the opposite happens. Becoming more cooperative helps children feel better about themselves because they're getting told off less, they're getting less irritation directed towards them, and they're getting more smiles and more appreciation. This helps children develop strong self-esteem. Cooperation helps children develop maturity and common sense. Over time the largely cooperative child internalises the parents' values so that eventually he learns to tell himself the right thing to do.

KEY CONCEPT

What sets this approach apart?

The key is cooperation – giving parents simple and specific strategies so that they never have to ask twice.

Every family has its own unique issues and 'flashpoints'. Some of the most typical ones parents mention are getting out the door on time in the mornings, bedtime battles, sibling conflicts, homework hassles and food and mealtime issues. The common theme in all of these challenges is a problem with cooperation. Lack of cooperation is actually just a habit that children gradually drift into. When you start using different strategies, your children will start to cooperate, and you can stop repeating and reminding!

Why repeating and reminding don't work

If we are in the habit of repeating ourselves, our children will gradually learn to tune us out, waiting (without their even realising it) for the repeated reminders. Only when we signal the importance of the matter by raising our voice or threatening a consequence, will our children take the instruction seriously. If we are willing to repeat an instruction five times, we will soon find that we need to repeat it six times! This phenomenon of children tuning us out explains why parents often report, 'My children don't take any notice of what I say until I get angry. Then they cooperate. But why do I have to shout and threaten before they will listen?' Don't despair. I'm going to be giving you strategies so that you'll never have to ask twice!

Another reason our children may ignore our instructions is that if we have not been consistent about *following through* on instructions and rules in the past, our children will not assume that we really mean it this time. So they will just wait and see what happens, which buys them more time to do what they feel like doing. The unpredictability of parents' responses leaves a lot of room for subtle testing and outright misbehaviour. Even children who are usually cooperative will test in situations where they sense, from their parents' initial reaction, that parents are uncomfortable about *following through*. They may try to 'bend the rules' without quite breaking them. This often happens in public, where children can see that the parents' embarrassment is keeping them from *following through*. Sometimes what we think of as being flexible about rules looks to the child as if we're giving in. The more consistently we *follow through*, the more our children will listen to us, take our instructions seriously and cooperate.

Our main job as parents

The basic premise of Calmer, Easier, Happier Parenting is that our main job as parents, in addition to loving and enjoying our children, is to transmit the values, skills and habits we believe are important.

Loving our children is the easy part of the job – it just comes with the territory. The hard part of the job is getting our kids into the habits that are important to us. This takes effort, determination, planning – and it takes knowing the strategies that work!

The five important habits all parents want for their children

Over the years I have asked parents from around the globe what values, skills and habits they want their children to develop. Regardless of geographical location, culture, religion or socioeconomic differences, these same five qualities are always mentioned:

1 Cooperation Doing what a trusted adult tells them to do, the first time they are told, and without a fuss.

2 Confidence Knowing and appreciating and using their talents, abilities and strengths; knowing and accepting and being willing to improve on their weaknesses.

3 Motivation The willingness to start, and to keep on doing, all the steps needed to reach a goal, even though they may not enjoy all those steps. (Homework, cleaning teeth, walking the dog, music practice and saving money are all examples of actions that often require motivation to overcome reluctance or resistance.)

4 Self-reliance Doing for themselves everything that they are capable of doing for themselves, rather than expecting or demanding or waiting for someone else to do it for them.

5 Consideration Caring about other people's feelings and understanding how their own actions affect others.

These five qualities are the building blocks for a calmer, easier and happier life in the present and also in the future. These are the traits that will help children to enjoy their families, to make and keep friends, to reach their potential at school and eventually to find satisfaction as adults in the areas of relationships, careers and leisure pursuits.

These five qualities or characteristics are not inborn, but they can be developed. They can become habits. And the beauty of learning how to develop these habits in your children is that you will be fulfilling two purposes: you will be influencing your children to show more of their best side as they grow up, and you will also be influencing them to show more of their best side as adults. That is why we call these five qualities the foundation habits. They are the foundation for a calmer, easier, happier life – for us and for our children.

If I were to ask a room full of parents which of these qualities is the most important, each of these habits would probably get a number of votes, because they are all so important. There is one, however, that is actually a stepping stone to developing the other four.

Cooperation: The gateway habit

At Calmer, Easier, Happier Parenting, we have found that the first of these five foundation habits – cooperation – is the gateway into the other four habits. Until children are cooperating, they won't be <u>willing</u> to do things for themselves (self-reliance) or to be polite most of the time (consideration) or to try new things (confidence) or to stick at a task even when it's difficult (motivation). When your children learn to be cooperative, they naturally become more confident, motivated, self-reliant and considerate. So rather than worrying about how you are going to train your children in all five habits, if you concentrate most of your training on that one habit, cooperation, the other four will follow quite easily and with much less effort.

Training

Some parents don't like the word 'training' when we're talking about children. They think the word is demeaning in some way and should only be used when we talk about training animals. But let's think about this for a minute. When you start a new job, you generally go through a training programme. That means you are taught new skills, and then there is a period of time during which you practise the skills until they become habitual, and you don't even have to think about them much any more. It's the same for our children. It's our job to teach our children how to do many things, and then, over time and with enough practice, the skills became habits. Toilet-training and tying shoes are classic examples of skills we keep training our children to do until they became habits. It's the same with the five foundation habits. For example, the more your children practise being cooperative, the sooner cooperation will become a habit. It's our job to train our children in the habits that are important to us.

KEY CONCEPT

Teaching vs Training

Teaching results in a child knowing how to do something.

Training gets a child into the habit of doing something, without needing to be reminded.

What family life is like with and without cooperation

Let's think about what family life is like when our children are cooperative, what it's like when they aren't, and what we usually do to try to get our kids to cooperate.

KEY CONCEPT

When cooperation is the norm, here's what we get:

Quality time together	More time – less rushing
Peaceful home life	Motivated children
Smiles and hugs	Confident parents and kids

KEY CONCEPT

Without cooperation, here's what we get:

Tension	Nagging	Negotiating
Frustration and stress	Arguments	Tantrums
Blame	Defiance	Criticism

Strategies that don't get us cooperation

Here's a list of some of the strategies parents use to try to achieve cooperation. When I show parents this list in a seminar, they often let out a loud groan because they have tried most or all of these strategies at some point, and they recognise that they aren't very effective:

repeat
remind
criticise
blame
give advice
reassure
threaten
lecture
question
distract
bribe
reason
negotiate
argue
give in

Of course, most parents don't do all of the things on this list – unless it's a really bad day! When I ask parents if these strategies are working, they usually shake their heads, 'No', or occasionally they say, 'Sometimes'. It's true that all of these strategies work some of the time, but I'll be teaching you positive strategies that work ninety percent of the time.

Wants vs Needs

As important as cooperation is, it is not what most of us consider to be our ultimate goal for our children. But lack of cooperation is what causes parents the most frustration and stress, so it's always the first issue that parents mention.

Sometimes parents say, 'I just want my child to be happy.' While it's completely understandable that we want our children to be happy, the problem with focusing on this as a goal is that it can gradually lead families down a slippery slope. When we set out to make our children happy, we find ourselves catering to all our children's <u>wants</u> instead of to their <u>needs</u>. Wants and needs often have very little in common. What our children need is more sleep, more vegetables, less television, more consistent routines, etc. What they want, however, is to stay up as late as possible, to eat junk food and to watch telly all day! The painful irony is that trying to make our children happy so often results in the very opposite: children who are unsatisfied, unmotivated and who don't value the possessions and treats they have.

So instead of focusing on what our children want, let's focus on what they need so we can give them the skills to help <u>themselves</u> be happier. The interesting thing is that the more we give our children what they need, the more they actually <u>want</u> what they need!

Confidence and self-reliance

What is it that we want for our children as they head out into the larger world? What skills do we want them to have so that they can lead productive lives and have rewarding relation- ships? The answer I hear the most is confidence, and there's a good reason why. Children who are confident enjoy the satisfaction that comes from doing things for themselves. They become more flexible so they have an easier time adjusting to new and different environments and handling any adversity they encounter. When they eventually leave home and go out into the world, they will have the necessary life skills to successfully manage the transition to adulthood.

Here is just a small sampling of some of the life skills that we want our children to learn:

- To be able to handle money responsibly.
- To be able to use public transport safely.
- To be able to keep their possessions organised and clean and tidy.
- To know all about, and feel confident with, food preparation.
- To feel comfortable in shops and restaurants and banks.
- To develop mature social skills.

All of these life skills add up to self-reliance. Self-reliance is a very important habit that goes beyond cooperation, which is usually the habit that initially preoccupies most parents who come to me for advice and coaching. When a child is cooperating, he is doing what we ask, the first time and without a fuss. But when a child is self-reliant, he no longer needs a parent or teacher to tell him what to do and how to do it. A self-reliant child or teen has reached the stage where he tells himself the right thing to do, and then he remembers to do it, ninety percent of the time.

KEY CONCEPT

> Self-reliance is the stepping stone to confidence.

As your children become more skilled, more self-reliant and more confident, life at home will be much more pleasant. And as your children become more able and more willing to do things for themselves, you will find yourself doing less and less for them, so you will have more time to call your own. And you will experience the satisfaction and confidence that comes from knowing that your children are actively learning the skills, habits and values that are important to you.

Of course, we all know that it is far quicker and easier to make the bed ourselves or load the dishwasher ourselves than it is to teach and supervise our child as he learns, bit by bit, day by day, to do it properly. But it's important to persevere! Teaching and training are investments that pay dividends much sooner than parents can imagine. When we continue to do things for our children that they could do for themselves, we are unintentionally robbing them of opportunities to become self-reliant and confident. Doing for our children what they can do for themselves also sends them a negative message that either we think they can't do it, or that they don't have to do it. Without even realising it, we can easily slip into the role of being an unpaid servant! So I recommend that whenever you're doing something for your child, always be thinking, 'What bit of this can he learn to do for himself?' and then start teaching him how. He'll be proud of himself, and you'll feel good about giving him one more life skill!

Self-reliance is the stepping stone to confidence. The more our children do things for themselves, the more confident they will become. The habit of cooperation is just the gateway – it helps our children to be less resistant to all the things we ask them to do, and it helps them become more willing to do things for themselves.

Who's in charge?

This is a rhetorical question, of course. We all know that we should be in charge. Being in charge means that we, the parents, are the decision-makers in the family. We decide the family's lifestyle, the habits, the rules, the routines and traditions. We get input from our children, but <u>we</u> decide because we have the necessary experience, maturity and wisdom to make better choices.

One downside of doing things for our kids that they can do for themselves and acting like unpaid staff, is that they start to lose respect for us. They may begin to order us around because it seems like it's our job to do things for them.

In many families, parents have unwittingly allowed their children to be in charge. As an example of what I mean, imagine a scenario in which you, and your partner if you have one, have decided that your child should be in bed with the light out, drifting off to sleep, by eight p.m. You know that is what is best for her health, her mood and also for your sanity. But more often than you would like to acknowledge, your child's delaying tactics at bedtime result in her finally settling down closer to eight-thirty or even nine o'clock. In that scenario, who is in charge? Your child is. Her goal is to stay up as late as possible, and she is achieving her goal. You are not achieving your goal. So being in charge is about making decisions and then *following through* on your decisions.

If you can relate to this example, you may be wondering, 'But how do I get her in bed by eight o'clock if she's refusing or dawdling?' And of course the scenarios in which a parent is no longer in charge are not necessarily only about bedtime. It could be delaying tactics at homework time; it could be dawdling over tidying up the toys; it could be refusing to eat the food you serve; it could be pestering you for sweets each time you go to the shops. The question is always the same, 'How do I get my children to do what I want them to do?'

The answer is that we cannot physically <u>make</u> our children do very much, although we may be able to physically stop them from doing some things, at least while they are still small. We cannot <u>control</u> what anybody else does, including our children. The more we try to <u>make</u> children do things our way, the more we annoy our children and cause them to resent us and resist us.

But we can <u>influence</u> our children. Influencing is about making it more and more likely that our children will want to do things the way we think they should be done. When we are focused on controlling, we become upset when things are not happening the way we think they should be happening. But when we are influencing, we can stay calmer and more positive because we know we have the strategies to guide our children into better habits over time. Of course we cannot know in advance exactly how long it will take to establish the good habits, but we know we will not give up so we know it will happen, sooner or later.

The skills and strategies that you will learn in this book will teach you how to influence – not control – your children so that they become more and more cooperative, confident, motivated, self-reliant and considerate. They will be less and less likely to misbehave. Family life will become calmer, easier and happier.

CHAPTER 3

DESCRIPTIVE PRAISE: THE MOST POWERFUL MOTIVATOR

I am falling in love with my kids again

I've got to share . . . I went to a Calmer, Easier, Happier Parenting talk last night but was not so convinced Descriptive Praise would work. One of my boys, Sean, constantly screams – happy, sad, it doesn't matter – he just looks me in the face, opens his mouth as wide as he can and lets out the loudest shrieks.

I just didn't see how acknowledging his quiet moments was going to make any difference. I had really gone to the seminar to come away with some new punishment techniques! I was so sceptical that I didn't even tell my husband about it. But I figured I had nothing to lose, so I tried it.

This morning I mentioned every small thing I could see that the kids were doing right. I waited through Sean's three screams, and whenever he had his mouth shut or was talking instead of screaming, I said, 'I notice how quiet you are, Sean. Now I want to listen to you'. And wow! Instead of screaming all morning, he was quiet.

He was also much quieter at preschool, and as I was picking him up, the preschool director took me aside and asked what happened differently this morning. I told her about the seminar and how it was working after just two hours of implementation.

You can bet that tonight I'll be sitting with my husband telling him all about my Calmer, Easier, Happier day!

Mother of two, aged 6 and 4

Descriptive Praise, the first core strategy

In all my years of working with families, I have found Descriptive Praise to be the single most powerful strategy for motivating children to want to cooperate and do their best. Learning how to use this new skill can transform your family life, improving your children's behaviour and guiding them to become the very best they can be. Just as you read in the story above, a lot of parents doubt that Descriptive Praise will make much of a difference in their child's behaviour because it just seems too simplistic to be very effective. Luckily, you don't have to believe it's going to work for it to work! Just start doing it, and you'll see the results.

So what is Descriptive Praise? Very simply, Descriptive Praise means noticing and then specifically describing what your child has done that pleases you. Once you have mastered the skill of Descriptive Praise, you will be well on your way to achieving a calmer, easier and happier family life.

How we usually praise our children

We've all heard that we should praise our children frequently to build up their self-esteem. What do you normally say when your child does something you're pleased about? If you're like most of the parents I ask, you probably say something like, 'Well done!' or 'Wonderful' or 'Fantastic' or 'Brilliant'. You're hoping that this praise will help your child become more confident and to feel loved and secure and special. Or maybe you want your child to try a new activity. Or you want to help her be more resilient and confident so she doesn't give up when a task feels difficult. We often praise our children to encourage them to do more of any behaviour that they might be feeling anxious about. You might say, 'You're doing really well!' 'You're so clever!' 'Keep up the good work!' 'Wow, that was amazing!'

Why praising with superlatives doesn't work

As well intentioned as this praise certainly is, the problem is that this kind of over-the-top praise doesn't really work. It is too general, too vague and, truthfully, it's also exaggerated. Parents tend to say 'Wonderful' and 'Terrific' and 'That's lovely' and 'You're the best' automatically. But your child can see that often we've barely glanced at the drawing or hand-stand or Lego construction. He can also see that the rest of the world is not saying how amazing and terrific he is, so he doesn't really believe these superlative statements. Your child concludes, rightly, that the overblown praise is not a true assessment of his behaviour or work, but an expression of your love.

What's wrong with that? Of course we want to tell our children that we love them frequently, but let's not do it with exaggerated and perhaps undeserved praise, as that will lead them to doubt our judgement and honesty. Furthermore, when we applaud a mediocre effort, the child may wonder whether we believe he's capable of doing any better.

There is another problem with this type of inflated praise. Current research in educational psychology, by investigators such as Carol Dweck, strongly suggests that praising intelligence or outcomes actually backfires and diminishes motivation as well as performance. What is effective for increasing motivation and the willingness to take on challenges is focusing praise on the child's effort, on what the child has done, not on an ability he can't control (such as intelligence) or on the final result (which he may not easily be able to replicate).

And finally, when we're talking about how we can motivate children to improve their behaviour, this superlative praise is too general to convey any useful information about what children can do in the future to get more parental acknowledgement and appreciation. For example, when we say, 'You're eating so nicely' or 'You two are playing together so beautifully', our children often don't really know what it is that we like about how they are eating or playing together. We intend the praise to be a teaching tool, showing our children that we like something they have done so they'll be motivated to do it again, but statements like this are far too vague to achieve that aim.

So I am going to ask you to avoid all those superlatives like 'amazing', 'wonderful', 'fabulous' and 'terrific'. Instead, I'm going to show you a new way to praise that has been proven to be much more effective at improving your child's behaviour, willingness and self-confidence.

What does work: Descriptive Praise!

Descriptive Praise is about noticing and commenting on exactly what your child has done that is right or just OK, or even what he hasn't done wrong. This means we need to momentarily stop what we're doing and really pay attention to what our child is doing and not doing. The very act of slowing down and paying attention gives us a valuable 'window', a little bit of time that we can devote to communicating our specific appreciation.

KEY CONCEPT

Superlative Praise = vague, exaggerated and ineffective

Wow, your homework is brilliant!

Descriptive Praise = specific, true and motivating

You answered all the questions on this worksheet, even though you weren't sure about some of the answers. You didn't leave any blanks. You challenged yourself and wrote something down for every single question.

If your child is eating his dinner without a fuss, just describe exactly what you like about his behaviour. 'You're eating your dinner without complaining about the food.' Or you could say, 'You tasted the peas; that was brave,' or, 'Even though your potatoes are touching your lentils, you didn't say "Yuk".' This is an effective way of communicating your values to your child, such as appreciating the meal instead of complaining, trying what's on his plate even if he thinks he won't like it and being flexible about foods touching each other on his plate.

If your children are playing well together, you might say, 'You're sharing the Lego, and there's no grabbing,' or 'No one's teasing,' or 'For ten whole minutes you two have been sitting there drawing quietly, and neither of you has come to me with any complaints about the other one.' This Descriptive Praise reinforces for your children that sharing, being considerate and working out sibling issues on their own are all important values in your family.

Because Descriptive Praise is so specific, it cannot be argued with; it is a fact. You're not making sweeping, over-the-top statements that can easily be disputed or discounted. Instead, you are describing, very specifically and in detail, what your child is doing that pleased you. Maybe he did the right thing, or maybe it was just barely OK, but it was an improvement on what he might have done. You can even notice and mention when your child is not doing anything wrong.

Descriptive Praise lets your children know exactly what you want them to do and not do. It is a huge relief to children not to have to try and figure out exactly what we mean when we say, 'Behave!' By telling your children exactly what they did right (or did not do wrong), Descriptive Praise gives them a blueprint for getting even more positive attention. With this new kind of praise, your children will see and hear, many times a day, that you are pleased with them. This motivates them to try even more to do what is expected of them. Descriptive Praise proves to children that they can do the right thing, since they just did it. The good behaviour will therefore seem easier to do again.

KEY CONCEPT

Descriptive Praise improves behaviour

The concept of Descriptive Praise is easy to grasp:

1 Notice a little thing that your child is doing that is right – or even the smallest step in the right direction!

2 Tell your child exactly what you notice. Describe the behaviour in detail.

3 Leave out the over-the-top superlatives.

You may be worried that Descriptive Praise will create a 'praise junkie', a child who only behaves to get his parents' approval. Fortunately, that is the opposite of what happens. At first children are motivated to do the right thing because they want to please us. But the more they hear about what they are doing right, the sooner they internalise these standards of behaviour. After a while, they will do the right thing because it feels right, because their conscience tells them to do it. Good behaviour becomes a habit.

As children become more confident that they can behave well, their common sense increases. They become more willing to monitor their own behaviour, rather than to react impulsively or defiantly.

Impressive attention to detail

My son Andrew, who is twelve, had just completed a practice test for an upcoming music theory exam, and I was grading it. Usually he misses several things, but this time he didn't miss any. I remember saying to my husband, 'Wow, Andrew did an amazing job on this practice test!' As I said it, I remembered about Descriptive Praise and took a minute to think about what was actually so 'amazing'.

I went to Andrew and said, 'I looked at your practice test, and that was the most thorough, careful work I've seen yet. I could tell that you went back and double-checked each section before you finished, and that you even caught some mistakes – impressive attention to detail! Guess what your score was?' He looked up at me with a grin and said, 'Ninety-five percent?' I shook my head and said, 'No, you got one hundred percent.' He beamed. That weekend he took the actual exam and scored one hundred percent.

Mother of two, aged 12 and 10

As you can see from this story, our natural reaction is to praise excellent achievement by saying it's 'amazing'. When you take the time to think about what was so amazing and describe it in detail, your child will then have some very useful information. This builds his confidence, leading him to think, 'That's how I did so well on the test; I can do that again.'

Descriptive Praise makes sense, but it may feel awkward at first. It isn't how we're used to talking to our kids. But it is far more effective than a vague and exaggerated 'brilliant' or 'amazing'.

PARENTS WANT TO KNOW

Q: *I think my preteen twins will look at me like I just landed from Mars if I start Descriptively Praising. How can I explain what I'm doing?*

A: At first your children, especially teens and preteens, may well think you've taken leave of your senses, but persevere. If something is right (in this case, both respectful and effective), it is right, even if it mystifies our children. You can explain, 'In the past I made a lot of mistakes as a parent (this will get their attention, though they may be disconcertingly ready to agree with you!). I used to point out your mistakes and nag or shout when I wanted you to do what I said. I can see now that it didn't work. It made you resentful and annoyed. And it made me feel bad too. So now I'm going to practise something different. I'm going to notice and mention the things you do right. I can't guarantee that I'll always be perfect, but I'm going to keep practising so I can improve.'

My three-year-old bit my bottom in the supermarket!

I had been practising Descriptive Praise for about a year when I was stunned by this incident. My three-year-old, Katie, and I were in the supermarket, and there was some food she wanted that I told her we wouldn't be buying. My strong-willed little girl reacted by actually biting my bottom. Apparently it was the nearest thing she could find and just the right height! I was stunned – and sore.

So the next time we were going to the shops, I talked with Katie about the right way to behave before we left – staying next to me, no biting, etc. As soon as we got to the shop, I said, 'You've been staying next to me, and you haven't bitten me on the bottom once!' Other shoppers looked at me like I was crazy, but the Descriptive Praise worked. She stayed next to me and didn't bite me.

Mother of two, aged 6 and 3

The Descriptive Praise helped Katie's behaviour to improve. Notice also that before this mother went back to the supermarket with her daughter, she made sure to clarify her expectations of how Katie should behave. In the next chapter, I'll be explaining how you can make sure your children know exactly what they should do, not just what they shouldn't do. This will help them to do more and more things right.

How to Descriptively Praise to get more of the behaviour we want: Mentioning small steps in the right direction

When we're looking for positive behaviour to praise, sometimes we have to use a metaphorical magnifying glass to find tiny things to praise. We have to capture the little steps in the right direction that we might ordinarily overlook. For example, your child might be sitting in front of his homework, with his pencil in his hand, but you can tell he's daydreaming. Instead of telling him to 'Focus!' you could say, 'You're holding your pencil; you're ready to write.' We need to mention these little positive steps.

Or perhaps your child isn't yet in the habit of doing something you want her to do every time, but she does do it right sometimes. Let's say that your daughter usually forgets to hang up her towel after taking a shower, but on this occasion she has remembered. You might not think of mentioning it when she does it right because you feel she should already be in the habit. But she isn't. So, instead of saying nothing, I suggest you say, 'I noticed you remembered to hang up your towel. You're helping to keep our house tidy.' Or perhaps you'd like your son to get into the habit of putting the toilet seat down. On the rare occasion when he does it, you can say, 'You remembered to put the toilet seat down. That was considerate.' In case you're thinking that Descriptive Praise won't be enough to get your children into good habits, you're right. I am not suggesting that Descriptive Praise will cure all problems. We have many other tools in the Calmer, Easier, Happier Parenting toolkit, and some or all of them may be needed to get the toilet seat put down or the towel hung up on a regular basis. But we need to motivate our children to be willing to pay attention to what we say so that the other tools will be effective. Descriptive Praise is the best motivator I know of.

PARENT PRACTICE
GETTING MORE OF THE BEHAVIOUR YOU WANT

More examples of Descriptive Praise for small steps in the right direction:

You've already got your underwear and one sock on! You're almost halfway dressed.

I told you it was time to clean your teeth, and you took a step towards the sink.

You put one of your sweet wrappers in the recycling bin.

As you've been reading these examples of Descriptive Praise, you may have noticed that there are no superlatives. You won't say it is fantastic or wonderful because your child knows it isn't actually wonderful to hang up a towel or put the toilet seat down. But your child will see and hear that you are pleased, and he will know exactly what he's done to deserve the appreciation. Because children naturally want our approval, they are more likely to repeat the actions that earned them the Descriptive Praise. Very quickly they become more and more motivated to do the right thing.

Getting my son to cooperate at bath time

What I like about Descriptive Praise is that it gives me a specific strategy I can use when I have trouble getting my children to cooperate. I started using Descriptive Praise on all the small things my children were doing right, and they responded immediately. It was amazing how much happier they all became, and they started to look for more ways to please me. They even made me breakfast in bed!

> *I also used Descriptive Praise to deal with a specific problem. When my son was three years old, I used to really struggle to get him out of the bath. One evening I decided to try Descriptive Praise. When it was time for him to get out of the bath, I said, 'Bath time is over. It's time to get out now.' I waited until he made even the smallest move towards the side of the bath and then immediately began to Descriptively Praise him. I said something like, 'You're coming right away. You're coming the first time I asked!' He gave me a huge smile and came out of the bath right away, without a fuss.*
>
> Mother of three, aged 8, 6 and 3

Descriptive Praise can reduce annoying behaviour

Parents are anxious to learn how to get rid of, or at least reduce, their children's annoying (or possibly even worrying) habits. Descriptive Praise is a powerful tool for this as well. Habits such as fingernail-biting, thumb-sucking, complaining, dawdling, squabbling with siblings, ignoring instructions – these are the sorts of negative behaviours we want to reduce. Here's what to do. Start noticing whenever your child is <u>not</u> doing the annoying habit, and Descriptively Praise the <u>absence</u> of that negative behaviour.

This is the opposite of how we usually react. In the past, we've probably noticed what our child was doing wrong and then asked her to stop. Now I am asking you to notice not just your child's major accomplishments, but also the smallest efforts, even when the result is not yet really satisfactory. At first you may need that metaphorical magnifying glass to help you to slow down and focus on the many times during the day when your child is not irritating you.

KEY CONCEPT

> When you Descriptively Praise the absence of an annoying
> behaviour, you'll soon see less of that behaviour.

Even when it feels as if your child is not doing much right at
the moment, you can foster goodwill and increase motivation
by talking about what she is not doing wrong:

You remembered not to grab. You're just looking with your eyes.

You didn't interrupt; you waited until I got off the telephone.

It's so quiet in the back seat.

You finished the first two sums without any complaining.

PARENT PRACTICE
DECREASING ANNOYING HABITS

More examples of Descriptive Praise to decrease annoying habits:

*You've stopped arguing, even though I can see you're still upset about
what I said.*

*Now you're remembering not to talk with your mouth full. That's
polite.*

You're not grabbing now. You're being considerate.

No one's shouting.

Even though it may not feel this way at times, most misbehaviour is actually minor, rather than major. It's just that if we're dealing with a lot of it, it feels major! Most misbehaviour is impulsive and thoughtless, and often it is over as quickly as it started, for example, grabbing, interrupting, stepping on a book instead of stepping over it or whingeing 'Why?' in response to an instruction. So a useful strategy, when your child does something annoying, is to wait a few seconds. As soon as your child stops, or even pauses for breath, jump in with Descriptive Praise! In the story at the beginning of this chapter, Sean's mother reduced his screaming by waiting until he stopped screaming and then quickly praising him for being quiet.

We tend to notice and mention a child's negative behaviour because it is so irritating. But even a child who is impulsive or defiant and who might do a lot of annoying things in the course of a typical day, is not doing those annoying or negative things all day long (although it may feel like it). So it's important to notice whenever he's not doing the annoying behaviour and Descriptively Praise him for not doing it. The more you notice and mention when your child is not arguing or complaining, the more cooperative your child will become. The more you notice when your child is not teasing or grabbing or fiddling with something, the more mature his behaviour will become.

But let's say that your child is in the middle of a marathon complaining session and you are wondering what you could possibly find to Descriptively Praise. Just be a bit patient because pretty soon your child will pause, if only to draw breath, and at that moment you need to jump in with Descriptive Praise and with a big smile say (through gritted teeth if necessary), 'You've stopped whingeing.' You may need quick reflexes to catch those few seconds of silence! Of course, your child may start whingeing again, especially in the first few weeks of this new strategy. He may be testing you. Again, just wait a bit. Praise him again for not whingeing. Sooner or later (it will probably feel like hours even if it's only a few minutes) your child will stop whingeing altogether, and it usually happens much sooner than you could imagine. And then you can say, 'You've stopped whingeing, and that's such a pleasant, friendly voice. Now I'd love to listen to you!' This may feel counter-intuitive at first, but it works!

Here's another example of an annoying habit – fingernail biting. If this isn't an issue you are dealing with, as you read you can mentally substitute some other annoying habit. The old way of trying to get your child to stop biting her nails would be to notice when she is doing it and ask her to take her fingers out of her mouth. You might explain all the reasons why she shouldn't do it: 'It's not good manners,' 'It's dirty,' etc., etc. In my seminars, whenever I ask parents if reasoning, explaining or pointing out what your child is doing wrong are working to reduce the annoying habit, the answer is almost always a resounding 'No'. Yet parents continue to point out the annoying behaviour, continue to explain and reason, even though that's not working, because they don't know what else to do. And besides, you might be thinking to yourself, 'This is how my parents did it, and I turned out OK, so what's the matter with correcting and reminding?' The problem with giving attention to undesirable behaviour is that it usually does not reduce it, and often it even makes the behaviour worse.

So instead, notice and mention whenever your child is not biting her nails. You could say, 'You're not biting your nails' or 'I haven't seen your fingers in your mouth all morning' or 'You've been remembering to keep your hands away from your face. That's very good manners' or 'Your hands are down'. Quite soon something very delightful will begin to happen. Your child will automatically start to put her fingers in her mouth, as she so often has in the past, but then she will stop herself and bring her hands down, without your having had to prompt her! This will happen because Descriptive Praise motivates children to remember our rules and instructions. You may not believe me, but try it, and you will see for yourself.

It's important to make this an all-out campaign. For a month, commit to noticing and mentioning all the times when your child is not biting her nails, not banging his fork on the table, not dangling the cat upside down by the tail, not correcting her sibling, etc. Any ongoing problem needs an ongoing solution!

Breaking the habit of lip-licking

After attending a Calmer, Easier, Happier Parenting seminar, we wanted to see how Descriptive Praise could help with Phoebe's bad habits. At the time she was three years old. She had started the habit of licking her bottom lip over and over until she had a big, red, chapped ring under her lip. I had told her lots of times not to do it. 'Don't lick your lip.' 'Phoebe, you're licking your lip.' 'Stop licking your lip.' But this wasn't working. She kept on licking her lip, and it kept on getting worse. So we decided to try Descriptive Praise and make it a campaign.

So when she was sitting and playing and not licking her lip, I said, 'Phoebe, you're not licking your lip right now.' I think I did this about ten times that day and ten times the next day – every moment I noticed she was not licking her lip. Three days later her lip was better. I said, 'Phoebe, your lip is getting so much better. I can tell you're breaking the habit.' Her face lit up; she was so pleased. Two days later her lip was totally healed, and she actually said to me, 'Mummy, look, I stopped licking my lip and it's all better.'

Mother of a 3-year-old

PARENTS WANT TO KNOW

Q: *I'm worried that Descriptively Praising my children when they're not misbehaving might remind them to misbehave. What can I do to stop this from happening?*

A: In the first few weeks, especially if your child tends to be impulsive, he may react to Descriptive Praise by occasionally doing the exact opposite of what you just praised him for. That's because the Descriptive Praise reminds him of the misbehaviour, and then his impulsivity gets the better of him. This is very annoying, of course, and it feels as if you are going backwards, so you may be tempted to give up on the Descriptive Praise. But keep Descriptively Praising even if the behaviour gets worse temporarily before it gets better. Persevere, and this phase will not last long. Soon he will naturally and automatically begin to try to control himself.

Reducing potty language and interrupting

I couldn't believe how much easier it was to get my four-year-old twins to do things like come to the car straightaway after childcare, when I Descriptively Praised them. However, I must say that I doubted that Descriptive Praise would work to stop annoying habits. But since pointing out the bad habits didn't improve anything, I thought I might as well try it.

So when the twins were going through an annoying stage of using potty language, I decided to try Descriptively Praising them for not using the potty language. The first time I praised them, they started using the potty language again straightaway. But I persevered, and after a while they just stopped.

> *At the same time I also used Descriptive Praise to stop them interrupting each other and raising their voices to make themselves heard, which they used to do all the time. After story time one evening I said, 'You're using kind words with your brother, and you took turns to talk to each other the whole day long. No one interrupted each other. Very considerate.' Both broke into enormous smiles, and I knew they were proud of their achievement.*
>
> Mother of twins, aged 4

It's natural that when you first start Descriptively Praising the absence of the negative behaviour, that your children may test you by impulsively doing it again, just as the twins did in the story above. They may be used to getting your attention by misbehaving, but when you start giving them positive attention for stopping, the annoying behaviour will soon stop. Persevere!

Descriptive Praise paragraphs

For maximum positive effect, turn your Descriptive Praise sentences into paragraphs. Sometimes a child who has been getting a lot of negative attention for misbehaving no longer really believes that he is capable of pleasing his parents. In self-defence, he may shut down, becoming 'parent-deaf'. His defences may be so strong that he barely hears or registers short Descriptive Praises such as, 'Thanks for putting your plate in the sink.' But when we take the time and make the effort to turn these one-liners into paragraphs, this child is far more likely to hear us. You might say, 'You remembered to put your plate in the sink. I didn't even have to tell you. That shows a mature sense of responsibility. You're not expecting people to do things for you when you can do them yourself.' At this point, your child will probably look around to see what else he can put in the sink!

Adding 'qualities' makes your Descriptive Praise even more meaningful

Descriptive Praise becomes even more powerful when you can summarise what you have noticed by mentioning a quality, as has been demonstrated in some of the examples and stories in this chapter. Here are some qualities that parents usually tell me they want their children to develop:

cooperation
respectful, friendly tone of voice
generosity
patience
consideration
self-reliance and independence
flexibility
honesty
courage
self-control
paying attention to details, doing their best
creativity
perseverance

The more often you mention that your child has shown these positive qualities, the sooner your child will be able to see herself as someone who is cooperative, considerate, honest, courageous, etc. For example, if you want your child to be more patient you could say, 'You were sitting so still while I rinsed the shampoo out. That took patience, and it really helps

me.' Or to encourage self-reliance you could say, 'You remembered our new bedtime routine, and you did some of it all by
yourself while I was on the phone. Very independent!'

KEY CONCEPT

> Adding 'qualities' to your praise helps your child absorb your
> values.

Sometimes we need to be reminded about our children's positive attributes and qualities. This is especially true if we've got
a child who has a more sensitive, intense or impulsive temperament, which can sometimes drive us crazy! One couple came
home from my seminar and wrote down a list of all the qualities they valued and wanted their children to develop. This
helped them have a focus for their Descriptive Praises. They
put the list on the inside of a kitchen cupboard as a reminder
to praise all those qualities whenever they saw even the slightest hint of them! The more you look for the good qualities in
your child, the more good qualities you will find, and soon you
will be adding new words to your list.

Descriptive Praise helped us deal with our son's impulsivity and defiance

*Our son Jack, eight years old, was very impulsive at home and at
school. He grabbed, hated to share, ate with his fingers, loudly
resisted homework and bedtimes. His teacher complained that he
chatted rather than doing his work and was too rough with his
classmates. In the first Family Learning Session with Noël, he kept
wandering around the room, interrupting, going into my handbag,*

pulling on his father's clothes to get his attention, repeatedly asking for what he wanted even after we had said no, sitting half off his chair, fiddling with whatever was available and looking away when people talked to him. This was typical. We were used to feeling embarrassed by his behaviour.

Our friends, neighbours and even his teachers had suggested that Jack might be suffering from attention deficit hyperactivity disorder because his behaviour was so different from other eight-year-olds.

Noël taught us to notice and mention every time he stayed in his seat even for a minute, whenever he waited even a few seconds without interrupting, when he wasn't going into my handbag or pulling on us for attention, whenever he sat up straight, didn't grab or made eye contact, etc. She also taught us to Descriptively Praise every tiny little step in the right direction at homework time and bedtime. As a result of this, and also because we made the rules clearer, homework very quickly started going better. It took up less time so Jack had more free time. It was amazing how much less tension there was. Jack fussed less at bedtime, so he got to bed earlier and fell asleep faster as he was less stressed. He was more rested and so he naturally had better impulse control.

In a telephone call with Jack's teacher, I also asked her to Descriptively Praise him when he wasn't chatting or calling out, when he kept his hands to himself, when he answered properly, when he wrote a bit more than usual, etc. The teacher was concerned that the other children would feel left out so I asked if she'd feel comfortable Descriptively Praising the other children as well. She was open to the idea. A few weeks later she said that Jack's behaviour had improved, and so had the other children's.

Jack's behaviour improved much quicker than I could have ever believed – he really wanted to please us and his teacher. Before we'd learned about Descriptive Praise we were reminding him and telling him off, which was worse than useless as it made him think he was always doing things wrong. He had given up even trying to control himself.

Sometimes, especially in the first few weeks, Jack would do the opposite of whatever we praised him about. But we remembered to wait and then Descriptively Praised him when he stopped, instead of telling him off or repeating what we wanted him to do.

For a while we had to be so careful to remember the Descriptive Praise. I knew I had to do it consistently as much as possible every day or else he would slide back into his old habits. But soon he started asking for praise and even praising himself. After a while we could praise him ten times a day, rather than ten times an hour.

Jack is now so much calmer and more sensible. He's even more mature. And all of us are happier.

Mother of an 8-year-old

PARENTS WANT TO KNOW

Q: *The idea of Descriptive Praise sounds great, but I'm worried it will sound false. I can't really see myself doing it, especially when I'm really fed up with the children and not feeling at all appreciative!*

A: Descriptive Praise does not come naturally at first, and it may seem false to you. But in fact Descriptive Praise is the opposite of false because you are observing and noticing exactly what you see. But it may feel awkward at first. So force yourself to Descriptively Praise, even when you are so annoyed that you do not feel or sound sincere. Even insincere Descriptive Praise is much more effective at improving behaviour than sincere correction and shouting. Eventually the Descriptive Praise will become second nature, and you will find that you are feeling sincere when you say it.

When you do not feel the slightest bit appreciative, it is hard to remember that going through the motions of Descriptively Praising will actually make you feel better. It helps to understand that we do not need to <u>feel</u> calm or positive. All we need to do is temporarily <u>act</u> calmer. This 'act' helps children calm down and start cooperating faster than our display of annoyance would. A delightful bonus of acting calm is that it often leads, sooner than one might imagine, to feeling calm.

Getting started – Your guide to success

Now it's time to put Descriptive Praise to work in your family.

How to phrase your Descriptive Praise

While the concept of Descriptive Praise is straightforward, putting it into action may feel awkward or uncomfortable at first. Because we are so used to saying 'Terrific,' 'Brilliant,' you may feel stumped by how to phrase your Descriptive Praise sentences.

A really useful way to start a Descriptive Praise sentence is with the words, 'I notice . . .' You could say, 'I noticed you put your napkin in your lap as soon as you sat down,' or 'I noticed that you put the milk away as soon as I asked.' Children perk their ears up when they hear us saying 'I notice . . .' because that's not the language we generally use when we are correcting or reprimanding. So when we say 'I notice' they soon expect to hear something nice about themselves, and they are motivated to listen.

Also, because with Descriptive Praise we are talking about what our child is doing, or what he has done, we can start most of our Descriptive Praise sentences very simply, with the word 'you'. As you were reading the examples earlier in this chapter, you probably noticed that most of them start with 'you'.

As you become more comfortable with 'catching them being good' you can start to experiment with injecting more variety into how you start your Descriptive Praises. In addition to smiling and looking pleased, you can say:

KEY CONCEPT

Sentence starters

You've been remembering to . . .

Three nights in a row now you . . .

Today, you didn't once . . .

I've noticed that you remembered to . . .

I hear you . . .

In the past week, you . . .

I remember that you . . .

In the past you . . . , but now you . . . .

You're still . . .

Yesterday, you . . .

Even though I could see you didn't want to, you . . .

Nowadays you usually . . .

I see that you . . .

What not to praise!

Focus most of your Descriptive Praise on the habits your children haven't mastered yet. Praising children for things they are already in the habit of doing correctly can feel insulting to them, especially for preteens and teens.

Before you begin practising Descriptive Praise

I strongly recommend that you commit to practising Descriptive Praise for two weeks before moving on to learning and then practising the other powerful skills of Calmer, Easier, Happier Parenting. Of course it's entirely up to you if you choose to stop here and practise Descriptive Praise or if you're so excited that you just can't wait to forge ahead and learn more strategies.

But it can be overwhelming if we tweak and change too many things at once. The skill of Descriptive Praise is extremely effective, so you'll want to give yourself time to become comfortable using it and to experience the positive results. Once you see the difference that Descriptive Praise can make, you'll feel more confident, and you'll be eager to learn the next strategy!

Here is an important point I want you to think about. What I'm talking about in this book is how to influence behaviour, how to change our children's habits. But first, in order to do that, we've got to change our own habits. We've got to alter how we're communicating with our kids. Learning any new skill takes a lot of practice and determination, so please give yourself time to be successful with Descriptive Praise. I'm going to give you more examples of Descriptive Praise in this last section, and I'll also answer some more of the questions parents typically ask as they begin putting this skill into action. And remember that you can use Descriptive Praise across all behaviour issues; you don't need a new skill for tackling each habit!

Putting Descriptive Praise into practice: Your Action Plan for the first two weeks

How to motivate your child so that you see more of the behaviour you want and less of the annoying behaviour:

1 Choose two annoying behaviours you'd like your child to improve, and write them down.
2 For each behaviour, notice and Descriptively Praise every time your child does it right or just OK or even just a bit better than before.
3 Notice and mention when your child isn't doing the annoying behaviour.

4 Avoid superlatives!
5 Make a goal of Descriptively Praising some aspect of the improved behaviour at least ten times a day.

Example of an annoying behaviour: Not doing what you ask the first time

Cooperation is a really useful habit to target first as it's the gateway to improving so many other important habits.

Notice the times each day when your child does what you ask, even if she does only a part of what you ask. You can also describe the absence of the negative behaviour. Here are several examples:

I asked you to shut the door, and you did it right away. That was cooperative.

An important tip: Be sure to praise the fact that the child cooperated, not just what she did. In the above example, the parent didn't say, 'Thanks for shutting the door.' The praise needs to be focused on the cooperation.

I noticed that when Dad told you to feed the dog, you hardly complained at all.

Even though you wanted to play longer, you came inside when I asked.

Three times today, when I asked you to do something, you did it the first time, without arguing.

I asked you to put on your jacket, and you got it off the hook.

You stopped arguing about turning off the telly.

You didn't roll your eyes when I told you to make your bed.

Example of an annoying behaviour: Whingeing
An important tip: Be sure to address your child's whingey, impatient or disrespectful tone of voice, even if the <u>words</u> he is saying are reasonable. As long as we're willing to answer our children when they're whingeing, they'll keep whingeing!

You stopped whingeing. Now I want to listen to you.

You used a friendly voice to ask for a treat.

For the past five minutes, you've been talking to me without any whingeing. What a respectful voice!

You started to whinge, but then you stopped yourself. That shows self-control.

It's so pleasant being with you when you use a polite tone of voice.

PARENTS WANT TO KNOW

Q: *This is all so new to me, the idea of praising all the time – how can I keep remembering to do it? Is ten times a day really necessary?*

A: There are two reasons why aiming for at least ten Descriptive Praises a day is so important. Of course one reason is that you want to improve your child's behaviour as quickly as possible. The second reason is that you are changing your parenting behaviour, and that takes practice.

So aim high and go for ten times a day or even more. If you do that, you'll find that within a week or two it becomes much easier to remember to Descriptively Praise, and you may well find yourself Descriptively Praising a lot more than ten times a day!

At first, you might find that you forget to say your ten Descriptive Praises. Don't worry. Here are some solutions that parents have come up with to help them remember:

1 When you are tucking your children in at bedtime, say all the Descriptive Praises that eluded you during the busy day.

2 Use mealtimes, when you have a captive audience, to catch up on Descriptive Praises.

3 Write 'DP' on Post-its and scatter them around your house – on the computer, fridge, kitchen cabinets, bathroom mirror, etc. Each time you see the note to yourself, it will jog your memory.

4 When the other parent comes home, or if you bump into an acquaintance, Descriptively Praise your child to the adult in the child's presence. He will be listening and absorbing, even if he seems oblivious.

5 Establish some new habits for yourself. For example, make a plan to say a Descriptive Praise each time you:

- get in the car.
- drop your child off or collect him from school.
- supervise bath time.
- see your child doing homework.

There is no doubt that Descriptive Praise makes a powerful, positive impact on behaviour, confidence, motivation and self-esteem. It is too powerful a tool not to use daily, many times a day!

Q: *I tried Descriptive Praise a few times, but it backfired on me. My son seems to hate being praised! He even stuck his fingers in his ears and started humming loudly to drown me out. So I stopped doing it. Why didn't it work?*

A: As excited as you may be about Descriptive Praise, don't expect your child to transform magically overnight! Your child may even argue with you about Descriptive Praise or become visibly upset or try to tune you out. This phase does not last long. Here are some possible reasons for the occasional negative reaction, and here is what parents can do to move through this phase as quickly as possible.

It can feel like an insult to children if we Descriptively Praise 'small steps in the right direction' for behaviours they have already mastered. To avoid this, we can Descriptively Praise the fact that the behaviour is becoming a habit. For example, instead of saying, 'Thanks for flushing the loo,' to a child who now usually remembers to flush, we can say, 'Most of the time you're remembering to flush the loo and wash your hands, and you don't leave the towel on the floor any more.'

Your child may be embarrassed to admit to himself that certain mature behaviour still needs to be reinforced by Descriptive Praise. He would like to believe that he has long since mastered certain habits, such as turning lights off when leaving a room, not drumming on the table, speaking quietly indoors, saying 'please' and 'thank you', etc. To avoid upsetting your child, you may be tempted not to praise. Don't give up on the Descriptive Praise. He will soon come to appreciate it and be motivated by it.

Sadly, boys are often labelled naughty, rebellious and oppositional. Boys are corrected more than girls are, both at home and at school. This often leads to negative attention-seeking and to the gradual development of a self-image of being bad, unlikeable or 'thick'. Because of this entrenched low self-esteem, it may take longer with some boys for the Descriptive Praise to start working. Persevere!

Your child may have been used to getting negative attention for misbehaviour for years. Positive attention can be unsettling at first. A child who has been told off a lot may not believe, at first, that you could possibly be pleased with him so many times each day. Your child might be so uncomfortable with his new persona that he even asks you to stop praising him. Don't stop praising him! Descriptive Praise is like medicine: it works even if we don't like the taste. It may even take a few months before he feels comfortable with getting positive attention for positive behaviour.

A child who is relatively more intense or angry seems almost to enjoy the excitement of seeing a parent get upset. It is not so interesting when you stay calm and positive. He may be hooked on the power to wind you up, a skill he has perfected to a fine art. When you keep mentioning the positive, the child can see that you are in charge of your emotions. This can make him angry. He may have come to associate parental love with the intense emotions that accompany shouting, arguing, telling off and smacking. So when you stay calm and positive, it may seem to the child as if you do not care about him any more. A child who is not very good at a lot of things (eg. schoolwork, sports, making friends) may come to feel that the only thing he is good at is making adults angry. When this child starts hearing a lot of Descriptive Praise, he may start panicking inwardly, worrying that he is losing his grip in the one area where he has felt successful and powerful. His self-image as someone who gets into trouble a lot is being shaken up. A child who has carved out a niche for himself by being 'bad' may worry that there will not be much that is special about him if he becomes 'good'. He may worry that no one will notice him. His familiar self-image may not give up without a fight.

I'm sure it's your goal to interact with your child in a more positive way, even if it temporarily upsets your child. And it's also important for you to be in charge of how you behave and to keep doing what you believe is right. So persevere, and soon positive attention will become the new normal in your home.

Summary

When you Descriptively Praise your children, taking the time to notice all the good and even the just OK behaviour, you will start to appreciate your children more and enjoy being with them more! You'll see better behaviour sooner than you can imagine.

It's OK to be sceptical. In fact, I've had many sceptics come through my courses, and when they see for themselves what a difference Descriptive Praise can make with their children, they become some of the biggest fans of Calmer, Easier, Happier Parenting.

Your children will become more confident because they are hearing far more about what they are doing right than about what they are doing wrong. And you will start to feel better and more confident about your parenting. As one parent told me, 'Now that I'm using Descriptive Praise, I feel, finally, that I'm a good mother.'

CHAPTER 4

PREPARING FOR SUCCESS: SIMPLE TECHNIQUES THAT PREVENT MOST MISBEHAVIOUR BY REDUCING RESISTANCE AND REFUSAL

My dawdler has been transformed

This morning, after only two days of practising Noël's Preparing for Success techniques, my previously recalcitrant, dawdling ten-year-old daughter woke up, got dressed, made her bed, made her own breakfast and brushed her teeth, all without a word from me. And I had done the 'think-through' about our morning routines just once. I never thought this would happen!

How is it that I studied family therapy during my psychotherapy training and never got skills like these? This is genius.

Mother of three, aged 8, 6 and 4

Preparing for Success, the second core strategy

Within a day or two of learning the Preparing for Success strategies, parents frequently contact me to share results like the anecdote above. We've even had parents tell us they were annoyed with themselves that they hadn't thought of these simple, common sense strategies themselves! Parents are surprised that slight changes in how we talk to our kids can create such positive results. The little girl in the story above had been diagnosed with attention deficit disorder. Her mother didn't really believe it would ever be possible to get her daughter into good habits. The mother assumed she would have to nag forever.

It's so easy to get caught in the trap of reminding and nagging. Even though that doesn't work to get us first-time cooperation, if we don't know a better strategy, we'll just keep doing what we've been doing. And of course we'll keep getting irritated because it doesn't work! That's a natural reaction, but it's time to learn a better way.

Preparing for Success is about some very specific techniques we can use to set our children up to succeed, to do things right. The alternative is waiting until things go wrong and then reacting with annoyance. When you start using these Preparing for Success techniques, you will vastly increase the number of things your child will be doing right, so you'll have far more things you can Descriptively Praise! These practical tools are effective at minimising almost all behaviour problems.

Preparing for Success is the best method I know for reducing our children's resistance to doing almost anything we ask of them. When you begin using the Preparing for Success techniques, you will soon be hearing your children say 'OK' instead of saying 'No' or 'In a minute,' or 'Why do I have to?' or every parent's favourite, 'You're not my boss!'

Why do our children say 'No'?

One of the main reasons our children resist cooperating is because it feels to them as if we are springing demands on them unexpectedly, and they are not prepared. Children are not able to transition from one activity to the next as quickly as we would like, especially when they are not particularly motivated to do the next thing!

As parents we have an agenda; we're often looking ahead to see what needs to get done next. Our children, on the other hand, are just trying to live in the moment. Their agenda is about having fun. So it's no wonder that their first response to a request or an instruction is often 'No' or 'Why should I?'

For example, you might be with your children at the park, and they are having a wonderful time until you tell them it is time to leave. Their response is likely to be quite predicta-ble. Depending on his age or temperament, a child might shout 'No', he might run off in the opposite direction or he might whinge or argue or plead for one more turn on the slide or two more minutes on the swings. But he is not going to say, 'All right, Mum, let's go home now. I know I need a bath tonight because I didn't have one yesterday, and we don't want to push bedtime back too late.' That is our agenda, but his agenda is the opposite – his agenda is to keep playing for as long as possible.

Since children often resist doing what we ask, it doesn't make sense for us to ask in the same way we have always asked and then get annoyed when they respond in the same resistant way. We've got to do something different if we want to get a different result.

Preparing for Success is about being proactive, not reactive. A proactive approach includes thinking about what went wrong in the past, anticipating what might go wrong in the future, and then being willing to do something different so that things are more likely to go right the next time.

Being reactive, on the other hand, means waiting until things go wrong yet again and then reacting in the same old ways that we already know do not motivate children to want to cooperate: repeating, reasoning, negotiating, bribing, threat-ening . . . or even shouting.

One of the delightful benefits of Preparing for Success is that the more we focus on preventing and minimising misbe-haviour, the fewer behaviour problems we will be faced with. Therefore we will need to do less crisis management, and we will need to give fewer consequences for misbehaviour and non-cooperation.

KEY CONCEPT

Focus on planning so that things go right, rather than reacting after things go wrong.

Preparing for Success Technique A: Using 'think-throughs' to help children remember rules and expectations and take them seriously

So how can we Prepare for Success to make it easier for our children to cooperate the first time we ask and to make it harder for them to forget or to ignore us or to argue back? Wouldn't it be great if there were one technique that would help our children understand what they need to do, remember what they need to do and actually do what they need to do, without reminders? There is one! A technique called a *think-through* is the key to achieving these goals.

A *think-through* is a powerful technique for helping our children remember and follow our rules and routines. It maximises the likelihood of your child cooperating by fixing the expectation or rule firmly in his long-term memory. But it is <u>not</u> a reminder.

When we're reminding our children about what they should

do and how they should do it, have you noticed that often they're not really listening? When we <u>tell</u> our children what we want them to do, we are hoping that they will take us seriously, think about what we're saying and remember to do it, without our needing to tell them again and again. Unfortunately, when we're talking, to kids it just sounds like another lecture – blah, blah, blah – and they easily tune us out.

But with a *think-through*, it is not you but <u>your child</u> who is saying what he has to do, and that has a powerful positive impact on his memory and also on his willingness. *Think-throughs* are a highly effective technique for improving any habit.

A *think-through* is different from a reminder in two important ways:

- A *think-through* happens before the misbehaviour occurs.
- In a *think-through*, your child is the one doing the talking, not you.

You can use *think-throughs* to establish new rules and to make them stick, as well as to help your children remember about existing rules and routines and to really take them seriously. I have called this technique a *think-through* because, as you will see, it requires both you and your child to think carefully.

How to do a think-through

Here are the basic *think-through* steps for helping your child remember and take seriously an existing rule or routine. Instead of waiting until your child breaks or ignores the rule, we need to be proactive and address the issue with a *think-through* earlier in the day.

1 **Choose a <u>neutral</u> time to do the think-through.** This is very important. Never try to do a *think-through* right after something has gone wrong. It won't work because you will be annoyed instead of calm and positive, and your child will be resentful and possibly rebellious. A neutral time means a time when neither you nor your child is in a hurry, and neither of you is annoyed. Look at your child and wait, smiling, until you have his full attention.

2 **Ask, don't tell.** Now ask your child several leading questions all about the behaviour you want to see more of. Remember, your child already knows the rule, so don't repeat it. Phrase your questions so that they cannot be answered with just a 'Yes' or a 'No'. You want your child to really have to think about how he will answer the *think-through* questions.

3 **Your child answers in detail, telling you what he should do.** Since you have chosen a neutral time, and there's no irritation and no scolding, your child will usually be quite willing to answer your questions. The more detailed your child's response, the more it will stick in his memory, so ask a number of follow-up questions. The only time you would switch from asking to telling is if your child's answer is incomplete or inaccurate. In that case clarify what you mean, and then ask some more questions until you are sure your child understands the rule or routine thoroughly.

You may be thinking that this technique sounds great for other people's kids, but that it would never work with yours!

This approach may be so different from what parents usually do that it's natural to think it won't work. You probably have a lot of questions at this point. For example, if your child isn't very cooperative, you might be wondering how you could possibly get her to answer your questions! Fear not; shortly I will be answering all the typical questions parents ask about *think-throughs*, as well as giving you some sample dialogues that you can adapt for your family.

Think-throughs in action

In this example, the behaviour the parents wanted to improve was table manners. They didn't want their son, Jamie, to complain about the food he was served, and they also wanted him to stay seated at the table until he was excused.

First the mother sat on the floor next to where Jamie was playing and chatted briefly about what he was making. Then the conversation went as follows:

Mother: *Jamie, I'm going to ask you some questions about dinner time. Tell me what you have to do at dinner.*

Jamie: *I have to be good.*

Mother: *I'm glad you know you have to be good. What will you do when you're being good?*

Jamie: (Long pause) *I have to stay in my chair . . . and not say 'Yuk'.*

Mother: *You remembered two of our rules. You're going to stay sitting down for the whole meal until what?*

Jamie: *Till I'm done.*

Mother: *No. You have to stay in your chair until Daddy and I say you can be excused. You have to stay until Daddy and I say what?*

Jamie: *Till you say I can be excused.*

Mother: *I can see you know that rule now. And why aren't you going to say 'Yuk'?*

Jamie: *Because . . . it hurts your feelings?*

Mother: *That's right. You don't want to hurt my feelings. What will you do if you have some food on your plate that you don't want, instead of saying 'Yuk'?*

Jamie: *I'll just leave it, and I won't say anything horrible.*

Mother: *Now that would be polite. That's what grown-ups do. You're getting more grown-up every day.*

KEY CONCEPT

Ask, don't tell

When your children tell you what they need to do, they are much more likely to remember to do it. But when you tell them, often they're barely listening.

The above *think-through*, which lasted about a minute, resulted in much better (although not perfect) behaviour. At dinner over the next few nights, both parents then made a point of Descriptively Praising Jamie for following the two rules that he had recently done the *think-through* about. They also Descriptively Praised a lot of other OK behaviours that had not even been mentioned in the *think-through*: saying the occasional 'please', using his napkin instead of his sleeve, not interrupting, keeping his legs down, not grabbing, sitting up straight. The parents reported that in subsequent *think-throughs*, Jamie mentioned as rules the behaviours that the parents had made a point of consistently Descriptively Praising. This is an example of how Descriptive Praise teaches children the appropriate ways to behave; we do not need to lecture or criticise.

Tips for effective think-throughs

- Spend no more than a minute on each *think-through*. In sixty seconds, you can ask and get answers to between three and eight questions, depending on the age of your child, how articulate he is and how willing he is. Keeping the *think-throughs* short helps children stay engaged.

- Do *think-throughs* with each child separately, even if you want to reinforce the same rule for more than one child. That way you can make sure each child answers each question, and you'll be able to tailor the vocabulary and concepts to the comprehension level of each child. Doing separate *think-throughs* for each child also eliminates the chances of your children reinforcing each other's complaints or ganging up to mock you.

- Remember to Descriptively Praise as your child answers the *think-through* questions. This will motivate her to want to answer your questions and to absorb your values.

- An ongoing problem needs an ongoing solution. So be willing to do several *think-throughs* a day for a week or so, especially if you have a child who is often uncooperative or who has a more inflexible temperament.

PARENT PRACTICE
TAKING CARE OF BELONGINGS

More examples of *think-through* questions:

When we get home from football practice, what's the first thing you need to do?

Where should you put your equipment bag?

What should you do with your clean clothes?

Here's another example. Let's say that bath time is a problem in your family. Your daughter loves to splash about in the bath, oblivious to the water that is landing on the floor. Understandably, you'd like less splashing so that more water stays in the bath! It is very tempting to say, 'Stop splashing' or 'You're getting the floor all wet' or 'If you keep splashing you'll have to get out'. The problem with those statements is that your child is having so much fun in the bath that she barely hears you. And because parents tend not to *follow through* on most threats, your child can safely assume that not much will happen if she ignores you, other than yet another instruction or reprimand that she can also ignore.

If this has been happening a lot at bath time, you can probably anticipate that splashing the water and ignoring your instructions are likely to happen again. It's time to get proactive! As I said earlier, if you've got an ongoing problem, you will probably need to do daily *think-throughs* to reduce the problem. Do two or three *think-throughs* about this every day, at completely neutral times, long before bath time. You can ask *think-through* questions such as:

When you're in the bath, where does the water belong?

How can you make sure that the floor stays dry?

What will happen if you keep all the water in the bath?

If there's water on the floor, who will mop it up?

What will you use to mop up the water?

By the time your daughter has answered sixty seconds' worth of questions like this, she will be much more likely to remember the rules and to cooperate. And then just before bath time you can ask her these same, or similar, questions again. You may worry that this seems needlessly repetitive, but repetition is necessary if we want to maximise cooperation. Notice that it is your daughter who is doing the repeating. This results in the important information being stored in her long-term memory. But if it were the parent doing the repeating, as is so often the case, all that is getting stored in the child's long-term memory is the thought, 'Mum's a nag'.

And be sure you give your daughter Descriptive Praise at bath time whenever the water is staying in the bath. Within days the problem will be much reduced, and within a few weeks you will hardly remember that water on the bathroom floor was once a problem.

PARENT PRACTICE
RREDUCING RESISTANCE TO GETTING IN AND STAYING IN THE CAR SEAT

Examples of *think-through* questions:

What do you need to do as soon as you climb into the car?

Who buckles your car seat?

Where should your arms be so Daddy and I can buckle you in?

When can you get out of your car seat?

KEY CONCEPT

Anticipate problems

To prevent problems, do *think-throughs* about the right way to behave. Do the *think-throughs* at neutral times, long before anything has had a chance to go wrong.

Five Ws and an H: The keys to effective think-throughs

Asking your child questions and having her answer them probably seems like a simple enough concept. But when you try to come up with *think-through* questions, you may find yourself getting stuck and falling back on the same kinds of questions again and again, for example, 'What do you need to do when you get home from school?' or 'What do you need to do to get ready for bed?' etc.

Here's something that can help you vary your questions so

that your child stays alert and engaged. Remember when you were writing English essays years ago, you probably learned about the 'six question words': who, what, when, where, why and how. These are considered the basics in information gathering. Answering these six question words will capture the full story.

In a sense, this is what we're doing with *think-throughs*. We're using questions to prompt our child to think about all the aspects of the behaviour that we expect from her. We want to make sure that she knows how to behave correctly in a particular situation. Notice that in the above example about keeping the water in the bath, there were three Ws and an H: where, what, who and how. A 'why' question might go something like this, 'Why does the water need to stay in the bath?' or 'Why will you mop up any water that lands on the floor?' So whenever you do a *think-through*, remember the five Ws and an H. This will make coming up with the *think-through* questions much easier.

Utterly amazed by how well this worked

The Calmer, Easier, Happier Parenting strategy that immediately resonated with me was Preparing for Success. It just made sense. I could see that the expectations I had of how our seven-year-old and two-year-old boys should behave were really only in my head. It seems so basic, but I had somehow overlooked the fact that I hadn't clarified the expectations with them. So how were they expected to know what they should do?

I first used the think-through strategy to deal with the problems we used to have when we got home after being out somewhere. Whenever we got home, chaos would descend. My older son would run through the house, dropping his coat on the floor, dumping his bag and shoes before disappearing off to play. So this time, when we were in the car on the way home, I explained what I wanted him to do when we got home. Then I asked him to tell me what he needed to do to make sure he understood.

My wife and I were utterly amazed by how well this worked. When we got home, he hung up his coat and started getting undressed for his bath without our having to tell him again. Since then we use think-throughs whenever we want to make a new rule or whenever we want to make sure that the boys remember what to do. Instead of hoping that they will do what we want them to do, we actually go over what we want to happen several times during the day, with them repeating back to us what's going to happen. And nine times out of ten it actually happens. It's freed up a lot of time that we used to spend repeating, nagging and losing our tempers.

Father of two, aged 7 and 2

Think-throughs for children who aren't very verbal yet

If you've got a young child who is not yet very good at answering questions, you're probably wondering if you can use this technique. The answer is yes, but you'll need to modify how you do it. You can ask the same types of questions, but instead of expecting your child to answer, at first you will answer for her.

Here's an example of a *think-through* you might do for a young child about being gentle with a pet. We might automatically phrase the *think-through* question in the following way, 'Do we bother Fluffy when she's asleep?' but there are two problems with this kind of question. The first problem is that we're putting our emphasis on the negative behaviour, on what she shouldn't do, which is bother the cat. But what we want her to be thinking about is what she <u>should</u> do. That's what we want to reinforce. The other problem with that question is using the pronoun 'we'. You are not the one bothering

Fluffy. It can be very confusing to our kids if we say 'we' when we really mean 'you'. Challenge yourself to shift this habit and use the correct pronoun so it's clear to your child who needs to do what.

Here's how your *think-through* could go:

You clarify and ask: *You can play with Fluffy as long as you touch her gently. How should you hold Fluffy?*
You answer: (Smiling) *Softly, gently. You have to be gentle with Fluffy.*
You ask again: *How should you hold Fluffy?*
You answer again: (Smiling) *Gently.*

Pretty soon you will ask this question and your child will say 'gently' because she has heard you say it a number of times. At that point, you can enthusiastically praise her for telling you the right answer. Whatever your issues are with your young child – resisting being buckled into a car seat, not wanting to get dressed, grabbing, playing with food – you can use these little *think-throughs*, where you ask the question and then answer it yourself. You'll be surprised how quickly your little one learns to respond.

Remember only to use this modification with children who are not yet very verbal. Older children, even if they're not answering you, are perfectly capable of answering, so let's not do their job for them.

PARENT PRACTICE
ESTABLISHING MEALTIME ROUTINES

Examples of *think-through* questions:

When I tell you it's time for dinner, what's the first thing you should do?

What kitchen chore do you need to do before we sit down?

When can we all start eating?

What needs to go in your lap before you pick up your cutlery?

PARENTS WANT TO KNOW

Q: *My son is thirteen and he doesn't even bother answering me when I ask him to do something. How do I get his attention so I can do a think-through?*

A: This is an important issue. Some children may be so used to their parents reminding and nagging that they don't even want to listen. They are expecting to hear criticism or a lecture. The way to shift this expectation is for parents to learn about and consistently use Descriptive Praise, the very first skill that we teach in the Calmer, Easier, Happier Parenting programme. Descriptive Praise motivates children to want to please us because they are hearing a lot about what they are doing right, instead of what they are doing wrong. You will be pleasantly surprised by how quickly your children become willing to listen and to respond positively once you make a habit of noticing and mentioning all the little OK things they are doing all day long.

You may find that you have to do a *think-through* about *think-throughs*! At a neutral time, here are a few questions you could ask, 'Gary, whenever Mum or I ask you a question, instead of ignoring us, what do you need to do?' and 'When do you need to answer us?' and 'How will you need to answer us?' And throughout the day, be sure to notice and mention whenever he speaks to you in a friendly or polite way, 'That was a polite tone. Very respectful.'

Clear rules and expectations

When something is continuing to bother us about our child's behaviour, often it's because we don't have a rule for it. Or maybe we did once have a rule, but over time we've let the rule slide so now our children don't really think they have to follow it. Having clear rules and expectations is another key aspect of Preparing for Success.

Before you can make a new rule to address a family problem, the first step is to get clear within ourselves exactly what we want the new rule to be. This first step is easily overlooked in the midst of our busy lives. If you have a partner, you both need to agree about what the rules will be, and we call this becoming a United Front.

When you and your partner are united, it will prevent many problems. And not being united causes many problems! It's important for all the adults in your home to agree on the rules so that you are all willing to <u>consistently</u> *follow through*. When parents don't agree, rules and routines will not be consistent, and far too much of the child's time and thoughts will go into testing, arguing, wheedling for exceptions and looking for loopholes.

It is not always easy for parents to agree. And unfortunately 'agreeing to disagree' is not a workable option because children react so badly to a lack of consistency. But as soon as parents realise how important consistency is for their children's well-being, they are usually willing to work at setting aside their differences and aligning their values. Even when parents disagree on many things, they do generally agree that the welfare of their children comes first. If you and your partner need help getting united on your rules so that you can function as a team, see Preparing for Success Technique E on page 116.

Once parents are united, the next step is to make sure that your children know and understand the rules and expectations, even though they may not like them. When children know exactly what they should and should not do, they are far more likely to develop the habit of cooperation and far less likely to keep testing you to see what they can get away with. And the more consistently you *follow through* on your rules, the more your children will respect you. I'll talk about how to *follow through*, which many parents find quite tricky, in Chapter 8.

You can change your rules whenever you need to

I give you permission to make a new rule any time things at home are not working as well as you would like. You can change rules any time you need to. You may worry that if you've been doing things a certain way, then you are somehow committed to that rule or routine forever for the sake of consistency. Break the pattern and make a better rule with these four magic words: *The new rule is . . .*

Using think-throughs to establish a new rule

1 Choose a neutral time and sit down with your child for one minute, just as you would when doing a *think-through* to revive an existing rule.

2 Start the *think-through* by saying, 'The new rule is . . .' or words to that effect. You might say:

Mum and I have made a new rule. Starting on Monday you can only turn the TV or computer on after your homework is finished to our satisfaction.

The new rule is that from now on Dad will read two stories at bedtime. You can earn a third story each night that you get into bed the first time we ask you.

The new rule is everyone makes their bed before breakfast, even Mum and Dad.

3 Once you or your partner have stated the new rule, stop talking! Wait for your child to respond. He might say 'OK' quite cheerfully. He might be responding so cooperatively because children generally are more comfortable when rules and routines are spelled out clearly. This is one of the reasons that most children behave much better at school than they do at home. On the other hand, he might be responding so positively because he doesn't really believe anything is going to change! Perhaps he has seen several new regimes come and go, so he doesn't feel he needs to take this new rule seriously. Whatever his deeper motives may be, you can Descriptively Praise him for accepting the new rule without a fuss.

Your child might say nothing at all, staring at you in fury, or he might try to ignore you, pointedly looking out of the window. His silence may be his attempt to block out the bad news. Or he may be mentally rehearsing a scathing rebuttal. Or he may be waiting for you to launch into justifying or lecturing. Don't! Just wait in silence for him to respond. He will respond, if you give him time.

The first few times you do a *think-through*, your child may complain, cry, argue about the new rule or even scream, 'It's not fair.' Do not fall into the trap of arguing back, lecturing, justifying or launching a counter-attack. Your child is entitled to his feelings. The most helpful response is to just listen and acknowledge his feelings, 'You're probably feeling angry that we're making this new rule. We've been letting you watch telly before homework, and you like it that way.'

Your child may attempt to negotiate and bargain. Don't even go there! Have the courage of your convictions. Stick to your new rule. Be firm. Your child knows what he wants, but you have the experience and maturity and wisdom to figure out what's best for your child.

Your child may storm out of the room, although this happens far less frequently than parents imagine it will. Remember that you will be asking the *think-through* questions at a neutral time, rather than telling him off after something has already gone wrong. So your child will usually be willing to listen and talk, especially if you are making a point of finding lots of OK behaviour to Descriptively Praise all day long.

But if your child does walk away, do not follow him. Quite soon he will want something. Children are always asking us questions or wanting something from us. Your child might want to know what's for lunch; he might want a ride to a friend's house; she might want you to help find the missing doll's shoe. When your child comes to you and wants something, you can say, 'I'll be glad to talk with you about that as soon as you answer my questions.' At this point your child will start to take you more seriously because you are *following through*. Pretty soon he will abandon the tactic of storming out because it will no longer be working to get him off the hook.

Your child may ask why you have made this new rule. Refrain from launching into an explanation. Most of the time when children ask 'Why?' it is not a genuine request for information. It is more likely to be a diversionary tactic or an attempt to find a loophole so they can argue their case. Our children usually know, or can easily figure out for themselves, the reasons for what we ask of them. Instead of explaining the reasons for the new rule, respond with, 'That's a good question. Why do you think we're making this new rule?' Your child may come up with a sensible reply, in which case you can Descriptively Praise by saying, 'That's the right answer, and I didn't even need to tell you. You came up with a sensible reason.' If, however, your child repeats that he doesn't know the reason for the new rule, require him to take a guess.

He may not want to take a sensible guess at first. That is because responding sensibly is the first step down the path towards behaving sensibly, and he may want to keep his options for misbehaving open!

PARENTS WANT TO KNOW

Q: *Knowing my son, I'm worried that if I ask him what he should do, he'll just shrug his shoulders and say, 'I don't know.' What do I do then?*

A: This may happen the first few times you do a *think-through*. Often children automatically answer, 'I don't know', even before they have given our question any thought because they have found that saying 'I don't know' is a great way to get parents to leave them alone. The solution to the 'I don't know' and 'I can't remember' habit is to require children to take a sensible guess. They do not have to know the right answer to your question, but they do have to use their brain and guess.

So if you ask your son what he needs to do to get ready for his karate lesson, he might answer, 'I don't know.' When you say, 'Take a guess,' he may reply, 'But Mum, I really don't know!' At this point, you might feel like screaming. But stay calm, so that you're setting a good example for your child. You can say in a friendly voice, 'You may not know the answer, but you do have to take a sensible guess.' Your child may whinge or argue or roll his eyes or complain about how stupid your question is. But just hold your ground. Don't do his thinking for him. Insist that he take a sensible guess, and be willing to wait longer than you would like, without giving a hint or clue. Eventually he'll answer you, and probably his guess will be correct, or almost correct, because it was not really a guess. Children know more than they let on! Find something in his answer to Descriptively Praise. Pretty soon, he'll drift into the habit of answering your questions sensibly.

Q: *My twelve-year-old complains that his life is just rules, rules, rules! I don't want him to grow up resenting me the way I resented my parents. How do I keep him from resenting new rules?*

A: Usually it is not the fact that there are rules that our children really mind; what they find so upsetting is grown-ups getting angry when they forget the rules. And it can feel very confusing and annoying when parents are inconsistent in their *follow-through*. Let's remember that school and sports and extra-curricular activities are full of rules, and our children generally accept those rules and thrive and enjoy themselves in those more consistent environments. Most children behave better outside of the home than they do at home.

The way to help our children feel good about rules is to be generous with our Descriptive Praise. Let's remember to notice and mention whenever they are following the rules. For example:

You remembered the rule about the computer. You finished all your homework and did your chores before you even asked if you could go on it.

You're remembering the rule about putting your napkin in your lap as soon as you sit down.

Such a friendly, respectful voice. You know the rule about being polite.

By being willing to give lots of Descriptive Praise, you can completely transform your child's attitude towards rules. Authority will no longer be seen as something he needs to kick against.

Why think-throughs are so effective

As I touched on earlier, telling our kids what we want them to do and then hoping they'll remember isn't very effective. It's a one-way communication. Since our kids' brains are not engaged, it's often a case of in one ear and out the other. However, with a *think-through*, the child is the one thinking about what he has to do and saying what he has to do, and that has a definite impact on his memory. The way the human brain works is that when we say something, we automatically visualise whatever it is that we are talking about. In fact, that's what we mean by thinking. So when we ask *think-through* questions and our child has to tell us what the right thing to do is, his brain has no choice but to create a vivid mental picture of himself doing whatever it is that he is talking about.

When children visualise exactly what they should do, and

where and when and why and how and with whom, they are far more likely to get into the habit of cooperation. But even so, *think-throughs* are not guaranteed to result in cooperation one hundred percent of the time. Making the rules absolutely clear is not a magic wand that will turn your child into an angel! But *think-throughs* will, over time, help your child's brain to take what you say seriously. *Think-throughs* significantly increase the likelihood of your child doing the right thing. And the more often you ask your child to say what he should be doing right, the easier it will become for him to naturally drift into the habit of doing things right. Without your child even having to make much of an effort to remember, he will splash less, argue less, whinge less and cooperate more.

Think-throughs require children to think for themselves about what they should do, and that makes it easier for them to do the right thing. You can use frequent *think-throughs* all day long to reduce your child's resistance to whatever you are asking of her, regardless of whether the resistance is coming from frustration, from anger, or even from anxiety. For example, to help your child become more responsible about putting things away, here are the kinds of *think-through* questions you could ask at a neutral time:

Tell me exactly what you should do with everything that's in your backpack when we get home from school.

Where should you put your homework when you've finished?

When you've finished your juice, where's the right place to put your cup?

What's the rule? Where do you put your football boots when you take them off?

In many families, mothers are the ones who are most involved in making and reinforcing rules. At school, most teachers are female. This often results in boys assuming that following rules, doing the right thing, being polite, cooperating in school, etc., are what women care about, but men are not really very concerned about those aspects of life. Children are genetically and culturally programmed to take very seriously whatever the same-gender parent does and says. So if you have a boy, make sure whenever possible that the father does many of the *think-throughs* about rules and expectations. Single mothers can recruit male family members or older male friends to share in the *think-throughs*. This will convey to a boy the importance of the mother's rules and values.

PARENTS WANT TO KNOW

Q: *There are some things I want my child to learn to do that I know he finds emotionally difficult, like looking people in the eye and saying 'hello' or asking the waiter for something in a restaurant. Are you saying that think-throughs will work even for real anxieties?*

A: Yes! Each time your child tells you exactly what he has to do and how and when and where and why, his brain is automatically creating a vivid mental image of himself doing just that. The more often he pictures himself doing it, the more comfortable he will become with that mental image, and the less worried he will be when the time comes for him to do it. To help children feel more comfortable with any rule or routine, do *think-throughs* numerous times every day. Out of the blue, completely unrelated to anything else, you could ask:

> *What do you have to do when someone says hello to you?*
> *Where do you have to look when you're answering Miss Walker's question?*

> *If you want another glass of water, what do you have to say to the waiter?*

At first your child may think these questions are odd, but don't be put off by that. *Think-throughs* work! Rehearsals are also very effective for anxieties like these. Act out these scenarios at home frequently, having your son practise eye contact and a big voice. Be sure to give him very specific praise for each tiny improvement.

Here's an example of how one family used *think-throughs*, along with the other Calmer, Easier, Happier Parenting skills, to make car journeys more pleasant.

Wild or noisy behaviour in the car is not only annoying, but it can also be dangerous. One family I worked with had three children, aged eleven, seven and four. When they were in the car together, the children frequently argued, screamed, poked, hit, teased and told on each other. The parents had got to the point where they dreaded going anywhere with their children.

The parents sat down with each child separately for *think-throughs* about the new rules:

'Quiet voices, friendly words, keep your arms and your legs to yourselves.'

They phrased their rules in the positive, rather than talking about what the children should not do. Next, the parents asked each child what he or she should do, and they didn't accept vague answers such as 'I'll be good' or 'I'll talk nicely'. They required each child to think carefully and to answer thoroughly. The parents also asked questions about how the children could solve the sibling problems that would inevitably arise.

The reward for the children following the rules was that the parent would keep driving. The parents asked each child what he or she thought would happen if any of the children forgot the rules. First each child replied with some version of, 'You'll tell us again'. When the parents said that they would not remind, each child then said, 'You'll stop the car'. The seven-year-old, a budding lawyer, said, 'But what about when you're in traffic and you can't stop?' The parents didn't rise to the bait; they just asked a follow-up question, prefaced with Descriptive Praise, 'I'm glad you're thinking about the new rule. What do you think we'll do if we can't pull over?' Their son answered that they would stop the car as soon as they could. He knew the answer to his own question.

The parents suspected that numerous *think-throughs* would be necessary to shift the habit of misbehaving in the car. So for a full week they did one or more *think-throughs* a day with each child. There were a few times when one of the children complained that the *think-throughs* were boring, but the parents stayed calm and determined. They knew that a one-minute *think-through* was not a terrible hardship.

In the past the parents had on numerous occasions threatened to stop the car but had rarely followed through. But now the parents felt more able to be consistent because they had decided together on the rule; it wasn't a threat blurted out in the heat of the moment. And because they were doing the daily *think-throughs*, they were absolutely sure that all the children knew the rule and the consequences.

The parents took advantage of the fact that the misbehaviour didn't usually start immediately. Each time they got in the car they made sure to Descriptively Praise each of the children several times for the absence of misbehaviour within the first five to ten minutes.

Within less than a week car journeys were transformed! The parents remembered to keep up the Descriptive Praise and occasionally did additional *think-throughs* just to reinforce the rules.

PARENTS WANT TO KNOW

Q: *I tried the think-through technique. After the first few think-throughs, my kids started getting annoyed. They don't want to answer. They say, 'I already told you. Why do I have to tell you again?' How do I get them to answer?*

A: What your children may really be finding annoying or uncomfortable about a *think-through* is that the options for misbehaving or for ignoring the rules are being systematically reduced. Your children can see that you are getting back in charge. If they are resistant to answering your questions, you'll need to do *think-throughs* about *think-throughs*! And remember only to do *think-throughs* with one child at a time, not as a group. Again, at a neutral time, you could ask:

> *What do you have to do when Mum or Dad or the teacher asks you a question?*
>
> *Why do you have to answer, even when you don't feel like it?*
>
> *Why do you have to answer the same questions day after day?*

This will lead your children to realise for themselves why they have to answer you, whereas if you explained or lectured they would most likely tune you out. It is important to remember that *think-throughs* are effective regardless of whether your children find them annoying at first. And let's remember that at school children answer questions without a fuss, even when they find the teacher's questions annoying, so they can learn to do the same at home.

Preparing for Success Technique B:
Preparing the environment to make it easier for kids to do the right thing

We've all discovered that there are certain things we can do that make it easier for our children to do what we ask and easier for them to remember the rules and routines. One important way we can Prepare for Success is to put some time, thought and action into preparing our children's environment. Instead of repeating and reminding, we can arrange the physical environment so that temptations to misbehave are significantly reduced. This helps children get into the habit of doing the right thing more and more often. This important strategy is common sense, but we often get so distracted by all the things we have to do in a day that it is easy to forget to prepare the environment.

You have already prepared your family's environment in many ways. When we put a cover over an electrical socket, we are preparing the environment. When we put a hook low enough for a child to hang up her own jacket, or when we bring games along in the car to occupy the children on a long journey, we are preparing the environment. Here are some more ways you can prepare the environment to maximise cooperation and self-reliance. All of the following suggestions have been tried and tested by numerous Calmer, Easier, Happier families:

- To prevent arguments about dressing warmly enough in the winter, remove all summer clothes from the children's cupboards and chests of drawers.
- Before homework time starts, remove all distractions, and make sure your child puts out on the table all the supplies he will need so there's less jumping up to get things.

- At the dinner table, seat siblings at diagonal corners so that they cannot easily poke or kick each other.
- Have labelled bins and uncluttered shelves so that kids have easily accessible places for all their belongings. This makes tidying up easier and less daunting.
- On school mornings, if siblings are in the habit of playing together or possibly squabbling when they should be getting ready, put each child's clothes in a separate room and have them each get dressed there.
- When your child wants to pour her own juice, get a small jug that she can lift more easily than the heavy container the juice comes in.

This technique of preparing the environment requires you to take a moment to reflect on what behaviour is bothering you, and then think about how you can rearrange things to make it easier for your child to do the right thing. But it's so easy to keep doing things the way we've always done them. We forget to think outside the box, as was the case with the family below, whose morning routine needed tweaking.

Preparing the environment helped our five-year-old tie his shoes!

Our younger son is five and has just learned to tie his shoes. His fine-motor skills aren't very well developed, so it takes him several minutes, as well as his full attention, to accomplish it! Our routine used to be that he put his shoes on after breakfast, but that's also when teeth need to be cleaned, hair combed, coats on, etc. It's a busy, noisy time of day and it was difficult for my son to concentrate, especially with his brother there providing additional distraction. All he heard from me was, 'Come on, hurry up. We'll be late for school!' which didn't motivate him at all. The nagging made him go even slower!

So the solution – and it sounds obvious now – was to have him put his shoes on before breakfast, when things are much calmer, so he can really concentrate on this task. And at that time his older brother is in another part of the house, practising the piano. This new plan works brilliantly, and now mornings are cheerful. There's no rushing, and it's much calmer and happier for everyone. It was such a simple solution, but we just hadn't taken the time to think about how we could arrange things to help him to succeed.

Mother of two, aged 6 and 5

Visual reminders

Having a list or chart that you can point to is a highly effective way of preparing the environment to help children remember the rules and routines. Visual reminders can keep you from falling into the trap of repeating yourself.

Mornings tend to be a difficult time of day for families. Parents feel rushed and stressed, trying to get the kids out the door on time, so it's often the time of day parents pick for having a chart. In fact, making mornings less stressful is such a priority that we've devoted an entire chapter to mornings in Section Two 'Transforming Family Flashpoints'.

Lists and charts can be created for homework, bath time, bedtime and even for activities that take place away from home, like birthday parties, church services, etc.

One family I worked with made an after-school chart to help their seven-year-old son get into a better homework routine and to keep the house tidier. Together the parents and the boy came up with the list of tasks, and the boy drew the chart. Here's what was on his chart:

1 Hang bike helmet on door hook.
2 Take out homework from backpack, and hang backpack on door hook.
3 Put homework on dining room table, with supplies (pencils, rubber, paper, etc.).
4 Eat a healthy snack.
5 Play outside for twenty minutes.
6 Sit down and do homework.

The mother liked that she could just point to the chart instead of nagging, and it also gave her a list of things she could Descriptively Praise. If her son forgot anything or got side-tracked, she would just say, 'You've already done one and two on your list, and with no reminders.' Then with a smile, she would silently point to the next task on the list. Sometimes her son seemed to be in his own little world, and she really needed to say something to get him back on track. She remembered to ask, not to tell. She just said, 'What's next on your list?' The chart took the place of reminding, and within several days her son had got into a sensible after-school routine.

Lists and charts work best when you sit down with your kids and decide together what items should be included. The children can contribute their ideas first, and then you can ask leading questions to prompt them to think of any steps they missed. Then give them a role in drawing the chart. This will help them to want to pay attention to the chart.

Make sure that the lists and charts are easy for your children to read and understand:

- Poster size at first
- Big print
- Legible writing
- Fewest words possible and lots of white space

- Pictures for non-readers
- Laminated for away-from-home activities.

Preparing for Success Technique C:
Planning your day realistically so you have enough time

Notice that I said planning your day *realistically*. We all think we can get more done in any given time period than we realistically can, especially when we've got children in tow. Children move at an entirely different tempo from adults. So we have to build in enough time for our children to do the things they need to do at a pace that is comfortable for them, without their feeling hurried and nagged.

In my seminars, I tell parents that there are four things I want them to never again say to their children. Those four things are: 'Come on,' 'Hurry up,' 'Let's go,' 'We'll be late.' This always gets a laugh and a big groan of recognition from the participants. It's easy to say these things automatically, without giving it much thought. But what actually happens when we're rushing our children? Does it make them move any faster? When I ask this question, parents say 'No!'

You may be wondering what else you could possibly say to get your children to move faster! If we want them to be motivated to do what we ask, we have to make sure we are not rushing them. That's because when children feel rushed and chivvied, they try to tune us out because being nagged feels so unpleasant. Sometimes children go even slower and start misbehaving, all because it feels very stressful to them when they are being rushed.

We need to remember that children move at a different speed from us. It is very easy to forget that children are mostly trying to live in the present, thinking about what they are doing right now. This is true of all children, but it is especially true of children who naturally have a trickier temperament. These children often become totally absorbed in their play. They find it extremely difficult to tear themselves away from whatever they are engrossed in to start doing the next thing on the parent's agenda, especially if they are in front of any type of screen.

In addition to the typical morning mayhem, children are often hurried along after school to extra-curricular activities, and then there's a rush to complete homework, have a quick dinner, bathe and get into bed. Being hurried does not bring out the best in our kids. Over-scheduling is not only stressful for them, but it also creates over-scheduled, stressed parents. That makes it harder for us to be our best selves! As our quality of life goes down, we become more easily irritated and more reactive.

To many parents this tight schedule feels inevitable. However, when parents are willing to pause for a moment and carefully examine how the family's time is being spent <u>and why</u>, it often becomes clear that the family isn't really enjoying or benefiting from these hurried days. 'Quality over quantity' is an important priority when thinking about our children's needs and our own needs.

As I mentioned earlier, the time of day that many parents find the most stressful is mornings because of the rushing and repeating and reminding. Since children do not move faster when we try to rush them, we need to do something different if we want to get them out of the door on time, having had a pleasant, relaxed morning. One thing we may have to do, temporarily, is get up earlier than we are used to. It may only have to be ten or twenty minutes earlier, but we need to make sure that children have the time to do what they need to do at a tempo that feels comfortable for them. And we also need to build in some extra time for children to have a bit of a fuss if something isn't going the way they want, and then get over it. This is particularly important if your children are not yet in the habit of doing what you tell them to do the first time you ask, or if they are not yet in the habit of doing for themselves everything that they are capable of doing for themselves, especially getting dressed.

When we allow a bit more time for each activity in the morning, we will feel less stressed and anxious, and that translates into our being less annoyed when things go wrong. And when we are feeling calmer, we can remember to Descriptively Praise every tiny step in the right direction. That will improve behaviour and habits even more. In Section Two, I'll talk more about how to help mornings go as smoothly as possible.

We felt like we'd become morning drill sergeants!

We were always running out of time in the mornings to get our boys, ages seven and five, off to school on time. We were trying not to do things for them that they could do for themselves, like helping them get dressed, because we remembered what Noël had said about how kids develop confidence by doing things for themselves. But there just wasn't enough time, so we were impatient as they dressed themselves, impatient during cello practice, rushing them through breakfast, etc. There was no quality to our time in the mornings – we had become morning drill sergeants!

My wife and I knew we had to do something different so we could get everything done and have a pleasant morning together. Our solution was to get up ten minutes earlier. We also had the boys set their alarm clocks for ten minutes earlier so they had more time to do the things they had to do, such as dressing themselves, making their beds and music practice. Just having those extra ten minutes meant less stress preparing school lunches, less of a rush with

morning music practice and more time for breakfast, cleaning teeth,
putting shoes on and getting out the door.

   Even though we weren't thrilled about having to wake up earlier,
what we gained made it all worthwhile. It transformed our morn-
ings. It was surprising that ten minutes could make such a
difference, but it did.

Father of two, aged 7 and 5

Preparing for Success Technique D: Scheduling frequent Special Time to enhance motivation

You may have heard the saying, 'Children spell love T-I-M-E.'
Every child <u>needs</u> to spend time alone with each parent. This
need is as strong as the need for food or water. And there's a
particular kind of time alone with each parent that children
need. It is quite different from just being in the same room
together, with parent and child each involved in their own
activity. It's also different from taking them out for a treat. The
kind of time with parents that children need and crave is what
I call Special Time.

KEY CONCEPT

Special Time

One parent with one child
Doing something you both enjoy
That doesn't cost money
That's not in front of a screen
Predictable
Daily, if possible
For a minimum of ten minutes

Daily, one-on-one Special Time has been shown to reduce a lot of resistance, negative attention-seeking and minor but exasperating misbehaviour, including whingeing and fussing when things don't go as the child wants. Special Time achieves maximum effectiveness when it is frequent and predictable and labelled as that, so that your child can anticipate it. One-on-one Special Time helps your child <u>want</u> to cooperate. It also awakens in your child the desire to imitate the positive habits and qualities and values of that parent.

Our children know that we love them and that if it came to it we would even die for them. But when we consistently arrange for this Special Time to happen, it shows our children that we not only love them, but that we also <u>like</u> them and want to spend time with them.

Special Time is <u>one</u> parent with <u>one</u> child. Even siblings who usually get on well together need and deserve each parent's undivided attention. And for siblings who may be in the habit of teasing, provoking or annoying each other, this Special Time alone with one parent is bliss. For a short while they can forget about the competition and rivalry. Children are at their best when they can relax, knowing that for a short time they do not need to share (or fight for) your attention.

In an ideal world, it would be nice if we could spend half an hour a day concentrating on each child, doing an activity we both enjoy. For most parents, who lead very busy lives, this would be impossible to manage. And what if there are three or four children in the family? It's unrealistic to expect a parent to carve out more than an extra hour from an already crowded daily schedule. This Special Time alone with each child can often be achieved, with some thought, by rearranging the family schedule. If you can't manage a half-hour each day, start with smaller chunks of time, like ten to fifteen minutes.

You'll usually notice straightaway how this time together strengthens the bond between you and your child. Because your child is getting something he needs, namely your undivided attention, he will become more and more cooperative, with less attention-seeking misbehaviour.

Parents also soon come to enjoy this Special Time and realise that they look forward to it and feel nourished by it. As a result, making the effort to carve out this time becomes less daunting. You will probably find that you want to arrange even more Special Time with each child whenever possible, such as at weekends and holidays. If ten minutes a day with each child is simply impossible, I encourage you to re-examine your daily schedule and think about what you can cut out or rearrange to reduce overwork and stress.

Special Time changed my relationship with my oldest child, eliminating a lot of negative attention-seeking behaviour

My husband was frequently away on business trips, and I was pretty overwhelmed taking care of three young children. My son was five, his sister was three, and we also had a new baby.

My son had started the irritating habit of bumping or swatting me whenever he walked past me in the kitchen. It was happening a lot, and he was getting an irritated reaction from me whenever he did it. I started thinking about which Calmer, Easier, Happier Parenting strategies I could use to help him stop. I realised that although I was spending a lot of time with my kids, I was almost always multi-tasking and wasn't really ever giving them my full attention during the day. I think my son's way of dealing with his resentment about the time I spent taking care of his siblings was to get my attention however he could.

I decided to carve out Special Time with him every day, and I knew that I needed to make the time sacred, as much as possible. I was already staggering the kids' bedtimes by half an hour, so this provided the perfect time slot for Special Time. After I finished reading a bedtime story to my daughter, my son and I would have our Special Time together, playing cards. Within a very short time, the bumping and swatting disappeared altogether.

I remember Noël saying to think of Special Time as food that a child needs, and that when we spend time alone with each one, it shows them that we _like_ them as well as love them. This really resonated with me and helped me to make it a priority. It's been five years now that we've had this predictable Special Time, and I feel really good knowing I'm giving my son what he needs. He's happier, I'm happier, and he doesn't have to get my attention in negative ways any more.

Mother of three, aged 10, 8 and 5

Carving out Special Time can initially feel overwhelming for parents. That's why I recommend starting with ten minutes; this can make it feel more manageable. Staggering bedtimes, as this mother did, can also be a very painless way to carve out that time. What soon happens is that we get hooked on Special Time for three reasons: our child starts cooperating more, doing less of the annoying and attention-seeking behaviour; we feel so much better as parents, knowing we're giving our child what he needs; and it's fun! Here are some other ways you can carve out Special Time.

Involving children in our activities

I often hear parents saying that they feel guilty because they don't want to play Barbies or Transformers or Spiderman, etc.

You don't have to! We assume that we need to play whatever game our child wants to play, but children also love to be involved in grown-up activities. What seems mundane to us, because we have done it hundreds of times, is still new and exciting to our children. So take the time to involve your children in all the ordinary chores and errands that you have to do, rather than thinking that you need to get those tasks out of the way before you can relax and play with the kids.

It's inevitable that involving one of the children in your own tasks will slow you down a bit. But you'll find that it's worth spending the extra time because you're taking care of three important responsibilities at the same time: you're completing the task; you're teaching your child valuable life skills that lead to self-reliance; and you're spending Special Time with your child.

Here are some examples of how parents who have attended the Calmer, Easier, Happier Parenting classes have successfully woven Special Time into their daily tasks:

1 Meal preparation Whenever you're cooking, give one child a job to do. At first make sure it's a short job so that the child doesn't lose interest, and also a very easy job, to boost confidence. To keep your child engaged, and to share your knowledge and skills without having to give lots of off-putting instructions, I recommend that you say aloud all the thoughts that you would ordinarily keep inside your head:

I wonder if we're out of onions. I'd better check.

This needs more liquid. I'll be careful not to put too much in.

I don't have a really big bowl, so I'll have to use two smaller bowls.

The vegetables should be ready by now. Let's test them and see.

Very soon your child will respond with his own comments and by trying to be helpful, handing you an onion or diving into cupboards looking for bowls.

A bonus of involving children in food preparation is that they will be much more willing to try foods that they helped to prepare!

2 Walking the dog This is a perfect opportunity to chat or just to be together in companionable silence. You can make a game out of noticing what you see: houses, shops, public buildings, animals, flowers and trees, etc.

3 Errands Whenever possible, take only <u>one</u> of your children with you on an errand, and then involve your child in the task. Before you leave the house for the shops, make sure your child knows that she will have a role to play, that there is something she will need to search for, choose, carry or ask for.

4 Gardening If you have a garden, or even a window box, involve one child at a time in planting seeds, pulling weeds, deadheading flowers, pruning, taking cuttings. If you have the space, start a little vegetable garden, and involve the children (again, one at a time) in maintaining it. They will become interested in watching their plants grow and also in harvesting vegetables or herbs for meals. And as children help with gardening chores they will start to understand what it takes to maintain a garden and property, and they'll respect their home and surroundings more.

5 Paying bills Most children are fascinated by money. Show them how you budget for and pay bills, and involve them in some part of the process. This will gradually introduce children to the realities of how much money comes into the household, from what sources, and how much money is spent, and on what. This will lead (but not overnight) to a more mature, more responsible attitude and to an appreciation of the family's finite resources and the need to prioritise and budget.

How to make more time for Special Time

Even if you cannot set aside as much time for this as you would wish, you can weave Special Time into your daily routines by utilising little bits of time when you are with your children anyway:

- Sit with your children at mealtimes, and chat with each one for a few minutes in turn.
- Whenever you are with just one child (in the car, on a bus, at the market, walking to school, waiting to collect another child, waiting for an appointment, etc.) use the time to focus on enhancing and deepening your relationship with this child. You can talk about what you see around you, what you have just done and what you are about to do. Show an interest in whatever your child is interested in, and also share your own enthusiasms.
- Take advantage of your younger child's naptime, not just to catch up on the housework but also to play for a few minutes with the older child.
- Stagger your children's bedtimes so that the youngest is put to bed earliest, then the next oldest, etc. I highly recommend this for a couple of reasons:

Being allowed to stay up later than his younger sibling shows the older sibling that there are some perks to being older. That helps make it worthwhile having to be the more sensible and responsible one.

Special Time is easier for the parent to manage when you do not need to keep an eye on the younger child, who is already in bed.

KEY CONCEPT

Special Time reduces negative attention-seeking behaviour.

Tips to make Special Time more effective

- Spend your Special Time together in ways that don't cost money. Otherwise you could easily get sucked into regularly taking children to the cinema, shopping or out for a meal for their Special Time.
- The oldest child will probably always need a bit more Special Time than the other children. This is because from the moment she was born until your second child came along, the eldest was queen of all she surveyed. She had an exclusive relationship with her parents, and she may continue to miss that, even years after the birth of siblings. That is one reason why the eldest is often the most jealous or competitive. The second and third children in the family are born into a world of children and always had to share their parents, and therefore they accept it as natural. So make sure that your eldest gets daily Special Time, even if she acts as if she doesn't want it or doesn't need it.

- Children need Special Time with both parents, but they especially need it with the same-gender parent. For a child, the most important person in her universe is the same-gender parent. This is the person your child assumes she will grow up to be. When the most important person in her world clearly wants to be with her, enjoys spending time with her and makes sure to schedule this Special Time, it does wonders for a child's confidence and self-esteem.

- But this can be a problem for boys, who often spend far more time with their mothers than with their fathers. Here is my heartfelt plea to dads: I strongly urge you, no matter how busy or stressed you are, to set aside even just ten minutes a day for Special Time with your son. If you regularly come home after the children's bedtime, maybe you and your son can wake up a bit earlier and spend ten minutes together in the morning before school. Take advantage of any extra time you have at weekends and holidays to squeeze in more Special Time. If you travel for work, arrange to communicate with each child daily by telephone, texting, emails or good old-fashioned cards.

- If, for whatever reason, a boy cannot have frequent Special Time with his father or step-father, I recommend that the mother arrange for a male role model to step in. This could be a relative, a family friend, a neighbour or even a teacher.

- Frequent, predictable and labelled Special Time benefits everyone in your family:

  o When the most important people in his world are demonstrating an on-going desire to spend time with him, your child's self-confidence, his enthusiasm for life, his willingness to tackle uncomfortable tasks and his motivation to please you will all grow steadily.

  o For both parent and child, Special Time results in a store of pleasant memories. This accumulation of memories

> makes it easier, during any potentially unpleasant confrontation, for you to remember your child's good qualities and for your child to remember your good qualities. Everyone stays calmer.
> - On a purely practical note, Special Time improves behaviour – ours as well as theirs! You'll notice less attention-seeking behaviour, less sibling rivalry and more cooperation.

Preparing for Success Technique E: Getting united on family rules and expectations

Why becoming a United Front is so important, and how to achieve it

Children thrive on consistency. Consistent rules and routines enable your child to feel comfortable because his environment is predictable and therefore emotionally safe. As I mentioned earlier, when rules and routines are consistent, your child will spend less and less time negotiating, arguing and testing.

Sometimes a parent may not want to live within consistent rules and routines because they are as binding on the parents as they are on the child, and it limits our freedom to be spontaneous! But consistency is what our children need. This is especially true of the sensitive, intense or emotionally immature child, whose natural rhythms are often quite inconsistent and unpredictable. He needs our help to get on an even keel and to stay there. The child who is constantly pestering us for an exception is the very child who cannot handle exceptions well. He stores the inconsistencies in his long-term memory and uses them at a later date as ammunition to try and get us to change our minds. He gets hooked on trying to get away with minor and major misbehaviours. Getting united with your partner will help you to become more consistent.

Why becoming united can be so challenging

Even in families where both parents work outside the home full-time, by and large mothers tend to spend more time with the children. Mothers usually do more of the day-to-day disciplining and keeping children on track with the routines of getting them out of the house on time, making sure music practice gets done, making sure they have a bath, etc. Therefore, it is easy for mothers to drift into the practice of declaring rules and handing out consequences unilaterally, without first consulting their partner. This is understandable, but it leads to problems, as I will show.

Agreeing isn't always easy, and here's one reason why. You've probably heard the saying, 'Opposites attract'. After having helped thousands of families become united, my experience is this: 'Opposites attract – at first. And then they annoy!' We are generally attracted to our opposites at first, but then we often find that we have opposite values or opposite approaches to raising children. A woman who is highly organised and detail-oriented might choose a partner who is more laid-back and therefore balances her personality. Then when they have children, the mother might be annoyed that the father is more flexible and spontaneous in his approach to raising the kids, while she is more consistent about adhering to schedules, etc. This can quickly lead to arguments between the parents.

When Dad comes home, he may be somewhat confused about the routines, a bit like an outsider. So he may hesitate to *follow through*, preferring to leave most of it to the mother.

Also, he may be reluctant to be seen as the 'bad guy' during his few precious hours with his children so he may let the children do things that the mother would not allow. The mother, in turn, may feel angry that the father is not 'backing her up'. This situation frustrates both parents and can turn the mother into a witch in the children's eyes and the father into a playmate who does not really need to be listened to. It can even turn the mother into an arbitrary, hysterical female in the eyes of the father. And, as we all know, children are quick to divide and conquer, taking full advantage of confusion, guilt and resentment.

The most basic aspect of a United Front is not arguing in front of the children. It takes two to have an argument so each parent needs to be responsible for not responding negatively if the other parent starts to bicker or complain or criticise. This becomes much easier to do if parents are willing to make the time to regularly sit down and talk through which rules and routines and which rewards and consequences they want to see implemented.

It's very important for you to back each other up. Sometimes parents are reluctant to do this because of the mistaken notion that the child may feel the parents are 'ganging up' on him and will feel intimidated. There is nothing unfair about a United Front! It sends the child a very clear message that both parents agree about the behaviour required and that both parents care enough to actively insist on that behaviour.

Quite often mothers tell me that even when they do make a point of sitting down with their partners and agreeing together on a rule, the husband then promptly forgets and doesn't *follow through*. One reason why this happens is that it was not actually a true discussion. What probably happened was that the father was trying to relax after work, reading the newspaper or watching the news, when the mother plops herself down on the sofa next to him and starts complaining about a problem that she has been dealing with for hours that day. The father is only half-listening because he has not yet really disengaged from whatever he has been doing or thinking about. The mother says what she thinks should be the solution, and the father says some version of, 'Yes dear, OK, that sounds like a good idea.' The mother assumes that this is a mutually agreed upon solution, but we can see that it isn't really. Coming up with solutions together requires the attention of both parents and no distractions. Interestingly, what is not needed is absolute agreement on what the problem is. What is needed is total commitment to finding solutions, even though to do so will probably involve compromise.

A strategy for becoming united

Solution talk

If you're finding the United Front difficult to maintain, set aside fifteen minutes, every day if possible, for what I call a *solution talk*. If one parent is out of town, the *solution talk* can take place over the telephone. During this sacred quarter of an hour, parents choose <u>one</u> area of confusion or conflict within the family, and both parents contribute ideas for possible solutions. To make your *solution talk* really work, it is important to follow these guidelines:

- Spend no more than fifteen minutes on it. Otherwise your focus will tend to drift away from solutions and onto talking about the problems.

- Spend no more than <u>one sentence</u> on describing the problem and then immediately focus on possible solutions. Otherwise, it is very easy to spend the whole of the fifteen minutes chewing over the problem (which usually includes apportioning blame) because we know the problem inside out but we do not yet know the solution.
- Each time you do a *solution talk*, take turns coming up with a problem, and that is what you will both be finding solutions for.
- Within the *solution talk*, alternate coming up with possible solutions, so that one parent doesn't monopolise the conversation while the other remains passive and possibly sceptical and resentful.
- Never criticise the other parent's suggestions.
- Both parents should write down all the possible solutions.
- Both parents need to commit to putting into practice all the possible solutions that are not mutually contradictory.
- Make sure not to do a *solution talk* after nine-thirty at night because a tired parent is an irritable parent.

One couple who were attending a Calmer, Easier, Happier Parenting course recorded this segment of one of their *solution talks*:

Mother: *Let's talk about breakfast.*

Father: *What's the problem? Don't make a problem when there isn't one.*

Mother: *There is. There is a problem. For me, because I'm here. They're too busy watching cartoons to eat properly. Tom takes forever to finish, and then he plays when he should be getting dressed. And Wendy . . .*

Father: *Wait. No more problems! Let's just solve what you said. We can talk about the other stuff tomorrow.*

Mother: *OK. Solutions. Umm . . . Really I know we should keep the TV off while they're eating.*

Father: *Why do they need to watch it at all in the morning? I would be happy if the TV didn't go on at all in the morning. Then you could actually have a conversation.*

Mother: *But, but . . . OK. They'll make a fuss . . . but I guess they'll get used to it.*

Father: *And then they can concentrate on their cereal.*

Mother: *One mum in the class said that now she makes her children get completely dressed before breakfast. Even put their backpacks by the door. And hair brushed.*

Father: *That wouldn't work with Wendy. She's such a slowcoach.*

Mother: *Stay positive!*

Father: (Groans) *OK. Positive. Let's try it.*

Mother: *For how long? Two weeks?*

Father: *Yeah. Two weeks. What if they don't finish eating and it's time to leave?*

Mother: *I'll get them up ten minutes earlier.*

Father: *OK. But let's tell them first. Otherwise it's not fair.*

Mother: *Let's give them a countdown that it'll start on Wednesday. So they have two more days of morning TV. Then no more.*

Father: *Hey, time's up! We stayed positive!*

Single parents do not, of course, have this problem of needing to maintain a United Front. But single parents do need support, and having frequent *solution talks* with a friend is an excellent way to get feedback and support. At a pinch, the friend need not even be a parent. A listening ear and a compassionate presence is often all that is needed to help shift the focus from complaining about problems to seeking and then implementing solutions.

Parents often ask how important it is to have a United Front between separated or divorced parents. Thankfully, children learn very early to compartmentalise. They soon realise that different behaviour is acceptable in different places. School, church, grandparents, friends' homes, dance class, etc. – all these different places have different rules. Children can take this in their stride. Of course, from the point of view of consistency, it would be preferable if parents living in different houses had the same rules and expectations, the same rewards and consequences, the same values. But it is not necessary. What is confusing for children is different expectations in the same location. That is why consistency is so important.

Putting Preparing for Success into practice: Your Action Plan for the first two weeks

As I mentioned earlier, my goal is for you to be able to put the Calmer, Easier, Happier Parenting strategies into practice immediately. Now I will demonstrate how to significantly reduce almost any annoying behaviour by combining the Preparing for Success techniques with Descriptive Praise. Whenever there is a new routine or habit you would like your child to develop, there are a number of crucial questions to ask yourself about the Preparing for Success techniques. Each question refers to a separate technique.

Now let's apply these questions to a new routine or expectation. Choose two behaviours you'd like to improve, then follow these steps. To illustrate how to use these questions, I've picked two annoying habits that parents often complain about:

Example: Children dawdling or making a fuss about getting dressed

1 Preparing for Success

- United Front: 'Do my partner and I agree about what the rule or expectation is?'

Decide, with your partner if you have one, what the rule will be. If you and your partner have trouble agreeing at first, then you will need to compromise. This is not always easy, but it gets easier with practice. Obviously, if you do not have a partner you can skip this question. But it often helps to talk the issue over with someone else anyway.

In this example, the rule could be: Before you go to bed, you have to lay out your clothes for the next day. And that's what you have to put on in the morning.

- Clear rules and expectations: 'Have I explicitly told my child what the rule is?'

Make sure that your child knows and understands the rule or routine; don't assume he knows it, even if it seems obvious to you. Remember, you can use the four magic words, 'The new rule is . . .' Then ask him to tell you the new rule.

You can skip this step if you are firming up an old rule, rather than introducing a new rule.

- 'Are we doing some think-throughs about this every day, asking several "W" questions (see page 83) about this rule and having the child answer in her own words?'

Here are some possible *think-through* questions that your child might answer:

Who puts out your clothes for school?

When do you have to choose your clothes for school?

What do you have to do before we read bedtime stories?

Why do you have to wear what you chose the night before, instead of changing your mind?

Your child needs to explain what the rule is and answer the questions <u>to your satisfaction</u>. At first he may give you an answer that is almost, but not quite, right. Clarify the rule if necessary, and then ask him again. Or your child may reply in an unfriendly tone of voice. If so, he needs to say it again in a respectful voice. When he does, remember to Descriptively Praise: 'That's exactly right. You remembered the rule, and you said it politely.'

- Preparing the environment: 'How can I make it easier for my child to follow the rule?'

For example, school clothes can be kept on low shelves or on a low rod so that your child can easily reach them. You can make sure that only seasonally appropriate clothes are available. If your child is overwhelmed when given lots of choices, limit his choices to two, either of which will be acceptable to you.

Visual reminders: 'How can I avoid repeating myself day after day?'

A chart for the bedtime routine can reduce stress and nagging. Another type of visual reminder is simply pointing at the chest of drawers or the clothes cupboard. The less we say, the more our children will listen when we do give an instruction.

- Plan realistically: 'Am I leaving enough time in the bedtime routine for laying out clothes?'

- Special Time: 'Are we spending frequent, predictable one-on-one time with each child?'

Over time, this will reduce your child's urge to misbehave to get your attention. Children become much less resistant to doing what we ask when they are getting regular time alone with each parent.

2 Descriptive Praise

- And now for Descriptive Praise: 'Am I noticing and mentioning every time my child remembers the rule or takes even a small step in the right direction?'

We need to reinforce positive behaviour, but sometimes this part is the hardest to remember. It's easy to take good behaviour for granted.

You've already laid out your socks and your shoes. And I only asked you once.

You didn't ask for a story yet. You're remembering there's one more thing you need to do.

You've got everything laid out that you'll need for school tomorrow. Very responsible!

Example: Whingeing

I used the example of whingeing in the Descriptive Praise chapter, but now let's add the Preparing for Success strategies to help reduce this annoying behaviour even more quickly!

1 Preparing for Success

- United Front: 'Do my partner and I agree on what the rule or expectation is?'

In this example, the new rule that is being introduced is: As long as you're talking to me in a respectful (or polite or friendly) voice, I'll answer you.

- Clear rules and expectations: 'Have I explicitly told my child what the rule is?'

- 'Are we doing some think-throughs about this every day, asking several "W" questions (see page 83) about this rule and having the child answer in his own words?'

Here are some possible *think-through* questions for your child to answer:

When you want to ask me a question, what kind of voice should you use?

Why do you have to use a respectful voice?

What will I do when you speak to me politely?

Who decides whether your voice is respectful enough?

When your child answers correctly, remember to Descriptively Praise: 'Yes, you remembered. I'll only answer when you speak to me in a friendly voice.'

- Preparing the environment: 'Am I making it easy for my child to do the right thing?'

For example, stocking up on healthy snacks and getting rid of sugary snacks will eliminate a lot of whingeing.

> **Visual reminders: 'Have I thought of a way to remind my child without repeating myself?'**
>
> This could be a chart, a sign or even a simple gesture; all these are friendlier and less emotionally charged than a verbal reminder.

- Plan realistically: 'Have I made sure that my child is not too hungry or too tired? Have I made sure that my child is getting plenty of exercise and fresh air?'

These factors make a big difference with whingeing.

- Special Time: 'Am I spending frequent, predictable one-on-one time with each child?'

Children whinge less when they have regular one-on-one time with each parent.

2 Descriptive Praise

- 'Am I noticing and mentioning every time my child remembers the rule or takes any steps in the right direction?'

What a polite, friendly voice! Now I want to listen to you.

You started to whinge, but then you remembered the rule and you stopped.

For the past half an hour, I haven't heard any whingeing, only a respectful, quiet voice!

PARENTS WANT TO KNOW

Q: *My son, who's ten, likes to annoy me on purpose, so he some-times gives me silly answers when I start doing think-throughs. How can I get him to take me seriously?*

A: Some children do like to wind their parents up and even become hooked on negative attention. Or the silliness may simply be the way your child is used to getting noticed in the family. If your son tries to make a joke out of the *think-through*, just smile calmly and say, 'You've got a good sense of humour. Now answer me properly.' If he repeats the silliness, just say, 'I can see you're not ready to answer sensibly. I'll ask you later,' and walk away. Pretty soon he'll come to you wanting something. At that point you can say something like, 'I'll be glad to talk with you about that, after you answer my questions properly.' It won't be long before your son sees that you are in charge, and he will respect you more and more. Remember that our children need and crave our positive attention. If you do not rise to the bait by getting annoyed, your children will soon see that it is easier to get your positive attention by doing the right thing than to get your negative atten-tion by doing the wrong thing.

Summary

When you Prepare for Success you are planning ahead, think-ing about what might happen based on your experience of what has happened in the past. You can then avoid potential problems by putting things in place that will make it easier for your children to do the right thing.

- Become a United Front with your partner, if you have one, so you agree on the rules and routines you want your kids to follow.
- Use *think-throughs* to clarify and reinforce rules and appropriate behaviour. Do the *think-throughs* throughout the day at neutral times, <u>before</u> any misbehaviour occurs. Make sure your child does the talking and that each *think-through* lasts only sixty seconds.
- Prepare the environment to make it easier for your child to do the right thing.
- Plan your day realistically to allow yourself and your children more time do things right and so it doesn't feel so stressful when things go wrong.
- Make time for Special Time as it vastly reduces negative attention-seeking and sibling rivalry.

The aim of all the Preparing for Success strategies is to make it easier and easier for our children to do the right thing and behave well more and more of the time. All of these techniques help children to become more cooperative, confident, motivated, self-reliant and considerate. As a result, we will have so much more to Descriptively Praise! Our children will be calmer, easier and happier, and so will we.

CHAPTER 5

REFLECTIVE LISTENING: HOW TO MINIMISE WHINGEING AND MISBEHAVIOUR BY DEFUSING FRUSTRATION, ANGER AND ANXIETY

Lecturing, reasoning and threatening just didn't work

When my son was six years old, he was on a football team. He had expected to be put on a team with all his friends, but unfortunately there was no space left on that team. The day came when his team had to play against the team with his friends on it. I thought it would be fun for him to be playing on the field with all his friends, but after about a minute of playing, my son came off the field looking sad, saying he didn't want to play.

First I tried encouraging him to get back on the field. When this didn't work, I tried lecturing him about how important it was to be part of a team. And then when that didn't convince him, I moved on to threatening him with no snack if he didn't go back and play. Nothing was working.

I realised that I wasn't making things any better, so I thought I'd try Reflective Listening. I didn't know exactly how to start so I said, 'It seems like you're not feeling too well.' He said, 'No, I'm fine.' So I tried again with, 'Maybe you're worried that you won't be as good as the other players.' He shook his head. I had him on my lap, and I was talking to him in a friendly way, rather than getting annoyed.

Then he opened up and tearfully explained that his friends were teasing him, saying he was on a loser team and that his team was 'going down', and he didn't want to play against them. I tried to listen to how he felt and said, 'It hurts your feelings when you're

teased, even though your friends think they're just having a bit of
fun.' He said, 'Yes'.

He seemed relieved that I understood, and he was then able to
get over being upset much more quickly than would have normally
happened. I felt better, too, because I knew I had really helped him.

Mother of two, aged 8 and 6

Now that you've been putting the first two Calmer, Easier, Happier Parenting strategies into practice, chances are that your children are starting to respond differently and their behaviour is improving. I'm not talking about perfect behaviour, of course, but much improved behaviour. Family life is steadily becoming calmer, easier and happier. That's because with Descriptive Praise you have a more effective way to motivate your children to want to behave well. And you have learned several Preparing for Success techniques that make it easier for your children to do things right, preventing a lot of misbehaviour. These two skills are inextricably linked: the more your kids are doing the right thing, the more you will find to Descriptively Praise!

As effective as these first two strategies are at reducing a lot of misbehaviour, parents still want to know what to do when things do go wrong. Your mind has probably been leaping ahead to, 'But what about when he's throwing a tantrum?' or 'What about when she stomps off and slams the door while I'm trying to talk to her?' or 'What about when he kicks his brother?' Don't despair. This is where our next powerful strategy comes in. And at the end of this chapter, we'll show you how to use all three skills together to solve most problems that are likely to come your way.

Reflective Listening, the third core strategy

When our children are feeling bad, they often behave badly. They may be reluctant to cooperate, or they may refuse altogether, like the boy in the story above. Our most natural reaction when children misbehave is to do exactly what this mother did. She lectured, explaining all the reasons why he should go back on the field, and then she started threatening.

It helps to remember that a lot of misbehaviour stems from a strong emotion your child is feeling. He doesn't know any other way to communicate how angry or disappointed or worried he is. But when kids are misbehaving, it's not surprising that it doesn't bring out the best in us! However, we can do what the mother in the story did. She took a moment to guess why her son was misbehaving. She saw that her son wasn't being deliberately uncooperative; he just didn't know what else to do with his intense feelings. When you learn about the third core strategy, Reflective Listening, you will have a way to help your children feel better and therefore feel like behaving better.

What is Reflective Listening?

Reflective Listening, or empathic listening as it is sometimes called, is an invaluable strategy for our parenting toolkit. It helps children (and adults too, for that matter) move through their uncomfortable feelings more quickly and easily, towards acceptance or towards problem-solving. Reflective Listening is a particular way of responding whenever we can see or hear or maybe even just sense that our child is upset or is experiencing an uncomfortable emotion. For some children, especially those born with a naturally more sensitive, intense or inflexible temperament, these upset feelings may erupt many times every day.

Reflective Listening helps defuse your child's upsets.

When do you Reflectively Listen to your child?

Now here's the challenge. The skills I've shared so far are quite straightforward – easy to understand and simple enough to use right away. As I explain Reflective Listening, you will see that it makes sense and may even seem simple, but what is challenging is knowing <u>when</u> you have to use it.

We need to use it when our kids are having a strong, uncomfortable feeling. But often kids can't articulate what they're feeling, so their big emotions may come out as misbehaviour – refusing, tantrums, hitting, whingeing. And we tend to react to our child's misbehaviour, instead of realising that we also need to address the feeling that is fuelling the misbehaviour. For example, if one of your children kicks the other, how do you normally react? You're likely to jump in and say, 'Stop kicking your brother right now! Go to your room!' Sound familiar? Or maybe your daughter is having a tantrum and screaming, 'I hate you!' Parents will often react by reasoning, telling off, shouting back or threatening a consequence. This is a completely understandable reaction, but unfortunately it won't really help the child. That's because our job at that moment isn't just dealing with the misbehaviour; we also want to help the child deal more constructively with whatever strong feelings triggered the outburst. When you learn Reflective Listening, which is a specific way to acknowledge your child's feelings more constructively, the misbehaviour and the tantrums usually clear up quite quickly.

The latest brain research can help us make sense of this. When our kids are in the throes of a big emotion, their 'emotional' right brain has taken over. We usually respond to their emotional outbursts with logic and reason, which are left brain characteristics. The bottom line is that these opposite sides of the brain can't work together in that moment. Children can't respond to left brain logic when they're in the grip of right brain emotions. However, when you learn a specific way to acknowledge the emotions, the two sides of the brain can work together. This often reduces the misbehaviour sooner than you might imagine.

Why we need to Reflectively Listen to our children

Knowing how to help our children deal with their emotions constructively is important, both for their sakes and also for our own sakes. Because we love our children, it is easy for us to become upset when they are upset. We want to help them to feel better as soon as possible, partly so that we can feel better. And the sooner our children feel better – less angry or frustrated or jealous or annoyed – the easier it will be for them to cooperate and behave better.

You may be thinking that you already know how to listen to your child. But Reflective Listening is more than being a sympathetic ear. It's about learning a specific way to respond to what you're hearing or seeing. It's about taking the time and making the effort to try to understand what your child is feeling at that moment, and then reflecting back to him in words what you imagine he is feeling.

What are the benefits of Reflective Listening?

Reflective Listening shows that we care about a child's feelings.

Of course, parents care about their children's feelings, but Reflective Listening actually <u>shows</u> that we care. You might assume that children already know this. But when we look at how we often respond to our children when they're upset, it's easy to see why our children might not believe that we do really care. Let's say your son comes home and says, 'The teacher's always picking on me.' You might respond with, 'Well, what were you doing wrong?' Or if your daughter says, 'Nobody likes me,' you might be tempted to reply, 'Don't be silly. Look how many people came to your birthday party.'

We are so anxious to help our children feel better that we can easily fall into the trap of dismissing and minimising their very real feelings. When we deny what our child is feeling or when we try to reason or argue him out of his feelings, we inadvertently give him an extra problem. His first problem is whatever he is upset about, and his second problem is that he is getting the impression from our response that he shouldn't be feeling that way. None of this helps him to move beyond his upset or to think constructively about solutions. Reflective Listening focuses on helping to change your child's mood, not on trying to change his mind.

Reflective Listening helps our children to feel heard and understood.

This is important because a lot of misbehaviour and negative attention-seeking occur when children are trying to make us see how awful they are feeling. They are trying to show us that they are really upset about something. If we respond in the usual way (with reasoning, lecturing, telling off, etc.) children get even more frustrated because it looks like we're not taking their feelings seriously. Reflective Listening demonstrates that we are trying to understand how upset they are feeling. When children feel understood, they experience a huge relief. This reassuring feeling can often defuse uncomfortable emotions and de-escalate potentially explosive situations. Only at that point can they start thinking constructively about how to solve a problem or how to improve a situation.

Reflective Listening helps our children, over time, to learn a vocabulary for expressing feelings.
As I have mentioned, children are often inarticulate about their feelings. Have you ever told an upset child, 'Use your words'? It's something a lot of parenting books recommend, but here's the problem with that advice. Often children don't know what words to use! So they tend to let parents know that they feel bad, not by talking coherently about the problem, but by whingeing or blaming or misbehaving. Reflective Listening changes that. Over time, Reflective Listening teaches children a rich and varied vocabulary for expressing their emotions. This helps children to recognise and understand their feelings (this is often known nowadays as emotional literacy or emotional intelligence). Children gradually become able to express their feelings in words, rather than by playing up. For a number of reasons, this usually happens sooner with girls and later with boys. Some of these reasons are cultural; some may be developmental. But both boys and girls can learn to understand their feelings and learn to express them more maturely.

When parents are willing to use this technique consistently, it always results (but again, not overnight) in better behaviour, more mature social skills and stronger motivation, as well as more confidence and cooperation. Listening in this way gives children the time they need to process their emotions, to feel them fully and then come out on the other side, calmer and saner. There are two common sayings that capture this process: 'Better out than in,' and 'The only way out is through.'

Entire books have been written about Reflective Listening because it produces almost magical results. What I will be doing here is breaking down how to Reflectively Listen into four simple steps to make it easier for you to start using this skill right away.

KEY CONCEPT

'Use your words'

Telling our kids to 'use their words' doesn't work. Kids don't know what words to use!

How to Reflectively Listen

I hope by now you're on the edge of your seat, quite keen to learn this new technique! First I'm going to give you a brief overview of the Reflective Listening steps, and then I'll expand on each step. The examples and the stories from parents will clarify this strategy so you can start using it straight away!

The Four Steps of Reflective Listening

Step One: Put your own emotions and wishes to one side
temporarily.

Step Two: Stop whatever you're doing, look at your child and
listen.

Step Three: Imagine what your child is feeling, and reflect that
back to your child in words.

Step Four: Give your child his wishes in fantasy *(optional).*

Step One: Put your own emotions and wishes to one side temporarily

As with so many things, the first step is actually the hardest! As I explained earlier, when we are trying to deal with a
child who is upset, we may be getting upset ourselves. We
may find ourselves feeling angry if they are behaving defiantly, or we might be feeling anxious or guilty because we
wish they weren't feeling so bad. It is completely understandable that our children's feelings and misbehaviour
often trigger a strong emotional reaction in parents. The
problem here is that our strong feelings can easily cloud
our thinking and lead us to react impulsively, rather than
taking the time to use each interaction to help our children
develop good habits.

So before we do or say anything, we need to make the effort
to calm ourselves down. For many parents, just having a tool
that they have found to be effective, like Reflective Listening,
helps them to stay calm. That's because it's when we feel stuck
and have no idea how to respond, other than reasoning, lecturing or shouting, that we feel stressed or even out of control.

Here's a way that has helped a lot of parents to stay calmer and more positive: visualise yourself scooping up your anger or worry or disappointment with both hands and placing that uncomfortable emotion at the side of the room. Picturing this can clear your mind. And your feeling will still be there, waiting for you, if you want it back later!

As silly as this strategy might sound, it has proved to be very effective at helping parents to stay calm in very trying circumstances. For example, if your child is crying and whingeing about long multiplication and complaining that he is stupid and that he will never be able to do it, this can feel like an arrow piercing a parent's heart. You naturally want to take this awful feeling away from your child as quickly as possible. But as you have probably discovered, it is just not possible to argue a child out of his feelings or to reason a child out of his feelings. So first you need to calm yourself down so that you can think clearly. Reacting will not help. You need to have a clear head.

Step Two: Stop whatever you're doing, look at your child, and listen

I know that this is easier said than done in a busy household. There seem to be so many demands on our time. But helping our children learn to deal with their feelings is a very important life skill, and we need to give it a high priority. And from a purely practical standpoint, taking the time to Reflectively Listen is a sensible investment because the sooner your children learn to deal with their uncomfortable feelings more constructively, the less fuss and misbehaviour you will be dealing with! You'll soon have more energy and time for getting things done and for having fun with your kids.

Sometimes our children are open with us about their feelings so it's relatively easy to listen. But it's also easy to get distracted. We need to look at the child and to show that we are listening. It helps to make 'listening noises', words and phrases such as, 'Hmmm ... Oh ... Really ... Goodness'. These responses make it easier for children to register that we are listening and that we really care how they are feeling. This will help them, over time, to open up more and more.

But what if your child isn't saying a word? That's when we need to 'listen' to her body language or facial expression or posture or gestures. Usually, you can instantly tell that something is bothering your child when you hear your daughter's surly or disrespectful tone of voice or when you notice that your son doesn't want to look you in the eye. You can tell from the scowl on your child's face or her slumped over, dejected posture that she is feeling bad, even though you may not have any idea what event may have triggered it. All these are cues for us to stop what we are doing and Reflectively Listen.

Step Three: Imagine what your child is feeling, and reflect that back to him in words

Children may say or do one thing, but mean something else. For example, 'I hate fractions,' usually means, 'I don't remember how to do these sums, and they look too hard.' Refusing to put toys away often means, 'I'm having such a good time that I don't want to stop.' Crying and whingeing and complaining might be how a child has learned to get your attention. Grabbing and shoving and hitting may be the only way a child knows how to get what he wants. It is all too easy to misread the code and assume that a child who is complaining or misbehaving is just doing it to annoy you. But a lot of inappropriate behaviour is caused by children not knowing, in the moment, how else to express their uncomfortable feelings of frustration, embarrassment, anger, worry, etc.

Ask yourself what feeling might be driving your child to do what he's doing or to say what he's saying. Just take an educated guess about what might be going on inside him, below the level of his words or actions. Then, rather than trying to change his thoughts with logic or reassurance or a mini-lecture, you simply reflect back to your child what you imagine he is feeling. The name of this skill, Reflective Listening, comes from this step.

Your guess about what the child is feeling may turn out to be accurate, or it may be wide of the mark. That's because, no matter how well we know our children, we can't read their minds. Fortunately, whether you guess correctly or not isn't the important thing. Even if your guess is wrong, your child will still feel respected and listened to. He will be learning that words are useful to describe feelings, and he will be learning which words go with which feelings. Even if you are perplexed about what your child is feeling or why, you can still take a guess.

It's useful to Reflectively Listen whenever you are tempted to repeat or remind. Here are several examples:

- Once you have told your child to put her toys away, instead of saying it again when she seems to be ignoring you, you could say, 'You really don't want to stop. You're having such a good time.' You'll find that Reflective Listening is far more effective than repeating or reminding or threatening. There is of course no guarantee that your child will immediately start putting her toys away, but she is more likely to do it sooner if you Reflectively Listen than if you repeat yourself or get annoyed.

- When a child is complaining that he can't do his homework, instead of saying, 'You can do it. It's really not hard,' you could say, 'You might be thinking this looks too hard. You don't want to get it wrong.'

- If you are at a birthday party and your child is hanging around you rather than running off to play, instead of saying, 'Don't keep standing here next to me. Go and play,' you could say, 'Maybe you're not sure if those children want to play with you.'

- If your child is getting more and more frustrated because he can't do something he's trying to do, instead of saying, 'Don't worry about it, dear,' you could say, 'It looks like you're feeling really frustrated. You tried so many times, and it's still not working.'

Tips for success in Step Three

- Resist the temptation to reassure, reason, justify or lecture. Instead, just imagine what your child might be feeling at that moment.

- Don't repeat back exactly what your child has said. Reflective Listening is not about repeating back to the child what she has just said to you. For example, if your daughter shouts, 'You're the meanest mummy in the whole world,' nothing is gained by saying, 'You think I'm the meanest mummy.' That is not what she really believes; this is simply the sort of thing children learn to say when they're angry and want to get a reaction from us. A Reflective Listening response might be, 'It sounds like you're furious because I won't let you wear your party dress to school.'

- Be tentative. We can never know for sure what someone else is feeling or thinking. Therefore we need to be quite tentative with most of our Reflective Listening in order for it to be effective. If we say, 'I know you feel sad' it comes across as more bossy than empathic! And that can feel so annoying that the child just clams up. Instead, we can say:

Maybe you're worried you won't get chosen for the team.

It probably felt uncomfortable on your first day of karate when you didn't know anybody.

- Avoid the 'but'. It's tempting to follow your Reflective Listening with a 'but', for example, 'You probably wish you didn't have to walk the dog, but you know it's your job.' When you add that 'but' it dilutes the effectiveness of your Reflective Listening sentence. As natural as it is to want to add 'but', it's unnecessary. Your child already knows he has to do it.
- Don't insist. With Reflective Listening, sometimes your child won't want to admit to a particular emotion, even though you are sure that is what she is feeling. Don't insist. It is fine if your child doesn't agree with you because the purpose of Reflective Listening is not to extract a confession. The purpose is to help children feel heard and understood and accepted. Reflective Listening also helps our children, over time, to feel comfortable with a wide range of human emotions and to help them feel comfortable using words, instead of actions, to communicate their emotions.

- Feeling words. Here is a short list of words that describe some uncomfortable feelings that your child may be experiencing on a fairly regular basis:

  afraid

  angry

  annoyed

  anxious

  ashamed

  confused

  disappointed

  envious

  frustrated

  jealous

  left out

  lonely

  misunderstood

  nervous

  sad

  sorry

  unconfident

  unsure

  upset

  worried

- Avoid using the words 'unfair' and 'hate'. Most children sooner or later pick up the word 'unfair' from their class-mates, and they use it indiscriminately, without really understanding what it means. When children use the word 'unfair', it usually just means they don't like something. So let's not use the word 'unfair' when we're Reflectively Listening, for example, 'It feels unfair to you,' even if the child uses that word. Instead, take the time to imagine and reflect back the feeling below the words.

There is another important reason why I ask parents not to reinforce a child's belief that things are unfair. As we all know, unfortunately there is a lot of very real unfairness and injustice in the world. Many children are living with poverty, hunger, sub-standard housing and even, sadly, disease or abuse. But most children whose parents are reading this book are not experiencing real unfairness. In fact, our children are amongst the most fortunate children on this planet. They have adequate food, clothing and shelter, plenty of affection and many opportunities. We can help our children develop a more balanced and realistic view of their lives by not talking about 'unfair'. But don't bother explaining to your children how lucky they are. It will just sound like a lecture or a telling off, and they are likely to tune you out.

I also recommend that parents not use the word 'hate', even though your child may. Reflective Listening is about helping children learn how to express their feelings, but 'hate' is often more a judgement than a feeling. And 'hate' seems more permanent, while feelings are very transitory. I am not suggesting that we correct children when they say 'hate' or that we try to ban the word, simply that in our Reflective Listening we rephrase it into an emotion, such as anger.

The more often you remember to use feeling words to defuse your children's upsets, the more familiar they will become with their own emotions, and the easier it will become for them to accept, and then let go of and move past, their uncomfortable feelings.

PARENT PRACTICE
IMAGINING WHAT A CHILD IS FEELING

More examples of Reflective Listening:

It's hard to leave the park when you're having such a great time.

It sounds like you're really disappointed that you didn't get a better score on that quiz.

You're probably feeling so angry that your little sister broke that toy.

Step Four: Give your child his wishes in fantasy (optional)

This last step is an extremely valuable strategy. It shows children that we are on their side. For example, if your child is hunched over his homework looking mutinous, you could say, 'Wouldn't you love a magic wand that you could wave over your homework, and it would correct all your spelling mistakes?' Obviously your child knows that this magic wand doesn't exist, but responding in this way injects a welcome note of humour and lightness into the situation.

PARENT PRACTICE
WISHES IN FANTASY

More examples of Reflective Listening:

Maybe you wish you could have all the video games that Miles has.

Wouldn't it be great if you could wave a magic wand that took away the taste of the peas?

Imagine if you had a robot that made your bed for you every morning!

I remember back when my son was eight, and I had to deal with his upset, angry feelings about not being allowed to eat, in one sitting, all the Halloween sweets he had collected. With a sympathetic expression and a friendly voice, I said, 'Wouldn't it be great if broccoli was bad for you and sweets were good for you?' I watched his angry face soften, and then he said, 'Yeah, and M&M's would have a lot of calcium!' Giving our children their wishes in fantasy shows that we don't only care about their behaviour. We also care about their feelings.

You may be wondering why we list this step as optional. That's because although it can make your Reflective Listening even more effective, it's not absolutely essential. But I do encourage you to use it often because you will see results!

He just needed to feel understood

When my son was three years old and was in the middle of toilet-training, bathrooms became a source of fascination for him!

We were at the park one morning, and he kept darting off towards the public rest rooms, trying to open the rest room door. I stopped him each time, telling him he couldn't go in because they weren't clean enough for him to use. He whinged and cried and kept running to the rest rooms.

I could see that reasoning with him just wasn't working. So I tried to think about what he was feeling. I said, 'You're so curious about that bathroom, and you really wish you could go inside and go potty. Why do you think Mummy said you can't go in?' He was quiet for a few seconds and then said, 'It's dirty.' I praised him and said, 'That's exactly right. You remembered what Mummy said.' Then I Reflectively Listened some more, 'You wish the bathroom were clean and you could go in.'

He stopped whingeing, his face cleared up, and he ran back to the playground. I couldn't believe how well it worked. He just needed to feel understood.

Mother of two, aged 6 and 3

Now let's think about what might have happened if this mother hadn't remembered to Reflectively Listen to her son. Probably she would have needed to carry her son away from the rest rooms, screaming, quite a few times. She probably would have continued to repeat herself as she kept re-explaining why he couldn't go in. Eventually she might have threatened to leave the park. It could have turned into a very unpleasant outing. Instead, she thought about what he might be feeling and took a guess. She gave him his wish in fantasy, and he ran back to play. This type of successful outcome happens most of the time when parents start using this skill!

At this point, you may have a number of questions. Here are some of the typical questions parents ask about Reflective Listening.

PARENTS WANT TO KNOW

Q: *This seems like a lot of steps. Why can't I just ask my child what's the matter?*

A: Most children have a hard time putting into words what they are upset or annoyed or worried about. Children do not usually know how to explain the complex mixture of emotions that are swirling around inside them. So when we ask, 'What's the matter?' they often respond with, 'Nothing' or 'I don't know.' Reflective Listening, over time, is more likely to help children understand what they're feeling and be willing to express their feelings in words.

Q: *If I Reflectively Listen when my daughter is misbehaving, won't she act up even more to get more of my attention?*

A: If your child were to get attention for the misbehaviour itself, then she probably would continue to misbehave. And in fact, that is exactly what is happening when we tell children off. In Chapter 7, I talk about how to deal with misbehaviour in a more effective way.

But the reaction you're concerned about doesn't happen with Reflective Listening because this strategy gets to the heart of the strong feelings that are fuelling the misbehaviour, so your child feels better and starts behaving better. To make sure that your daughter is getting the positive attention she needs and craves, remember to Descriptively Praise her many times a day, and arrange to have Special Time with her every day, even if it's only for ten or fifteen minutes.

Q: *At what age can I start Reflectively Listening to my children?*

A: Even before children understand language, they respond very well to the calm, empathetic tone of Reflective Listening. Although this book is focusing on children aged from three to thirteen, this skill is certainly effective with even younger children. Toddlers, just like older children, do not respond well to repeating and reminding, which we tend to say in an increasingly impatient tone of voice. Even by the age of eighteen months, most toddlers will probably understand language well enough to grasp the gist of what we are saying when we Reflectively Listen.

Small children have very strong emotions, and usually the only way they know how to express them is by crying, whingeing, throwing things and hitting. Recently a mother told me about her eighteen-month-old son, who was looking very distressed and was starting to whimper louder and louder because he desperately wanted to play with a toy train that his older brother was playing with. The mother very wisely stayed out of the potential conflict. She just said to the toddler, 'Your brother is playing with that train, and you really wish that you could be playing with it right now.' The mother was surprised and delighted to see that her toddler's face cleared, he nodded, and then he walked away and started playing with something else. What was even more important to the little boy than playing with the train was that his mother understood what he was feeling.

Q: *How can I get my son to talk about his day at school? I rarely get more than monosyllables. Sometimes I can tell from his face when I collect him that something is upsetting him. But when I ask him what happened, he just says, 'Nothing,' or he shrugs his shoulders. Can Reflective Listening help him to open up?*

A: The answer to this question is yes and no. Of course parents are interested in what happens at school each day. Unfortunately, asking questions is usually <u>the least effective</u> way of finding out. Asking questions often makes otherwise very chatty children suddenly go silent.

First, let's accept that sometimes our children don't want to talk about their day. For one thing, so much happens over the course of a single day at school that it may take a number of hours to process all the events of the day before they are ready to communicate. And the social interactions in the playground can be complex and confusing, hard to articulate. Sometimes children don't want to answer because the questioning makes them feel anxious, as if they have to come up with the right answer.

Reflectively Listen to whatever your child says about his day, and if he doesn't say anything, you can even Reflectively Listen to his body language. But discipline yourself not to ask.

Instead of quizzing your child, make a point of sharing something about your own day, including how you felt. Make sure to mention more good things than not-good things so that growing up to become an adult seems like an attractive proposition!

One father told me that most mornings, while he is doing his exercises, his son comes in to keep him company, and that is when the boy talks about what happened the day before. This father has learned not to probe, just to wait, and then to show lots of interest in whatever his son wants to tell him – at his son's own pace.

I know this may be hard to believe, but you will find out more, and you will find out sooner, by not asking. If you don't rush your child, if you wait and give him time, he will begin to feel more comfortable and more confident and more willing to share his thoughts and feelings.

Q: *I'm worried that when my kids are feeling upset about something, Reflective Listening will be like rubbing salt in the wound. Won't Reflective Listening make them feel worse?*

A: The empathy of someone who cares about us can sometimes bring to the surface painful feelings that were buried just below the level of our conscious awareness. When those feelings rise up, it might seem as if the Reflective Listening is what caused the upset. But in reality the Reflective Listening just released the upset and allowed it to come to the surface. This is a good thing, even if it is painful temporarily. These feelings are better out than in.

Q: *When my children are upset, my natural inclination is to reassure them that everything will be OK. Why won't this work?'*

A. It is completely natural to want to help our children feel better as soon as possible. As parents, we often fall into the habit of trying to fix our children's problems or trying to convince them that they don't really have a problem. Unfortunately, reassuring children rarely helps them feel better.

Paradoxically, reassuring children can give them the impression that something has gone wrong that they need to be reassured about. When we try and reassure our child out of her upset, she can come to the conclusion that this situation (whatever it is she is upset about) must indeed be terrible, and that we think the pain of it is too great for her to bear. That is the very opposite of what we want our children to learn. We want our children to develop emotional resilience and stamina so that they can bounce back from life's inevitable and frequent upsets, rather than being discouraged and thrown off course by them.

When we attempt to reassure, we often unintentionally give children the impression that their upset should not be happening, that life should always be easy and fun, that there should be no problems, no mistakes, failures or upsets. Children may start to assume that if they are upset, something isn't right. This view of life sets children up for even more upsets because all of us, every day, experience setbacks, frustrations and disappointments, whether large or small.

And lastly, reassuring rarely reassures! In fact, sometimes reassurance drives children to make an even bigger fuss in an attempt to get their feelings heard. Generally, children appreciate the honesty of Reflective Listening. This new way of responding helps children to trust parents.

Reflective Listening makes establishing new rules and routines easier

As you begin using the Calmer, Easier, Happier Parenting strategies, you will probably realise that in order to Prepare for Success, you will have to make a number of new rules. Or you may need to reinstate some old rules that you haven't been consistently *following through* on. One thing that stops parents from being clear and firm about rules is worrying about how the children will react to the new rule. Parents are pretty sure their children will be upset and may cry or have a tantrum. So as you're telling your child the new rule, be ready to Reflectively Listen.

Let's say that your daughter is in the habit of watching television before doing her homework, and you have realised that consequently she is leaving her homework until too late and then rushing it, not doing her best. You may now decide, as many parents have, that screen time will be a reward for completing her homework to the best of her ability. She won't be happy about this new rule! Depending on her age and temperament, she may whinge, complain, talk disrespectfully, shout, walk away or worse.

Here's how to introduce the new rule. Remember not to spring it on her right when she gets home from school. Instead, at a neutral time, do a *think-through* to tell her about the new rule.

Reflective Listening in Action

Think-through: At a neutral time

Dad: *Jenny, starting on Monday, there's going to be a new rule about when you can watch television on schooldays.*

Jenny: (Scowls silently at her father)

Dad: *Starting Monday, you can have an hour of telly or computer every day, but only __after__ you finish your homework. You probably won't like this new rule. Mum and I have been letting you watch TV __before__ homework, and you probably like things the way they are.*

Jenny: *That's so mean. Why are you doing this? I'll miss my favourite programmes. It's how I relax after school!*

Dad: *I'm glad you're thinking about why Mum and I made a new rule. Why do you think we're making this new rule about homework?*

Jenny: *I don't care.*

Dad: *I can see you're feeling cross. This new rule probably feels awful.*

Jenny: *Yeah.*

Dad: *Why do you think we're making this new rule?*

Jenny: *Because I watch too long?*

Dad: *You guessed right. Yes, and it's so hard to stop once you start watching. And why is it good to do the things you have to do before you do the things you want to do?*

Jenny: *So I get my work done earlier.*

Dad: *That's right. That's a sensible way of looking at it – 'worst first'. So tell me now, what's the new rule?*

Jenny: *I have to do my homework first, then I can watch TV.*

Dad: *That's brave of you to say the new rule, even though you might really be annoyed about it.*

This example of a *think-through* shows how you can incorporate Reflective Listening into your conversation when you are setting a new rule. Notice that this father Reflectively Listened right after he told his daughter the rule, even before she had a chance to react. This type of pre-emptive Reflective Listening is highly effective at reducing upset whenever you want to make a new rule or whenever you anticipate that your child may be annoyed or upset about what you expect from her. Notice also that this father Descriptively Praised Jenny for guessing and for answering sensibly.

Unhappy or upset?

As I mentioned, parents often worry about their children being unhappy. It's one reason parents avoid making necessary rules or find themselves giving in, rather than *following through*, when children make a fuss, throw a tantrum or cry. At those times our children seem so unhappy, and naturally we don't want them to be unhappy. This is something almost all parents worry about, whether your child has an easy-going temperament or a more sensitive and intense temperament.

There is a very important difference between children being upset and children being unhappy. I use these two words to differentiate between two very different states of mind. Upset is a temporary emotion, a reaction to a specific situation or circumstance. Unhappy is an ongoing feeling; it's how we feel when some important part of our life just isn't working right. Most of the children whose parents are reading this book are not unhappy. Their lives are fine. But they will of course get upset, probably several times a day, when they aren't getting what they want or when they have to do something they don't want to do. And depending on their temperament, some children may get upset many times in a day.

And when children are upset, it feels huge to them. They may make a big fuss, and it looks as if they are truly unhappy. So we need to keep remembering the distinction between unhappy and upset. Unhappy is rare. Upset is common and absolutely natural. Let's not try to take away our children's upset, because they will learn a lot from being upset and realising that the world doesn't just stop and give in.

Whenever we make new rules or clarify our expectations, we can be pretty sure that our children won't always be thrilled. No one likes change. So let's accept that our children will be upset at first when they don't get what they want. The best response is to let them know that you care and understand by Reflectively Listening.

Tweaking your Reflective Listening for a child with a more sensitive, intense or inflexible temperament

If you have a child with a trickier temperament or a special need that is neurological in origin, you may be concerned about how he's going to react when you start using this new technique. Reflective Listening does work, regardless of temperament type. But you might find that you need to make some adjustments to how you Reflectively Listen.

A result that was truly miraculous

My seven-year-old, James, was resentful about a weekend homework project. He had to do a character analysis that required very detailed and complex colour-coding, etc. He was feeling really frustrated and couldn't find his blue crayon to colour-code. I was in the bathroom when I heard him screaming,

'I can't find my blue crayon! Get in here and find my blue crayon.'

I closed my eyes and took a deep breath, because what I wanted to do was to reprimand him for his screaming and disrespectful voice. But I knew I needed to practise Reflective Listening and to listen to the feeling. He came into the bathroom and said angrily,

'Get in here and find my blue crayon!'

I looked at him and said, 'You must be so frustrated that you have to do homework on a Sunday.'

I literally saw his face soften. All he wanted was to know that I understood the frustration he was feeling. He paused and said quietly, 'But I am not a nice kid, and I didn't ask for that crayon politely.'

And I looked at him and said, 'I think you're a pretty nice kid.'

And then he looked up at me and said, 'Mum, can you please help me find my blue crayon?'

So I did, and we found it, and he finished his homework with no more complaining. It was so amazing because my instinct was to argue with him and say, 'But it's just homework. Just get it done! Get it out of the way and then we can do what we want to do!' That's what's natural for me, but by taking that second to pause and to think, 'If I were feeling like he's feeling, how would I want somebody to react to me?' I got a result that was truly miraculous.

James has high-functioning autism, and I love that these techniques work just as well for kids with special needs. It's so easy for us to blame his behaviour on his diagnosis, but we still need to know how to help bring out the best in him. The Calmer, Easier, Happier Parenting techniques help us do that, and I know that whenever behaviour is becoming an issue, it's because I've stopped using one of these techniques. As soon as I change, he changes.

Mother of a 7-year-old

There's no doubt that parenting is more challenging when you have a child with a more sensitive or intense temperament. Here are some questions about Reflective Listening from parents with children who tend to be more sensitive, intense and easily upset.

PARENTS WANT TO KNOW

Q: *My son has always been very sensitive. Nothing seems to calm him down when he's in the middle of an emotional outburst. Why doesn't Reflective Listening work with my son?*

A: This isn't uncommon. With some children you may need to delay your Reflective Listening until after the tears have dried or the tantrum has run its course.

For some kids the cooling down process may take just a few minutes; for others you might need to wait an hour or more before they are rational again. Once the emotional hurricane has largely blown over, and they are able to process what you're saying, that's when it's helpful to Reflectively Listen.

You may already know what helps your child to calm down. For one child, a hug may be calming. For another child, the best thing may be to sit near him, saying nothing. Some children prefer to be left alone. In Chapter 7, 'How to Stop Misbehaviour in Its Tracks', I give some tried and tested suggestions for calming major upsets.

As you practise all the Calmer, Easier, Happier Parenting strategies, you will see that the tantrums become shorter, milder and less frequent.

Q: *My twelve-year-old daughter asked me to stop talking in 'psychobabble'. She keeps saying it doesn't help her feel any better when she's upset. What should I do now?*

A: Initially it can be painful for a more sensitive, intense child to face her feelings. She may also feel like she is losing control because she is no longer getting the intense, emotional reaction from you that she is used to. But you will need to persevere with the Reflective Listening in order for it to be effective. For one full month, commit to Reflectively Listening every time you see or even sense that she is upset or even just mildly annoyed. She will soon appreciate that you care, that you are trying to understand how she feels, and that you are on her side.

Q: *What should I do after I Reflectively Listen? When can I move on to discussing a solution? My daughter is pretty inflexible and can go on moaning for hours. She even brings up complaints from a few years ago!*

A: There are times when a child seems to be stuck in a feeling. It may feel to you as if no amount of Reflective Listening will ever help heal her anguish. It may even seem like she is just playing on your sympathy, milking the situation for all it's worth.

Often the long-drawn-out crying or complaining is not only about whatever your child thinks she's upset about. The tears or whingeing or tantrum may really be a response to an accumulation of several days or maybe even many weeks of upsets that have not yet been acknowledged and so have continued to fester and multiply.

This is more likely to happen with children who have an inflexible, sensitive temperament because they are the ones who tend to get told off and corrected a lot, both at home and at school. This understandably breeds resentment and sometimes even a desire for revenge. It is not always easy to recognise just how upset this child can be because the uncomfortable feelings may manifest as defiance or as sulky, withdrawn behaviour. It <u>seems</u> as if she just doesn't care how her behaviour affects others, and that makes parents even angrier!

Focus on practising Reflective Listening and the other Calmer, Easier, Happier Parenting skills, instead of repeating and reminding and lecturing and finding fault. This will help tip the scales towards a more positive attitude. You will soon find that your daughter is able to let go of and move through her upsets more and more quickly. A lot of the negative attention-seeking will disappear within a few weeks.

But this won't mean you can stop Reflective Listening. You'll need to keep using this skill as long you are a parent! Once you begin experiencing the benefits, you will see how powerful this technique is, and you won't want to stop doing it.

Here's an example of how Reflective Listening helped one couple improve the difficult behaviour of their sensitive and over-reactive daughter:

Heather was thirteen years old. She complained almost daily that she had more chores to do than her younger siblings, that her teachers were boring, that the other girls in her year were mean to her, that her hair was curly and she wished it was straight, that nobody ever listened to her, etc.

The mother's usual response to all the complaining was either to try and reason her daughter out of what she was feeling or try to ignore the litany of complaints because what Heather was saying was so often clearly not true. But Heather was relentless so she usually managed to get an irritated reaction from her mother. The father, on the other hand, tended to feel sorry for Heather. He tried to make up for the mother's seeming indifference by bending the rules for Heather or giving her special little treats. The mother and father frequently argued over the best way to handle Heather.

At first, the mother could not really believe that any strategy existed that could possibly help her sensitive, intense and easily upset daughter to feel more positive about her life. But the mother had nothing to lose, so she decided that for a fortnight every time

Heather complained about something she would stop everything and Reflectively Listen for a few minutes. The first few days were very hard because Heather complained even more once she saw that her mother was really listening. But even so, the mother found that this new strategy didn't take any extra time because previously she had been responding in a way that often led to a prolonged argument. With Reflective Listening there were no more arguments because she was not trying to convince Heather that she was wrong.

The mother had to consciously put her irritation to one side so that she could stay relaxed and empathetic. This became easier with practice. Sometimes the mother was confident that she knew what her daughter was feeling: unappreciated, envious, left out. At other times the mother didn't have a clue what Heather was feeling so she had to guess. She was surprised to find that Heather didn't seem to mind when the guess was incorrect. Heather still appreciated that her mother was listening and not reasoning or arguing or denying her feelings.

At first, the father was very sceptical about Reflective Listening, feeling that it was too artificial and contrived, so he was unwilling to practise it. However, long before the fortnight was over, he could see that the atmosphere at home was much better. There were fewer arguments between mother and daughter, more cooperation from Heather and much less complaining. He became willing to Reflectively Listen as well, and this United Front led to a reduction in the bickering between the parents. Within a month, several members of the extended family, and even Heather's teachers and some neighbours, had commented that Heather seemed not only more mature, but also happier.

Reducing fears and anxiety

Reflective Listening is very effective for helping children move through their anxious feelings. Dealing with anxiety in our children often feels emotionally difficult for us as parents. We desperately want to make our children feel better, but simply reassuring them will not help them get past their anxious feelings. So the first thing we need to do, and it can be difficult, is set our own emotions aside so that we can listen to their upsets and still stay calm.

Reflective Listening is actually the basis of most forms of psychotherapy. When our children are feeling anxious, we need to communicate empathy and understanding for what they are experiencing and not try to take the feeling away or minimise it. It's a very real feeling for them. Reflective Listening opens the door for deeper communication, which is crucial for a child dealing with anxiety. If your child says, 'I don't want to go to school today,' resist the temptation to lecture, reassure or dismiss. Instead try, 'Maybe you're worried about your geography test today.' Even if you didn't guess right, this way of responding shows that you care, that you are trying to understand and that you will help your child move on to problem-solving. He will become less anxious, less defensive and less prone to meltdowns when you respond in this empathetic way.

Defusing sibling conflict

Watching anger melt away

Our boys were twelve and ten when this incident happened. I was sitting with my older son, Tyler, after snack time, and he was telling me about his homework, when my younger son, Nick, came in with a very angry look on his face and started aggressively kicking his brother's chair. I was surprised since Nick is usually pretty easy-going, but that day he was obviously furious. I told him he had to stop immediately and let us finish talking. He glared at me and stormed off to his room.

After he left, I said to Tyler, 'Wow. Nick must be <u>really</u> angry to act like that and kick your chair.' Tyler looked at me rather sheepishly and said, 'Well, we were eating a snack, and he's not supposed to have seconds of yoghurt . . . right?' Ah, then I understood what the problem was. Tyler had been telling Nick what he could and couldn't eat for a snack. I asked Tyler whose job it was to say what they can and can't have for snack, and he said, 'Yours and Dad's.'

I went into Nick's room. He was still furious and said in a loud, angry voice, 'I don't want to talk to you!' I stayed calm, nodded and said, 'I didn't come in to talk with you; I just came in to tell you something.' He wasn't sure what to say then, so I continued and said, 'It must have made you furious that Tyler was being bossy about what you could eat at snack time. And maybe it seemed like I was on his side because I asked you to leave the room.' His angry face started to change very quickly. We were both quiet for a minute, and then I left his room. Pretty soon he went about his life and engaged himself quietly in a book. Just acknowledging his feelings made so much of his anger melt away.

What my husband and I like about Reflective Listening is that it gives us a specific way to show that we care about their hurt or angry feelings, but we don't get involved in the argument. There's no refereeing or trying to solve, just acknowledgment of their upset. It's surprising how well it works.

Mother of two, aged 12 and 10

Sibling arguments can make even the most patient of parents lose their cool. The usual way we respond when siblings fight is to jump in and intervene, to become referees and try to solve their conflict for them. In the previous story, Nick wasn't deliberately being uncooperative. He was in the grip of his very angry feeling towards his brother, and in the moment he didn't know what else to do besides kick the chair! If his mother had punished him instead of taking the time to Reflectively Listen, it would have bred more resentment and more anger, possibly leading to additional misbehaviour and consequences. With Reflective Listening, the ticking time bomb of Nick's anger was defused.

KEY CONCEPT

Squabbling and telling tales soon lose their appeal when we don't get involved or become referees. Show you care by imagining how they are feeling, and don't try to solve the problem.

When one child comes to you complaining about the other, or when you can see a dispute becoming more heated, I ask you to resist the urge to find out what happened or to try and solve their problem for them. Although that response feels so natural, it actually reinforces the arguing by giving a lot of attention to it.

Telling on each other soon loses its appeal if we stop trying to find out who's to blame, if we stop scolding or punishing or trying to fix it. Instead, just be willing to acknowledge their feelings by Reflective Listening. Your children will calm down sooner than you think.

Getting started – Your guide to success

Now it's time to put Reflective Listening to work in your family.

How to phrase your Reflective Listening sentences

As I said earlier, because we can never be absolutely sure what our child is feeling, our Reflective Listening needs to be tentative. When parents first start using this technique, they generally tend to start their sentences with, 'I know that you're feeling . . .' This won't be as effective. It can sound presumptuous, and that's definitely not what we want. We want to convey empathy.

Here are some effective ways you might phrase a Reflective Listening sentence:

You look as if you're feeling . . .
You seem to be feeling . . .
You probably feel . . .
You might be feeling . . .
You may feel . . .
It looks like . . .
Seems like you're . . .
It sounds like you're . . .
I can see/hear/tell from your face that . . .
Maybe you're feeling . . .
I guess this feels . . .
I imagine you're feeling . . .
It can feel . . . when you . . .

Before you begin practising Reflective Listening

Reflective Listening is not intuitive. It's just not the way most of us respond when our children are upset. We want to fix the problem, solve it, make it go away. Reflective Listening is like a new language, and it's not always so easy to learn a new language. Plus, we often have to use this new skill at the most trying of times – when our kids are misbehaving! It's going to take practice. So keep looking at these sentence starters. Reread the parent stories to inspire you. Start practising Reflective Listening throughout the day, with your child's milder upsets at first: a sad or disappointed look, a whinge when things don't go the way he wants. This will start to build your confidence as you develop this skill. The more you Reflectively Listen, the more benefit you will see, so the more confident you will feel about using it for bigger misbehaviour, such as defiance, tantrums or even physical aggression.

Putting Reflective Listening into practice: Your Action Plan for the first two weeks

Reflectively Listen whenever:

- Your child seems to be experiencing a strong emotion, such as anger, anxiety, frustration, worry, etc., even when the emotion is accompanied by misbehaviour, such as resistance, reluctance, refusal, hitting, name-calling, etc.
- You're making a new rule or reinstating an old rule.
- You're tempted to reason, repeat, scold, lecture, fix, threaten or shout.
- Your child exhibits negative attention-seeking behaviour: complaining, blaming, showing off, etc.
- Your child's body language or tone of voice alerts you that he is even slightly annoyed.

Now let's look at a few examples of how we can combine the three powerful strategies of Descriptive Praise, Preparing for Success and Reflective Listening. As I mentioned at the beginning of this chapter, Preparing for Success and Descriptive Praise can be used proactively, but Reflective Listening is about how we react, so this Action Plan section will be different. There is one time, however, when we <u>can</u> be proactive in our Reflective Listening, and that is when we make a new rule or reinstate an old rule (see page 75). To be on the safe side, we can always start by assuming that our child might have a negative reaction to the rule so we can Reflectively Listen even while we're telling them the rule!

Combining Reflective Listening with Descriptive Praise and Preparing for Success

Example: Think-through for making a new rule about a chore

Think-through: At a neutral time

You: (Tell your child the new rule and Reflectively Listen) *Mummy and I have decided to give you a new job to do. It's something we've been doing for a long time, so it might seem like it shouldn't be your job. Starting this Saturday, it will be your job to feed the cats twice a day.*

Your child: *I already do a lot of chores.*

You: (Acknowledge, Reflectively Listen and ask a *think-through* question) *You do a lot of things for yourself, and you're probably annoyed that we're adding another one. What's the new rule?*

Your child: *I have to feed the cats.*

You: (Descriptively Praise, Reflectively Listen and ask another *think-through* question) *That's right. And you told me, even though you probably didn't want to say it. Why do you think we're asking you to be responsible for feeding the cats?*

Your child: *Because you like making me do stuff.*

You: (Reflectively Listen) *That's probably what it feels like. Take a sensible guess.*

Your child: *To help.*

You: (Descriptively Praise) *That's right. You know the reason.*

Reflective Listening examples for reacting to strong emotions

Example: Nine-year-old child slumps in frustration during piano practice

Your child: (In a crying voice) *I can't do this. I'm terrible at this. I can't do it!*

You: (Reflectively Listen with an empathetic expression) *You sound so frustrated. Maybe you feel like you'll never get this sequence – it just seems too hard.*

Your child: (Face softens and she stops complaining, or may even burst into tears)

At this point, it often helps to give your child a hug. This will probably help her to calm down. Once she's calm, you could brainstorm together about how to break down the difficult sequence into smaller parts to make it easier for her. But when she's upset, she won't be in a frame of mind to be able to think rationally. Reflective Listening will help defuse her frustration and move her towards problem-solving. The natural reaction in this situation would be to reason with your daughter and try to talk her out of her very real feelings. 'You're amazing at piano! Just keep working at it and you'll get it – I know you can do it!' As understandable as this reaction is, it won't build her confidence or help her move past her frustration.

Example: Your thirteen-year-old son comes home from school, goes to his room and slams the door

You: (Open his bedroom door)

Teenager: *Go away! I don't want to talk to anyone!*

You: (Reflectively Listening) *Something really upsetting must have happened at school today.*

Teenager: *I'm quitting football!*

You: (Reflectively Listen) *That game must have been really frustrating.*

Teenager: *It wasn't frustrating, it was stupid! Nobody follows the rules.*

You: (Reflectively Listen) *You have such a strong sense of justice; it really bothers you when kids don't follow the rules.*

Teenager: *It's so unfair. Our team should have won.*

At this point you could just sit near your son and let him vent, if there is anything else he wants to say. Continue to Reflectively Listen and resist the urge to make suggestions or problem-solve until he's ready.

PARENTS WANT TO KNOW

Q: *I tried giving my child his wishes in fantasy. I said, 'Wouldn't it be great if you could wear the same clothes every day because I know you love this shirt so much,' and he answered me in a very belligerent tone, 'Yeah, why can't I?' I'm wondering what I did wrong.*

A: It sounds like you did nothing wrong. This kind of angry question is not a genuine request for information. The child can answer that question for himself because he has probably heard the reason from you numerous times. And even if he has not been given a reason, children are capable of figuring out for themselves much more than we give them credit for. So do not get sucked into giving an explanation or a mini-lecture that your child will not even be listening to. Instead you could say, 'Take a guess. Why won't we let you wear the same clothes every day?' Or you could just Reflectively Listen some more, for example, 'You're so annoyed!'

Q: *When I start to Reflectively Listen, my child usually launches into a long tirade about how it was all somebody else's fault. How do I help him to focus on his own part in creating the problem instead of always blaming someone else?*

A: The more you practise Reflective Listening, the better you will get at this skill, and the more comfortable your children will become with accepting their feelings and expressing them in a constructive way. To wean a child off complaining and blaming, we need to stop trying to argue or reason him out of what he is thinking and feeling. If your child says, 'They won't play with me. They won't even talk to me. They're so mean,' it doesn't help to reply, 'Well, nobody wants to play with the same people every day. Maybe they'll play with you tomorrow. Or maybe they were annoyed with you. Did you do something to upset them? Were you being bossy? You know you're bossy sometimes.' As true as all that may be, your child cannot absorb your words of wisdom when he is in the grip of his upset.

With Reflective Listening, you focus on how your child might be feeling, and you put that feeling into words. You could say, 'You were probably feeling really left out,' or 'It sounds like that hurt your feelings.' Expect a child who is in the habit of blaming to continue to blame, instead of instantly becoming more mature and taking responsibility for his part in the problem. Resist the temptation to interrupt and set him straight. Just wait until he stops talking, and then reflect back to him again whatever you imagine he might be feeling. This will help you to stay calmer than if you were trying to find an explanation or a solution. And you can be pretty sure that an upset child is going to shoot down your excellent insights and advice.

To help a child move beyond the natural human tendency to blame others, we need to make sure that we discipline ourselves so that we ourselves very, very rarely give in to the temptation to blame, accuse, tell off and threaten. We need to lead by example. Additionally, you can help your child explore how he could handle upsetting situations differently by using the *think-through* strategy I talk about in Chapter Four.

Q: *When I Reflectively Listen, my son just changes the subject or walks away. Why doesn't he want to talk about it?*

A: It takes time for children to start feeling comfortable with hearing about emotions and then talking about emotions. Particularly for boys in our culture, feelings can be very unfamiliar territory. Because children are hard-wired genetically to imitate the same-gender parent, for boys it is especially important that the father or a father-figure regularly demonstrates Reflective Listening and talking about his own feelings.

Reflective Listening addresses how your child is feeling, but of course you will still need to address any misbehaviour. Whenever a child is breaking a rule, naturally we want him to stop as soon as possible. Reflective Listening alone may be enough to achieve this, but not always. Chapter 7 'How to Stop Misbehaviour in Its Tracks' gives you some useful strategies for this.

In Chapter 4, 'Preparing for Success', I mentioned that ongoing problems need to be addressed by making a rule. In time, your child will get into the habit of following this rule, and the rule will become a routine. However, there are a lot of little annoying things that children say and do that may not be specifically covered by an existing rule. Chapter 7, 'How to Stop Misbehaviour in Its Tracks', shows how to handle both the minor, irritating things children do and also the more serious misbehaviour.

Sometimes the rule breaking has already happened so there is no misbehaviour we need to stop right now. But we still want to take steps to minimise the recurrence of that misbehaviour in the future. Chapter 8, 'Rewards and Consequences', talks about how parents can prevent future misbehaviour.

Summary

Reflective Listening is the most helpful way I know to respond when children are experiencing any kind of upset, from mild all the way to severe. Our natural reactions when our children are upset and misbehaving may be to reason with our child, dismiss what they're feeling, to justify, lecture or threaten. But these typical reactions don't help our children behave better or feel better. Of course it takes practice and determination to stay calm and to be willing to spend a moment imagining the feeling that's behind the misbehaviour.

When you commit to practising this new skill for a minimum of two weeks, you will soon see that Reflective Listening works to help children and teens (and husbands and wives as well!) move through strong, uncomfortable feelings more quickly, so that they can move towards problem-solving if necessary.

You have now learned three core Calmer, Easier, Happier Parenting strategies. Each one works with the others. Reflective Listening is an invaluable tool for helping children accept rules and routines. It helps to significantly reduce sibling rivalry. It enables you to help your child work through upsets and strong emotions more quickly, which reduces resistance, reluctance and refusal. And when you combine Reflective Listening with Preparing for Success and Descriptive Praise, you can transform the day-to-day life of your family.

CHAPTER 6

NEVER ASK TWICE: THE SIX-STEP METHOD THAT TEACHES CHILDREN TO DO WHAT YOU ASK THE FIRST TIME YOU ASK

I felt like a tape recorder!

Nag! Nag! Nag! It felt like that was all I was ever doing with my boys, who were three and five years old. I used to have to repeat myself so many times when I wanted them to do something – even a simple task – I thought I might as well just press the repeat button on my recorder and turn the volume up until they did what I asked. I couldn't think what else I could do to get my children to listen to me.

So when I went to Noël's seminar and learned about the Never Ask Twice method I couldn't wait to try it on my boys. Could it really work?

I found out the next morning. When it was time for my eldest son to stop playing and put his shoes on for school, I went to where he was playing. I stood right in front of him, told him what I wanted him to do, and then I waited. I didn't repeat myself. I just waited patiently and remembered to follow the Six Steps.

On the first day I had to wait a bit, though not as long as I normally would have when I'd be repeating myself. And when he realised I wasn't going to go away, he did put his shoes on. Each day I did the same thing, and it got easier and easier, and I had to wait a shorter time before he went to put his shoes on. The truly amazing thing was that by the third or fourth day my son came and found me in the kitchen and said, 'Mummy, look at my feet.' I did, and sure enough he had his shoes on.

'But I didn't even ask you!' I said.
'I know,' he said with a big smile, 'I read your mind!'
I was really shocked that the Never Ask Twice method worked so well. And now I use it whenever I want my kids to do something. I don't need that tape recorder any more!

Mother of two, aged 5 and 3

For many parents, one of the most frustrating things about family life is how many times they have to repeat themselves before children eventually cooperate. Often parents tell me that it is only when they finally lose patience and start shouting that their children comply. Not only is this frustrating, but we don't want our children to cooperate just to keep us from shouting. And all the repeating and raised voices don't add up to a Calmer, Easier, Happier family life.

Why children don't do what they're told the first time we ask

When we ask our children to do something and they just ignore us, it may seem like they are being deliberately uncooperative. But this isn't always the case. As I mentioned before, our agenda is very different from our child's agenda. Our minds are focused on what needs to get done next. Our children, on the other hand, are happily absorbed in whatever they are doing at the moment. So it's not surprising that they don't immediately switch gears when we ask them to do something. They may ignore us or they may complain and resist.

KEY CONCEPT

The more we are willing to repeat ourselves, the more times we'll have to repeat ourselves.

When this happens, you may be tempted to repeat your instruction, possibly a bit louder and a bit more impatiently. But what happens when you drift into the habit of repeating yourself? What message does all this repeating and reminding send to your children? The message is that they don't have to listen the first time. Consequently, your children won't take you seriously the first time you give an instruction. They will start to tune you out because they know that you will say it again and again. If we are willing to repeat ourselves six times, we will soon find that we <u>have to</u> repeat ourselves six times. Children won't think they have to pay attention until they start to hear that familiar rising pitch of hysteria in our voices. There is a better way to achieve first-time cooperation, and that is the Never Ask Twice strategy.

Never Ask Twice, the fourth core strategy

The Never Ask Twice method is a simple and effective six-step strategy for getting your children to cooperate ninety percent of the time, the first time you give an instruction <u>and</u> without a fuss! No more nagging, no more repeating, reasoning, negotiating or shouting, which, as you've probably discovered for yourself, don't get you the cooperation you want. The Never Ask Twice method is a strategy that does work. It helps children achieve the important habit of cooperation more effectively than any other strategy I know. By following these Six Steps you will have another tool in your toolbox to get cooperation from your children so that you never have to ask twice!

When to use the Never Ask Twice method

You can use the Never Ask Twice method whenever you would like your child to stop doing one thing and start doing something else. This is called a 'start behaviour'. To make myself clear, I need to explain the difference between 'start behaviours' and 'stop behaviours'.

A 'stop behaviour' is what is happening when your child is misbehaving or breaking a rule or doing something annoying. You want her to stop doing it. I will teach you some strategies for how to deal with 'stop behaviours' in the next chapter. But with a 'start behaviour', your child is not misbehaving or doing anything wrong. It is simply time for her to wrap up whatever she is doing and start doing the next thing, such as put the puzzle away and go upstairs to clean her teeth, or stop playing with the bricks and go wash her hands for dinner. As you can see, there is nothing wrong with what your child is doing at the moment, but you now want her to move on to the next activity or task on the schedule.

KEY CONCEPT

Start behaviour
Your child is not misbehaving but needs to transition to the next activity.

Stop behaviour
Your child is doing something wrong or something annoying, and you want her to stop.

We all know that some children can be trickier, even from birth. The good news is that the Never Ask Twice method works even if you happen to have a child who has a more sensitive or intense or impulsive temperament. If you have quite easy-going children who are already cooperative most of the time, you may not feel you really need this method. But it is still useful. What I hear over and over again from parents is that even if you have a relatively cooperative child, the Never Ask Twice method increases the level of cooperation because it is an extremely respectful and positive way to make transitions easier for any child.

At what age can I start using the Never Ask Twice method?

You can use the Never Ask Twice method with children from the age of about three. By this age, most children are old enough to understand what you are asking them to do and are able to concentrate for long enough to follow simple instructions.

When not to use the Never Ask Twice method

There are two situations in which I do not recommend using the Never Ask Twice method:

1 **If your child is in front of any type of screen.** This could be computers, hand-held game devices, mobile phones, television, etc. Screen activity can be very mesmerising and addictive. So in order to be successful using the Never Ask Twice steps, you'll need to get all electronics switched off

before you even begin Step One of this method. If getting your child to unplug from screens is a battle in your family, I'll be showing you in Chapter 12, 'Screen Time', how you can get back in charge so that screen activity becomes a positive element in family life.

2 When you're feeling rushed and need to get out of the house quickly. Start practising this method when you know you have enough time to *follow through* with all Six Steps, if it becomes necessary.

Overview of the Six Steps

You can use this positive and respectful method when your child is not doing anything wrong, but you want her to start doing the next activity. Six steps may seem like a lot at first, but as you start practising this, you'll need to do fewer and fewer of the steps because your children will start cooperating sooner and sooner. First I am going to tell you the Six Steps, and then I will explain why each step is so crucial. You might be surprised to discover that with this method you don't even give the instruction until Step Three. And usually the first three steps are all you will need to get cooperation!

Step One Stop what you are doing, go to where your child is, and stand and look at him.
Step Two Wait until your child stops what he is doing and looks at you.
Step Three Give your child the instruction – clearly, simply and only once.
Step Four Ask your child to repeat the instruction back to you – accurately, thoroughly and in his own words.

Step Five Stand and wait.

Step Six While you are standing and waiting, Descriptively Praise every step in the right direction, no matter how small, and Reflectively Listen to how your child might be feeling.

The Six Steps in detail

You've probably got a lot of questions after reading this brief overview, but hold on because I'm going to explain each step in more detail.

Step One: Stop what you are doing, go to where your child is, and stand and look at him. How often do you call up the stairs to your children to get dressed? Or call out of the kitchen window to tell your kids to come inside for homework or dinner? Or ask a question when you are in one room and they are in another? If we want our children to listen and take in what we say, we must not call up the stairs or from one room to the next, or even from one side of the room to the other. It is just too easy for our children to ignore us when they are not looking at us. If we do not take what we are about to say seriously enough to stop what we are doing and go to our child and look at him, we mustn't be surprised if our child doesn't really take us seriously either. Standing and looking at him demonstrates our serious, firm intention.

When you stand very near to a child, he cannot block you out for long, even though he may be trying to ignore you. Standing (when one could sit) demonstrates that 'this is important', whereas sitting conveys a more relaxed attitude. Occasionally a parent is concerned that standing very close will be experienced by their child as intimidating or as an invasion of 'personal space'. That might be true if you were looking annoyed or saying something critical. But the Six Steps are all very positive, as you will see.

Step Two: Wait until your child stops what he is doing and looks at you. You need to make sure your child is ready to pay attention to what you are going to say, and Step Two does exactly that. It helps your child to focus on what he is about to hear.

Step Two is how you capture your child's attention. It is the opposite of what so often happens. We frequently give an instruction while the child is still focused on his drawing or book or cards so he may not even be listening. Even if your child does hear you, he may forget what you have said very quickly because he is not in the habit of taking you seriously. When you are willing to stand and wait until he looks up at you, you will see that your child's attitude changes dramatically.

Some children are very aware of what is happening around them. These children are likely to look up as soon as you walk into the room. Other children, particularly those with a more inflexible temperament, are harder to engage. They may become so absorbed in their book or train set or pretend play that they are oblivious to their surroundings. For these children, you will need to stand very close to them before they even register your presence.

At first your child may seem determined not to look up at you. But when he doesn't hear the expected nagging or criticism, he relaxes, and he will look up to see what's happening. And if you have been doing lots of Descriptive Praise, Preparing for Success, Reflective Listening and Special Time, by now he will be feeling more appreciated and respected and less resentful, and he is likely to look up quite soon. You will find that the more often you use this extremely positive, respectful and friendly method for 'start behaviours', the more your child will want to look at you and listen to you.

While you are waiting for your child to stop what he is doing and look at you, you can show a friendly interest in whatever he is doing, and you can find something to Descriptively Praise. Remember that the Never Ask Twice method is for 'start behaviours' only so he will not be doing anything wrong or annoying at that moment. You will certainly be able to find something to Descriptively Praise. This will motivate him to return your eye contact and will help him to feel friendlier and more willing to listen and cooperate. For example you could say:

That puzzle has a lot of pieces. And you haven't given up.

Those blocks are balanced so carefully. That's a tall tower.

You're halfway through that book already.

It looks like you're having fun organising your rock collection.

This positive attention will help your child want to please you even more.

You might be tempted to call your child's name to get his attention, but I don't recommend doing that. A child mostly hears his name when adults are telling him to do something or not to do something. He tries to tune this out, so calling his name rarely gets his full or immediate attention.

During the time it takes you to accomplish Steps One and Two, you will have the time to consider carefully: 'Is this instruction worth saying?' 'Do I have the time and determination right now to *follow through* if necessary?' Steps One and

Two will give you the time to focus on becoming calm, friendly and polite and to think about how to phrase your instruction positively. We want our children to learn to be polite, so it's important that we practise leading by example.

If you are feeling just too stressed at that moment to be able to practise being calm and friendly, <u>stop yourself</u> before you get to Step Three. Leave the room and focus on calming yourself or on getting support. An irritated, annoyed tone never helps children become willing to cooperate.

Step Three: Give your child the instruction – clearly, simply and only once. Once you have given the instruction clearly and simply, do <u>not</u> repeat yourself. If you repeat the instruction, you are unintentionally sending the message that your children don't need to listen the first time, or possibly even the fourth time! In the past you might have been tempted to repeat yourself, thinking that maybe your children didn't really hear you the first time. But with the Never Ask Twice method, you know for sure that your child has heard you because in Step Two you waited for him to look at you.

These first three steps are so different from what we've been in the habit of doing, and they are so positive and respect-ful, that it's likely your children will do what you've asked with a minimum of fuss.

Here are a few additional tips that you might need for Step Three, depending upon the temperament of your child. It might happen that as you are telling your child what to do, his attention wanders and he looks away. If that happens, stop talking instantly, and remain standing and waiting. When he looks back at you (which he will, if only to see why you suddenly stopped talking) Descriptively Praise him for looking at you. Then you can start talking again. As long as you stay positive and respectful, your child will find it easy to listen to you. Keep your instruction short so that restlessness does not set in.

Children can get very absorbed in whatever they are doing, and it can feel like a painful wrench when they have to shift gears quickly, especially if they are having to shift from an activity they are enjoying to one that is not so appealing. We can ease the transition by giving a *countdown:*

In five minutes it will be time to put the Lego away.

Many parents do this type of *countdown* for some 'start behaviours', particularly the very problematic transitions, such as turning off the computer or sitting down for homework. However, I am asking you to give a *countdown* <u>whenever</u> you sense that your instruction might be met with resistance. You may think that you do not have the time to give a *countdown* ten or twenty times a day. In fact, all these *countdowns* will <u>save</u> you time, as well as hassle and frayed nerves.

If you know from past experience that your child will not take the *countdown* seriously, you need to be willing to <u>stay with your child</u> after you give the *countdown*. For a child who has a more intense, easily fixated or inflexible temperament, give several in-between *countdowns* at three minutes and then at two minutes and then at one minute. Each time your child hears what he will soon be doing, his brain automatically begins to create a mental picture of the next activity. Without his even realising it, his brain is getting used to the transition. By the time you say, 'Time's up,' or the timer goes ding, your child will already have got used to the idea that he needs to do whatever you have asked. Parents are amazed and delighted to see that their child will often begin to transition even before all the allotted *countdown* time has expired.

Most children, most of the time, will cooperate after Step

Three, and you will not even need Steps Four, Five and Six. If you are the parent of a child who often resists or simply ignores you, you are probably finding it hard to believe that these first three steps will result in cooperation ninety percent of the time.

At this point you may be thinking, 'But my child is different. He's much more rebellious (or sensitive or argumentative or mischievous or manipulative). Noël obviously hasn't met my kid! This method won't work with him.' You are basing that assumption on how your child has been reacting to your <u>old</u> ways of getting him to do things. But the Never Ask Twice method is radically different. This new method is friendly and respectful. It does not hurry the child. And it gives parents the time to calm down and think about how to be more effective. This method works to build the habit of cooperation much sooner than you might think possible. (And, by the way, I <u>have</u> met your child, as well as many children whose behaviour was much more problematic!)

Remember to Descriptively Praise as soon as your child makes a move in the right direction. But for those times when your child is not cooperating after Step Three, luckily we still have three more steps left for mopping up the opposition.

Step Four: Ask your child to repeat the instruction back to you – accurately, thoroughly and in his own words. You might say something like, 'So what do you need to do now?' or 'Please tell me what you have to do next.'

Essentially, Step Four is a mini-*think-through*. As your child tells you what he should do, his brain automatically creates a clear, vivid mental picture of himself doing that activity. And having that vivid mental picture makes it much easier and much less painful for your child to transition to the new activity, even if he was feeling resistant at first.

And when your child hears himself saying what he has to do, he starts to take ownership of it. He takes the instruction far more seriously than when it is just you who is doing the telling. In a subtle way, your child feels morally obligated to do what he himself has said he would do, whereas he may be in the habit of disregarding what the adults say.

When you ask him what he should do next, your child may test you to see if he can get away with, 'I dunno,' or 'I forgot.' Ask him to take a sensible guess, and Descriptively Praise anything remotely correct. Wait until he 'guesses' what he has to do. He will soon realise that his old ploys are no longer working to rile you or get him off the hook, and he will experience that your Descriptive Praise feels good.

It's important not to let him simply parrot back the words he has just heard you say. Many children are able to do this without really registering what they need to do. Your child's brain will respond very differently, however, when he has to put the instruction into words of his own choosing. This is when his brain forms a clear mental picture of himself doing whatever he is talking about.

When your child tells you, in his own words, exactly what he has to do and how and when, you have indisputable proof that he has heard you and that he understands. And he knows that you know that he knows. This eliminates a lot of excuses.

Some children, especially children with a sensitive, intense temperament or children who are full of resentments and complaints, will at this stage grudgingly go and do what they have been told to do, but they really don't want to have to say what they have to do:

Why do I have to say it?

OK, OK, I heard you!

Leave me alone!

I'm not an idiot, you know.

Or they may just get up silently and comply without answering your question. Having to say what they are supposed to do seems to these children like an admission of defeat. They are thinking this is a battle, probably because of having been told off a lot in the past, either at home or at school.

It is a mistake to assume that all that matters is that your child cooperates. When you ask a question, you need to receive an answer because otherwise your child will assume he can ignore you. Here is what I recommend if that situation arises: Wait for the cooperation, Descriptively Praise everything you can think of, and only then ask him to answer your Step Four question. He will, of course, think this is unnecessary because in his eyes the question is no longer relevant once he has complied. Explain (during a *think-through* at an earlier, neutral time) that he has to answer your questions, just as he answers his teachers' questions. And if he asks why, don't launch into a mini-lecture that he will probably just tune out. You can say, 'That's a good question. Take a guess. Why do you have to answer Mum and Dad and your teachers?'

If you arrange your child's day so that it is largely governed by predictable routines, soon a very delightful thing will start happening more and more. After doing Steps One and Two, even before you give your instruction in Step Three, your child will pre-empt you. As you approach him, he may say, 'I know, I know, it's bedtime,' or 'Is it dinner time?' You will find that often you can skip straight from Step Two to Step Four. This gives your child training in using his common sense, rather than relying on an adult to tell him what to do.

Step Four usually takes care of any remaining resistance. When you use these four steps, non-compliance is rare. Again, remember to Descriptively Praise when your child does eventually cooperate, even if it takes longer to achieve than you would like.

But there will of course still be a few occasions when she has not yet followed your instruction after Step Four. Now is the time to move on to Step Five.

Step Five: Stand and wait. If your child has not yet started to do what you ask after Step Four, be willing to stand and wait. Waiting is very powerful. It shows that you mean what you say. This is one of the reasons it's so important not to use this method when you're in any kind of a rush. If you get to Step Five, you need time to *follow through*.

Standing and waiting may seem impossible because in a busy household there is always something you need to be doing, some mini-crisis to defuse. But if you have a child who is not yet in the habit of cooperating ninety percent of the time, this is the mini-crisis that needs your attention more than any other! Think of the time you spend standing and waiting as an investment that will very soon pay off in a Calmer, Easier, Happier family life.

You may be imagining that you will have to stand and wait for hours! Probably you are remembering all those times in the past when your child kept disregarding what you said. So in frustration you may have resorted to repeating, nagging, threatening and maybe finally shouting. It might be hard to accept that it is those very understandable, very natural parental reactions that contributed in the past to a lot of the ignoring or defiance. When we practise staying friendly, respectful, calm, clear and determined, our children naturally want to please us more and more of the time. So Step Five almost always results in cooperation.

KEY CONCEPT

Waiting is very powerful. It shows intentionality – that you mean what you say.

A mother in one of our Calmer, Easier, Happier Parenting classes assumed that when she started the Never Ask Twice method, she would have to wait hours for her rebellious teenager to comply about unloading the dishwasher or sitting down to do her revision. She was worried that all the standing and waiting would be bad for her varicose veins so she invested in a pair of support tights. When she got up the courage to use the Six Steps, she found that her daughter cooperated, albeit with bad grace, within ten minutes (which seemed like ten years at the time), so the support tights turned out to be a wasted purchase!

To make the standing and waiting less stressful for you, make a point of starting all your routine activities a bit earlier so that you have some time to spare, rather than feeling that you are always hurrying to beat the clock.

And for the very rare occasions when your child <u>still</u> has not cooperated after Step Five, we have one last step.

Step Six: While you are standing and waiting, Descriptively Praise every step in the right direction, no matter how small, and Reflectively Listen to how your child might be feeling. Remember, the more Descriptive Praise we give our children all day long, the more motivated they will be to cooperate and to show us their best sides. Here are a few examples of Descriptive Praise for a tiny step in the right direction during Step Six. You could say:

You stopped arguing.

You've put your paintbrush down.

You're closer to the door.

You haven't walked away, and you're being respectful.

You're not complaining.

I see you've found your shoes.

We can even Descriptively Praise <u>past</u> good behaviour:

You're getting quicker and quicker at doing what you're told.

I hardly heard you screaming today.

You were so gentle with the baby yesterday.

Reflective Listening will show that you understand your child doesn't want to stop what he is doing and move on to the next activity. Remember, don't bother arguing back, justifying or lecturing – it doesn't usually work! Instead you might say:

You're having so much fun building with your new set. You don't want to stop.

It's no fun having to put everything away when you just want to keep playing.

It sounds like you're really angry. You don't want to get up. You probably wish you could stay in bed for a few more hours.

Maybe it feels embarrassing to say goodbye to our guest. You wish we didn't have that new rule.

It's not easy to do what someone else tells you to do.

It took you so long to set up your fort exactly right. You wish you didn't have to dismantle it before dinner time.

You don't need to worry that empathising like this might mislead your child into thinking he does not need to comply. The Six Steps make it very clear that your instruction is non-negotiable. And the word 'wish' clearly conveys that it is a fantasy, not a real option.

And for maximum impact, you can combine Descriptive Praise and Reflective Listening:

Even though you probably wish I would just leave you alone, you're not arguing, and you haven't told me to get out of your room.

I can see you're really annoyed that it's homework time already, but you're not shouting or saying anything rude.

I can see how angry you are by the way you threw that lorry into the toy box, but you did put it in the right place. You are tidying up, even though you're showing me how angry you are.

When you commit to standing and waiting and Descriptively Praising and Reflectively Listening, it won't be long before your child responds positively.

So keep persevering with Step Six until your child cooperates, which will happen, and sooner than you think. The reason that the Never Ask Twice method always works is because there is no Step Seven that says, 'After a while, give up'!

When your child finally cooperates, even if it took all Six Steps, remember to Descriptively Praise. Next time it will be a little bit easier and a little bit quicker. Soon you will need only the first three steps.

Watching resistance melt away

After learning the Calmer, Easier Happier Parenting skills, we realised that a lot of the things we had been doing when we were trying to get our sensitive seven-year-old son to cooperate and change direction were patently off-base, primarily because we were barking orders and shouting instructions from another room. If another adult does that to me, I'm likely to feel irritated and resistant, so I can't say it should be different for a child.

So doing that first step and going to the room where my son was and being right with him was really paramount for success with the Six Steps. And once we did that, my wife and I realised that our son didn't actually have a problem with his hearing! What we now grasped was that he often felt like we were springing these direction changes on him, and so his natural reaction was to resist. This all made sense. It was unrealistic to think our son should be OK about having whatever he's doing stopped suddenly and a new activity or job started. I know most adults wouldn't react very well to that either. It was only fair to give our child the same respect we would give another adult.

We were able to tie in Preparing for Success with the Never Ask Twice method. It made the transition into the Six Steps a lot easier for us. We began giving our son a fair warning about the upcoming transition ten minutes in advance of starting the Six Steps so he wasn't surprised and knew exactly what was coming. Our son is a pretty sensitive and intense child, and we found that giving him that respect of a ten-minute countdown has really cut down on his resistance and made it pretty much a Steps One, Two, Three deal instead of having to get to Four, Five and Six.

Father of two, aged 7 and 2

PARENTS WANT TO KNOW

Q: *If I use the Never Ask Twice method, how long will it take before my kids are cooperating most of the time?*

A: Of course the Never Ask Twice method will work to achieve the habit of cooperation more quickly with some children than with others. It will usually take a child with a sensitive or intense temperament longer to get into the habit of cooperating the first time and without a fuss. Similarly, when a child has been angry and resentful for a long time, it will take parents longer to earn back his trust and respect. And when a child has become used to unclear rules and routines and inconsistent *follow through*, it is understandable (although irritating) that he will test again and again, in the first few weeks, before he finally accepts that you are now in charge and that this new method is here to stay.

   But I can promise you that this method works with <u>all</u> children who are old enough to understand and remember what we are asking of them. So use the Six Steps for all 'start behaviours'. Your children will soon see that you mean what you say, and they will <u>want</u> to please you by cooperating.

Q: *I can see how the Never Ask Twice method might work if I had all the time in the world. But what do I do when we're running late and I'm trying to get everyone out of the door in the morning? It's just too hectic a time to stand and wait.*

A: If your child is not yet in the habit of ninety percent cooperation the first time she is told, it's very possible that at first the Never Ask Twice method may take longer than you would wish. But these Six Steps are an investment that will <u>save</u> you time very soon. And let's remember that repeating and reminding also take up a lot more time than we would wish.

And, in addition, repeating and reminding end up reinforcing the child's habit of disregarding what we say, so nothing improves.

Guiding children into good habits does take time. There is no shortcut around that. So you have to be willing to make the time to be able to *follow through*. It helps to plan your day realistically so that you are not rushing. You may need to get yourself or the children up earlier for the first few weeks. Quite soon your children will see that you are determined to *follow through*, and they will cooperate more and more quickly. If you are wondering how to plan your day more realistically in order to give yourself more time, please re-read Chapter 4, 'Preparing for Success'.

Q: *I don't want to micro-manage my children. Why do I have to make such a big deal about each little thing I want them to do?*

A: By 'micro-manage' we usually mean trying to dictate all the little details of how someone carries out a task. The Never Ask Twice method does not ask you to do that. This method assumes that your child already knows how to do what you ask, and that what is needed now is training in cooperation.

Maybe your question is really asking why six steps are needed when you could just give your instruction in one quick step. If that is working to achieve first-time cooperation in your family, then there is no need to learn a new strategy.

But the usual way we tell children what to do too often results in resistance, either quiet or noisy. Then the parent gets sucked into repeating and reminding and eventually threatening and telling off in an attempt to get the child to pay attention and take the instruction seriously. To reduce these unpleasant reactions (yours as well as theirs), something more than just giving an instruction is usually necessary. What you are calling a 'big deal' (the Six Steps) will actually keep a much bigger and more unpleasant deal (refusal, rude-ness, tantrums) from developing.

And remember that most children, most of the time, will cooperate after Step Three because this approach is so calm, friendly and respectful and because it shows you are in charge. Paradoxically, the more willing you are to *follow through* with all Six Steps whenever necessary, the fewer steps you'll need.

The Six Steps and my 'no-time listener'

After hearing about the Never Ask Twice method at a Calmer, Easier, Happier Parenting talk, I couldn't wait to try it. It just made a lot of sense.

We were having problems getting our six- and eight year-old boys to wash their hands for dinner, and there was a lot of repeating and then annoyance from me. So this time, I went to the room where they were and looked at them. When they looked up, I told them to wash their hands and come to the table, and my eight-year-old popped up from the couch and did it exactly right, without a fuss. I was shocked and couldn't think of what Descriptive Praise to say, so I blurted out, 'You're a first-time listener.' My younger son then said, 'I'm a first-time listener too,' and rushed to wash his hands as well. I hadn't expected those words and those simple first three steps to have such an effect.

I also didn't expect what happened the next day. My six-year-old washed his hands and came to the table before I even asked him and then announced that he was a 'no-time listener' because he did what he was supposed to do without being asked!

In the past I hadn't used praise as a motivator, but more as an attempt to build self-esteem. Now I know that I can use Descriptive Praise as a tool to help my boys cooperate and combine it with this respectful Six-Step method.

> *A year later, both boys still like being 'first-time listeners' but are also looking for opportunities to be 'no-time listeners' and get the satisfaction of surprising us.*
>
> Mother of two, aged 9 and 7

Before you begin practising the Never Ask Twice method

A really important key to the success of the Six Steps in the Never Ask Twice method is using your Descriptive Praise and Reflective Listening skills effectively. The more you can practise these skills and the more comfortable you feel using them, the easier you will find it to put the Never Ask Twice method into action. You may be longing to try out the Six Steps on your children immediately, and of course you can, but I do want you to remember that it will be easier, feel more natural, and work more effectively, the more you have practised Descriptive Praise and Reflective Listening.

Another useful tip is to write up a brief list of the steps and have it with you when you first practise this! Parents of three-year-olds to thirteen-year-olds have all done this to help them remember to stick to the steps as they begin using the Never Ask Twice method.

Putting the Never Ask Twice method into practice: Your Action Plan for the first two weeks

Use this method for:

- 'Start behaviours' – when you want your child to stop doing what he's doing and start doing something else.

- Children who are three years and older.

Do not use this method for:

- 'Stop behaviours' – when your child is misbehaving
- When your child is in front of a screen
- When you're in a rush and don't have time to *follow through*.

Identify two 'start behaviours' you want your children to improve. Now I'll walk you through two typical scenarios.

Example: Stopping playing and starting music practice
Let's say that your child is playing, and now you want her to put her toys away and start doing her music practice. This is a 'start behaviour'; she has not done anything wrong, but it is time for her to start doing the next activity on the family timetable.

Here is Step One. You might be in the kitchen, but you resist the temptation to call to your daughter, who is in the other room. Instead, you turn down whatever is bubbling on the stove, and you go to her and just stand near her and look at her. Remember to smile!

In Step Two, you wait until she stops what she is doing and looks at you. This will happen sooner if you find something to Descriptively Praise about what she is doing, such as: 'You've been playing by yourself for ten minutes, and you didn't need me to help you with anything.' Then you just stand there and wait until she looks up at you. She will!

Now you come to Step Three: When she looks up, smile. You could say something like, 'Now it's time to put your dolls away and get your music out.' If she complains or argues or whinges, resist the temptation to explain why or to repeat yourself. Just zip your lip and wait until there is a pause in the arguing. Let just a few seconds go by and then say, 'You've stopped arguing' or 'You're not whingeing now'. You may find this hard to believe, but most children will comply at Step Three, <u>but only</u> if you haven't skimped on Steps One and Two.

But if your child still hasn't started to cooperate, continue to Step Four, which is asking her what she needs to do. You could say, 'What did I just say you need to do next?' Your child may or may not answer you at this point, but she probably will do what you have told her to do. Once she has, remember to Descriptively Praise, and then have her answer your Step Four question.

In the unlikely event that she still has not started to cooperate, go to Step Five, which is to stand and wait. That usually does the trick. It shows the child that you are serious. You are not walking away to finish cooking the dinner. You are not getting distracted. Standing and waiting shows that you mean what you said.

By this time, the strong likelihood is that your child will have started to cooperate. But if not, go to Step Six, which is: While you are standing and waiting, Reflectively Listen and Descriptively Praise. You could say:

It looks like you wish you could keep playing. It's so much fun.

You're not arguing.

Keep persevering with Step Six until your child cooperates, which <u>will</u> happen, and sooner than you think.

Example: Starting to get ready for bed – using the countdown
In this example, your children are happily absorbed in a game of Monopoly, but it's nearly bedtime. You want them to stop playing and start getting ready for bed.

In Step One, you go to your children's bedroom where they are playing.

In Step Two, you wait for your children to stop playing and look at you.
Think of something positive to say about how they are playing. You could mention how nice it is to see them playing together quietly. You could praise them for using teamwork to make decisions even though they both want to win.

Now comes Step Three. Give the instruction.
Tell your children that it is nearly time for them to finish playing and put the Monopoly away before getting ready for bed. Give them a *countdown* of five minutes to finish what they are doing. Set the timer so that you don't have to keep track of the time, and stay in the room with them, Descriptively Praising what they are doing and talking about what they will be doing next. Because your children have been given some time to wrap up their activity, when the timer goes ding they will probably be ready to follow your instruction and go to the bathroom to clean their teeth.

But in case they don't start putting the Monopoly away, move to Step Four. Ask them to tell you what they are meant to do now.
That is usually all that is needed.

But if necessary, stand and wait, which is Step Five.

If you find yourself standing and waiting for more than a minute or so, go to Step Six. Whilst you are standing there, Descriptively Praise every small step your children are taking to stop their play. And Reflectively Listen to show that you understand how difficult it is to have to stop their fun.

PARENTS WANT TO KNOW

Q: *What should I do if my child tries to distract me by talking about something else while I'm doing the Six Steps? She's a master at distracting me.*

A: Trying to change the subject is a very common diversionary ploy. Your child may be testing to see if she can get you to change your mind or to forget your instruction. She may even be trying to upset you. Don't let yourself get sidetracked. Persevere with the Six Steps. Don't talk about anything else until your child has cooperated. Don't tell her not to talk; just Descriptively Praise her when she stops chatting about something else or whingeing. For example, at Steps Three or Four your child might say something like, 'Can we go to the park today?' Instead of answering with 'Yes' or 'No' or 'Maybe', just pause for a few moments and then Descriptively Praise when she stops talking. You could say, 'You're not talking about anything else now. I'll be glad to talk about the park after you do what I ask.' Your child will soon see that you are in charge of your reactions.

Q: *What should I do if my child walks away while I am doing the Never Ask Twice method? If I don't follow him won't he feel like he has won?*

A: Parents of children who often storm out of the room may find it hard to believe that children rarely walk off during the Six Steps. This calm, friendly approach usually brings out the best in children. But if your child does storm off or run away during any of the Six Steps, <u>do not</u> follow him. Who is in charge if you follow your child? Your child is! Don't feel you need to stay rooted to the spot; just go about your life. Practise being calm and determined; wait until your child comes to you for something, which will happen sooner than you might think. Children love to interact with parents, so it probably won't be long before he comes back wanting something:

What's for dinner?

Can I have a biscuit?

Susie tore my mask.

Want to hear a joke?

Miss Smith said my graph was very good.

Or your child may simply come near you and hang about, waiting for you to notice him. Resist the temptation to talk about anything else with your child. When he asks for something, you can say, 'I'll be glad to talk with you about that after you do what I said.' Then start the Six Steps again from the beginning. Your child will soon see that nothing is gained by flouncing off so he will be less and less tempted to do it as time goes on – <u>if</u> you stay consistent.

By the way, most children will not leave the room if parents have remembered to clarify a rule about this during a *think-through* at an earlier, neutral time by saying very firmly and clearly, 'When I am talking to you, you have to stay. You may not walk off,' or words to that effect. Let's remember that most children would not dream of walking away while their teacher is talking to them.

Q: *My son usually cooperates without too much of a fuss, but he is so absent-minded that he forgets most of what he is supposed to be doing before he is halfway through. How do I get him to stay focused?*

A: There are a number of reasons why a child who is completely willing to cooperate might lose focus partway through the task. One or more of these reasons may apply to your child:

- Some children are naturally far more easily distractible or impulsive than other children of the same age. When something interesting catches this child's attention, it temporarily drives every other thought out of his brain. Over time we can help this child to develop more mature habits, but there is no point in getting annoyed with him for doing what comes naturally to him.
- Some children have quite immature short-term memories, especially for what they hear, so the instruction evaporates quickly. In this way these children are similar to a much younger child.
- Some children listen to the first part of the instruction and start thinking about that, so don't even register the rest of what the parent is telling them to do.

To improve your child's ability to focus, you will of course need to Prepare for Success throughout the day, not just when you are telling him to do something:

- Descriptively Praise all day long whenever you see the tiniest bit of evidence that your child is focusing, remembering or *following through*.
- Never talk about this child (even if you think he can't hear you) as forgetful, dozy, dreamy, distractible, a space cadet, etc.
- Whenever you are tempted to say 'You forgot,' say 'You need to remember.'

Here's what I suggest to help your son stay focused and remember what he's supposed to do:

- Break each instruction into several stages, and give each stage as a separate instruction. Don't ask this child to put his Jedi warriors away, get into his pyjamas, clean his teeth and choose a story. Just focus the Six Steps of Never Ask Twice on the tidying away. Then do the Six Steps for getting into his pyjamas, etc.

- When your child goes to do what you asked, go with him, rather than assuming your job is done. Your presence will help remind him of what he needs to do without your having to repeat it. And staying with him will give you lots of opportunities to Descriptively Praise him for remembering, for not getting distracted, for putting something in the right place, for any evidence of focus or organisation.

Q: *My daughter is only twelve, but she's been acting like a sullen teenager for years, and I know she would hate the Six Steps and would feel I was being patronising. What can I do instead to get her to be more cooperative and responsible?*

A: Although most teens and preteens don't exactly understand what the word 'patronising' means, they soon discover that accusing their parents of being patronising is very powerful. It shuts parents up or gets them desperately justifying and back-pedalling.

Interestingly, teens don't ever accuse parents who are nagging or shouting of being patronising. The word only seems to be applied to parents who are staying calm, friendly and in charge! Children who are used to getting away with too much often prefer to deal with an angry parent, one who is much easier to provoke or distract, rather than with a parent who is calmly and quietly focused on achieving cooperation. So persevere with the Never Ask Twice method, and you will notice your daughter becoming less and less sullen and reactive, and you will notice her becoming more and more cooperative, confident, motivated, self-reliant and considerate.

Q: *How do I use the Never Ask Twice method when I'm trying to get all three of my children to transition to the next activity? They tend to gang up against me, getting noisier and wilder when I try to talk.*

A: First, you need to address the reasons why your children are often noisy and wild. There are a number of possible explanations, one or more of which may be true for your family:

- If your children are not spending enough time out-of-doors to burn off a lot of their energy, they will have no alternative but to get rid of their excess energy indoors, where it can be highly irritating.
- There may not be clear rules in place that tell your children what they can and cannot do and where and when.
- The *follow-through* for remembering the rules (especially Descriptive Praise) may be inconsistent. The *follow-through* for not remembering the rules may be inconsistent. I will talk more about this in Chapter 8, 'Rewards and Consequences'.
- The wild play may be a form of attention-seeking. In a noisy, busy household, children soon learn that wildness, silly noises, provoking siblings, resistance and refusal are all very effective ways to get noticed.
- Out of revenge, siblings may take delight in winding each other up.
- The children may not have been trained in the habit of playing or talking quietly.

- In a noisy environment, children will become ever noisier in an attempt to be heard over the din.

To rectify this annoying state of affairs, it is not enough to react differently in the moment, as important as that certainly is. You will also need to Prepare for Success by using the skills you read about earlier:

- With each child individually, do lots of *think-throughs* all day long so that they know what you expect:

When Mum or Dad or the teacher tell you to do something, what do you have to do?

How do we talk inside the house?

Where is the right place for play-fighting?

- Give lots of Descriptive Praise all day long whenever your children are the opposite of noisy and wild – whenever they are calm, quiet, focused, cooperative:

You're playing by yourself.

You did what I said so quickly.

Such a quiet voice! I like listening to that voice.

You're not bothering your brother.

You remembered the rule about walking in the house. You're walking, not running.

You're not swinging on the handle.

You're waiting patiently instead of grabbing.

I can see you're being careful not to spill.

The more you Descriptively Praise all day long, the more children will remember the rules and take them seriously.

- Don't use screens as a way to keep noisy, active children quiet or out of mischief. It may work temporarily, but it does nothing to teach them how to play less wildly. See Chapter 16, 'Playing Independently', for ideas on how to teach children to play quietly by themselves.

Now I want to talk about how to use the Never Ask Twice method when your children are being wild or noisy or silly:

- Whenever a transition needs to happen, Prepare for Success by leaving plenty of extra time so that you are more likely to stay calm.
- Don't try to shout over your children. You may (or may not) succeed in getting their immediate attention if you raise your voice, but in the long run they will learn to be even noisier to drown you out.
- Consistently make sure that all your children know that you will play a game with them as a reward whenever they all cooperate so quickly that the extra time you have built into the routine is not needed.
- When you use the Never Ask Twice method, target the ringleader! Parents often direct their instructions to the child who is usually most cooperative in the hope that the others will follow that example. If that works for you, by all means keep doing it, but I am assuming from your question that you have not found that to be effective. That is usually because the least cooperative child has become an expert at getting negative attention, which can be very addictive. So start the Six Steps with the child who is likely to give you the most trouble.
- If one of these wild, noisy children is under three years

old, don't expect cooperation from him when he's overexcited. Simply lead him by the hand away from the
melee, Descriptively Praising as you go.

Q: *My child has learning difficulties. Will the Never Ask Twice
method work with her?*

A: Yes, as long as she:

- understands what you want her to do
- knows how to do it
- has the language comprehension, attention span and
  memory of at least a typical three-year-old.

Children with various learning difficulties often exhibit what
educational psychologists call a 'spiky profile'. This means that
some of their brain functions may be approximately average,
some may be slightly below average, some may be very low,
and some may even be way above average. In particular, short-
term memory, sequencing and the understanding of relatively
complex sentence construction are often weak.

Don't make the mistake of asking your child to do something she doesn't really know how to do. The likelihood is
that a child with special needs will require a great deal more
teaching to make certain that a skill, especially the sequence
of actions that make up a skill, is firmly embedded in her
long-term memory. Only then would you use the Never Ask
Twice method to establish the habit of cooperating the first
time and without a fuss. In the meantime, if her memory is
weak, instead of expecting her to remember your instruction,
be willing to do it with her. If she is very easily distracted,
follow the guidelines I outlined in my earlier answer about
helping a distractible child learn to focus.

When it comes to the Never Ask Twice method, start by
expecting a child with special needs to respond as if she is the

age of her lowest cognitive functioning. With consistent use of the Six Steps, not only will the habit of cooperation improve, but so will her brain functioning. That is because Steps Three and Four teach children how to listen and visualise more accurately and how to think more clearly and carefully.

Summary

Over the years, you may have grown accustomed to your child ignoring your instructions or arguing back. Even though you fervently want your child to respond more positively, you may find it very hard to believe that these six simple steps, or indeed any strategy, can, in a very short time, achieve calm cooperation. Perhaps you may also be worried that you don't have enough time in your busy life to devote to the Six Steps. But commit to doing it for one month. When you practise this method, very soon you will see for yourself that it works. And you will see how much hassle, and therefore how much time, you actually save when your children are in the habit of cooperating the first time they are asked and without a fuss most of the time.

CHAPTER 7

HOW TO STOP MISBEHAVIOUR IN ITS TRACKS

If you have just picked up this book and are flipping through it, you might be surprised to find that the chapter on stopping misbehaviour would be towards the middle of the book. Shouldn't it be at the beginning? Isn't that what this book is all about?

The answer is yes – that is what this book is all about! But really, the most effective way to stop misbehaviour is to prevent it in the first place. So that is what I have been addressing in the preceding four chapters. I explained several very effective strategies you can use to motivate your child to do the right thing and to prevent most misbehaviour from even happening.

Descriptive Praise will motivate your child to want to listen to you and do what you ask. The Preparing for Success techniques will help your child do more and more things right, preventing a lot of behaviour problems and dissolving most resistance. Reflective Listening will defuse the emotional upsets that trigger so much misbehaviour. The Never Ask Twice method will help your children cooperate and transition to the next activity.

After you have been practising each of the core strategies for two to four weeks, you will find that you are dealing with less and less misbehaviour. You won't need to refer to this chapter on stopping misbehaviour as often as you might think. This may be hard for you to believe, especially if your child is misbehaving a lot right now.

When parents first come to Calmer, Easier, Happier Parenting, it's usually because their children aren't listening or cooperating. Lack of cooperation, even about little things, is so frustrating because it seems to make everything else so difficult.

You may have a child who seems to make a fuss about everything. This child probably has a more difficult temperament. Parents may describe this child as intense, sensitive, inflexible, impulsive or defiant. Parents are often at their wits' end, not knowing how to discipline when nothing seems to be working, even punishments. These parents feel desperate, and they are worried about what their child's future will be like if he doesn't learn self-control.

Children who have developed the habit of defiance can get completely hooked on negative attention. If that sounds familiar to you, let me reassure you that no matter how problematic your child's behaviour is right now, it can change! Families who have committed to using the Calmer, Easier, Happier Parenting strategies have experienced huge transformations, even families where the children had very serious behaviour problems. You will read some of their stories in this chapter and the next.

There's a very important distinction we need to make between stopping misbehaviour when it's happening and taking action to prevent and minimise future misbehaviour. These are two very different goals, but we don't always realise it. Because we are so preoccupied with misbehaviour when it is happening, we are often reacting in the heat of the moment and not really thinking about what we are trying to achieve in the long term. Are we just trying to get the misbehaviour to stop right now? Or are we also trying to prevent it from happening again in the future? Each of these goals requires a different set of tactics!

Of course we want to stop the misbehaviour right now, but

we also need to know what we can do or say to teach our child not to do it again in the future. The purpose of a consequence is to affect future behaviour. In this chapter, I will show you what you can do to stop misbehaviour when it is happening. We'll look at what works and what doesn't work to stop misbehaviour.

In the next chapter, I'll explain how parents can use Rewards and Consequences to maximise cooperation and minimise misbehaviour in the future. Parents often tell me that their child doesn't respond to consequences; in fact their child may even see consequences as a challenge and may react by becoming all the more defiant. Thankfully, when the focus is on rewards rather than on consequences, children are far more motivated to improve their behaviour. That is why in the next chapter, 'Rewards and Consequences', I emphasise the role of rewards and talk about only two consequences.

Our son was hooked on attention for bad behaviour

Our four-year-old son was extremely challenging – active, highly impulsive, very physical, aggressive and explosive. He had outbursts literally all day long, so we were reacting to misbehaviour non-stop. We had tried it all: shouting, threatening consequences, taking things away and, in really bad moments, even physical punishment. Nothing worked. It's fair to say that we were at our wits' end when we first learned the strategies of Calmer, Easier, Happier Parenting at a seminar.

These strategies made complete sense, so we were excited and ready to start using them. But the moment we came home from the seminar, the outbursts flared, and all we could do was react. The strategies and skills were all so new that we weren't sure which ones to use for what!

We wanted our son's behaviour to magically change at the snap of a finger, and when it didn't, we were frustrated. But we recognised that we were stuck in our usual pattern of reacting negatively to his behaviour. It took us a week or two to shift from being reactive to being proactive, using think-throughs and other Preparing for Success strategies. Once we changed, he changed, but it was a process and not a five-minute instant fix. These were issues that we'd been dealing with for several years, and we had to learn to approach them differently, but at least this programme gave us the tools to do it.

Our son was hooked on attention for bad behaviour, and we saw that we had to reverse course and get him used to attention for being good, so he would start craving the positive attention more and more. The concept of Descriptive Praise was logical, but truthfully, there was very little to find that was good in his behaviour so we had to stretch and look for the smallest little things!

The most illuminating example of the power of Descriptive Praise was when our son was very angry and raised his arm to hit me. Noël had taught us that even during the most trying of times, we had to catch him before he would hit and praise him, so I said, 'I can see you're very angry, but you're not hitting. You're showing so much self-control.' His arm slowly came down, and his face softened. We were stunned that it worked. It made us realise that he had never before been praised for having self-control. This was the beginning of him being able to see himself as someone who could control his impulses.

Our son hasn't hit in several years now. He has so much more self-control, self-confidence and self-esteem. It really is a miracle that he has come this far. We all had to work hard to change our habits, and I credit so many of the Calmer, Easier, Happier Parenting tools for this transformation. Our family life was pretty disastrous before we were introduced to this programme. We feel like these skills saved our son's life and saved our family.

Mother of a 7-year-old

Stopping Misbehaviour: What works and what doesn't work

When our children are misbehaving we want to know what we can do to stop the misbehaviour as soon as possible. Whether your children are ignoring your instructions, whingeing or crying when they don't get what they want, begging to be bought something each time you go to the shops, climbing on the furniture, throwing things in anger, being aggressive (physically or verbally) with you or with siblings or breaking some other rule, these 'stop behaviours' can make parents feel intensely frustrated. We want to stop the misbehaviour now!

First, let's look at what doesn't work to help our children stop misbehaving right now and why it doesn't work. Then I'll talk about what does work.

What doesn't work and why

Shouting

Shouting 'Stop that,' or 'No!' or 'Don't do that!' or simply calling the child's name sharply when your child misbehaves may be what comes naturally, but it isn't reliably effective, and it certainly isn't positive. None of us responds well to an exasperated tone of voice. It doesn't encourage cooperation. Instead, shouting tends to intensify a negative situation.

Ignoring and giving in

Pretending that you don't notice the misbehaviour or giving in 'for a quiet life' doesn't actually get you a quiet life! When children are allowed to break one rule, of course they will continue to test our other rules. They will also respect us less and less when they see that we are not *following through* consistently.

Repeating, re-explaining, bribing and threatening

None of these work in the long run. These natural parental responses will undermine your authority and make you more and more 'ignorable'. Your child may eventually comply, but she is learning that she does not have to cooperate the <u>first time</u>. And of course, when we bribe for behaviour, our children focus on the bribe and not on doing the right thing.

Arguing and negotiating

Decisions about proper behaviour need to be made by parents based on our values. When we allow ourselves to be drawn into an argument or a negotiation, the child gets the mistaken impression that our values are negotiable and that he should not have to do what we ask. If your child asks you, 'Why do I have to?' it is rarely a genuine request for information and most likely a diversionary tactic. If your instruction is a sensible one, your child will usually understand why he should do it, or he can easily figure it out for himself.

Following your child if she storms out

If you follow your child, she is in charge. Let her leave the room; she will be back, usually within minutes. When she returns, she may try to act as if nothing has happened in the hope that you will have forgotten all about it. In the next chapter, 'Rewards and Consequences', I will tell you a strategy you can use, when she returns, that will help prevent further storming off in the future.

Assuming your child will continue to refuse
If your child says 'No' or screams 'I won't' or throws himself on the floor in fury, it's natural for us to have a strong emotional response – it may look like the end of the world! But take heart: the drama is much less serious than it sounds or looks. Usually it just means that he does not enjoy being thwarted. When you stay calm and use your new Calmer, Easier, Happier Parenting skills, the storm will quickly blow over, and you will be able to reawaken in him the motivation to please that exists in all human beings.

'Control yourself!'
A child who is relatively more impulsive, sensitive and intense will have a harder time controlling himself. He may know <u>how</u> to control himself, but has not yet developed the <u>habit</u> of controlling himself, probably because in the past his misbehaviour got him plenty of attention or enabled him to do what he wanted for a bit longer. You will know if your child is capable of controlling himself by noticing what his teachers say about him. School is full of frustrating experiences. If a child can manage a six-hour schoolday without tantrums or misbehaviour, this is solid evidence that he knows how to control himself and could do so at home. He just does not think that he has to at home. If this is the case, it is the parents' job to ease the child into calmer, more considerate and more mature responses. All the skills in the Calmer, Easier, Happier Parenting programme will help you achieve this.

Smacking
Smacking is a controversial discipline strategy. Recent research reveals that three out of four parents admit to having smacked their children at some point. Most of these parents feel guilty because they know they smacked in a moment of stress,

impulsivity and desperation. Sometimes it's because the parent doesn't know a better way. But more often the parent does know, in theory, what to do differently, but doesn't know how to stay calm enough in the face of persistent misbehaviour to do it consistently. Without getting into a moral argument, here are a few reasons why smacking is an ineffective strategy:

- Smacking can generate a distrust, and possibly even fear, of the parent.
- Children imitate their parents, so smacking sets the example that it is acceptable to use force, violence or intimidation as a solution to problems and as a way to get what you want. The child who identifies with the parent's power may become a bully.
- If the smacking is infrequent, as is usually the case, then by definition it is an inconsistent method of discipline. When repeatedly faced with inconsistent consequences, children respond by continually testing. They need to be able to predict how we'll react. Children feel secure and can make sense of their world when they know the limits.

Now let's talk about what does work to help our children stop misbehaving. There is so much we can do to influence our children – to keep the misbehaviour from escalating, to defuse an emotionally charged situation and to help them stop themselves from continuing to misbehave.

Here are a number of positive strategies that will help you to achieve these goals.

What does work to stop misbehaviour and why

Keep it friendly

This might feel impossible when you are dealing with misbehaviour, but after you have been practising the Calmer, Easier, Happier Parenting strategies for a while, you will feel calmer because you now have effective strategies that you didn't have before. Knowing something you can do that works can help you to stay calmer and friendlier. So our first guideline, which is to stay friendly, may initially be the hardest. Practise speaking in a low, calm voice, even if you are feeling stressed or annoyed. Friendliness on our part often calls forth willingness from our children, and they are far more likely to meet us halfway, gradually becoming less antagonistic and more willing to cooperate. Knowing this, we can spend a moment or two being friendly, showing our appreciation for any tiny positive part of whatever they are doing.

Find something to Descriptively Praise

For example, we could say:

Those ornaments are so pretty and shiny, and you're being so careful. Now it's time to put them back.

Use your metaphorical magnifying glass to find some tiny bits of OK behaviour or even a momentary pause in the misbehaviour. For example, if your child has just spoken disrespectfully, you can wait a few seconds, until she pauses for breath, and then say:

You're not being rude (or disrespectful) now.

I can hear you're upset, but now you're controlling yourself.

You're using your words, not your body, to show how angry you are.

You will be delighted to find that Descriptive Praise, just by itself, is often enough to get kids back on track.

Get close

If your child is still misbehaving after you have Descriptively Praised him, immediately stop whatever you are doing and go to where he is and stand very close to him. You may find that your very close presence, <u>standing,</u> is enough to get your child behaving properly again. In fact, many parents report that as they are in the act of crossing the room, their child, who a moment ago seemed oblivious to everything except what he was doing, either stops the misbehaviour altogether or de-escalates it considerably. When this happens, it gives parents the opportunity to Descriptively Praise some more. You could say:

I didn't even need to tell you to stop ripping that piece of paper. You stopped all by yourself.

You realised you were breaking a rule, and then you stopped – so fast!

And you could mix in some Reflective Listening:

I can see from your face that you don't want to stop. But you're doing the right thing now.

If, by the time you are standing <u>very close</u> to your child, he still hasn't stopped the misbehaviour, you will probably be tempted to tell him to stop. But wait! When you give your child an instruction, you need to be pretty sure that he is likely to comply. Otherwise, your child will probably ignore you or defy you. So – only give a direct instruction when you are almost certain that your child will cooperate.

Give clues

Instead of giving a direct instruction to a child who seems unlikely to comply, you can give a little clue to help your child figure out what to do. Plant a seed so that her brain can work out what she needs to do. Let's say your daughter is jumping on the bed, but there is a rule in your house about not jumping on the furniture. She will probably have stopped jumping by the time you have walked over to her and waited for a few seconds. But if she is still jumping, don't say, 'Stop jumping!' or 'Get off the bed!' or 'How many times have I told you?' Simply say in a calm, friendly voice:

You know the rule about where you can jump.

This generally makes children pause momentarily in their misbehaviour, so you need to seize that moment and Descriptively Praise and Reflectively Listen:

You're remembering the new rule.

You probably wish we didn't have this new rule.

Offer alternatives

When we need to stop our children's fun, it is often helpful to offer an alternative activity. You might say:

I can see you want to hold that sharp knife, but you know the rules. We do not play with knives. But tonight you can help me cut the quiche. I know you want to be very careful, and I will be there to help you and make sure everyone stays safe.

Make it a rule for everyone
It can also help if we depersonalise our instruction by stating it as a family rule that applies equally to all family members. For example, you could say:

We have to use our indoor voices when we're in the flat. We all have to talk quietly, even Mum and Dad.

This family has a very important rule, no hurting or frightening the cat. We are gentle with our pets.

By now your child will probably be cooperating – although you may not believe me!

Empathise
Another very effective way to help our children want to cooperate is to show them that we understand how frustrated and annoyed they feel when we interrupt their fun. This is the strategy of Reflective Listening that I explained in Chapter 5. We imagine how our child might be feeling, and we reflect that feeling in words back to the child:

You've got so much energy, and you love jumping. You wish you could jump on the sofa. What's our rule about where you can jump? (Your child tells you.) *That's right. You can jump on the trampoline, but not on the furniture.*

Offer limited choices
Give your child an element of choice whenever possible. To simplify your life, limit the choices to two:

I can see you'd like to keep playing with that. You probably wish our rule was different. Would you like to hand it to me, or would you like to put it back on the shelf by yourself?

Phrase it in the positive!
It's possible that your child may continue to misbehave even after you have planted a seed and used these other techniques, especially in the first few weeks of your using these new strategies. In that case you will need to tell him exactly what he has to do. It is far more motivating for children to hear what they <u>should</u> do, phrasing it in the positive, rather than what they <u>should not</u> do.

'Put the salt shaker down, please' is an easier instruction to follow than *'Stop playing with that'.*

'Talk quietly, please' is likely to get a better response than *'Stop shouting'.*

Model the behaviour you want to see
It also helps if you can demonstrate the appropriate behaviour while you are telling them what to do. For example, if your child is holding the guinea pig too tightly and half-strangling it, you can say:

Stroke him gently – very softly – like this. You're being so gentle now. That's just what Squeaky likes.

Get united
Part of being a United Front is parents backing each other up. If one parent is running into problems with misbehaviour, the other parent needs to give strong support. Often it's enough for the other parent to go over to where the problem

is happening and say, 'Do what your mother (or father) says,' in a very calm, serious voice. Children will not usually ignore or defy this United Front, although at first they may test to see what they can get away with, especially if parents have not been consistent in the past. A United Front sends children a very clear message that both parents agree about the behaviour expected and that both parents care enough to actively enforce it.

Always follow through with action

Following through consistently results in our children knowing that we mean what we say. So if your child does not start to stop within five to ten seconds of your giving a direct instruction, resist the impulse to simply repeat your instruction louder. Instead, <u>take action</u>. This is usually either removing an object from the child or removing the child from the situation. We do this naturally when a child's safety is in danger or when it looks as if property is about to be damaged. But *following through* immediately with action is just as important when the issue is not safety but cooperation.

As soon as you start to make a move to *follow through* with immediate action, your child will probably see that you mean business and will comply quite quickly. At this point, you may forget about *following through*, reasoning that your child has complied so it does not seem as if you need to do anything else. But now is the perfect time to reinforce the cooperation by *following through* with Descriptive Praise.

Show how pleased you are with a pleased tone of voice and a pleased expression on your face. You could say:

You really wanted another biscuit, but you only took two because that's what I said, 'only two'.

I'm so glad I didn't have to put the puzzle up on the shelf for the rest of today. You stopped throwing the pieces so quickly. I only had to say it once.

If, however, once you remove the object from your child or your child from the situation, you are faced with a very angry child, let him have his feelings. Let him cry or complain or argue. Rather than trying to distract him or reason with him, take a few minutes to Reflectively Listen. Offer a hug if you think that might help. And of course Descriptively Praise any glimmers of positivity.

Important tip: Adjust your expectations for children with trickier temperaments

Of course, our aim with all these strategies is to get our child to stop the misbehaviour straightaway. But we need to recognise that for some children this is just not possible, even when they are very motivated to comply. In general, children tend to have a slower reaction time than adults, particularly for things they don't want to do. And that is especially true of many children who have more sensitive, intense temperaments. Such a child's movements and reaction time can be very speedy, even hyperactive, when he is doing something he wants to do. But he is often very slow and distracted and even lethargic when he has to do something he does not want to do. This delay may seem deliberate, and sometimes, of course, it is. Or the slowness may be a habit, or it may be a combination of the two. But more often than parents realise, this slower reaction time is also part of his temperament.

So your goal, when dealing with 'stop behaviours', is for your child to stop as quickly as he personally is <u>able</u> to stop. Depending on his own innate reaction time, a child who wants to cooperate will start to stop within a few seconds. But with some children it might take up to ten seconds. If you have a child with this temperament, be willing to stand and wait a bit longer than you really want to.

I've shared a number of strategies for getting your child to stop misbehaving if it seems like a simple 'Stop!' is not likely to be effective. From long experience I know that most children, most of the time, will respond positively to these strategies. Additionally, children are far more likely to respond positively when they are:

- well-rested
- eating healthy food
- getting regular exercise
- not being rushed in the mornings or evenings.

Thinking about how to manage and improve all these lifestyle issues may feel quite overwhelming! So in Section Two, I'll be making suggestions about how you can incorporate lifestyle changes into your daily routine using the core Calmer, Easier, Happier Parenting strategies you have been learning.

Taming tantrums

> **I thought these methods only worked for easy and calm children**
>
> *I attended a workshop for Calmer, Easier, Happier Parenting a few years ago, and had seen the skills work brilliantly with children who seemed to be 'easy and calm children'. When a crisis arose in my five-year-old grandson's life recently, I did not think the same skills would work on a very impulsive and defiant child suffering from recent emotional trauma. But threatening, arguing, shouting and time-outs weren't working at all (actually they were just making his behaviour worse), so we decided there was nothing to lose by trying these skills.*
>
> *Now I know how well they do work. I was dumbfounded to watch the resistance and defiance we have experienced for years either dissolve or be completely avoided using these positive strategies. He is now, in just a few weeks, respectful, cooperative, happy, and more self-confident most of the time. He is also enthusiastically engaged in school and a joy to be with.*
>
> Grandmother of a 5-year-old

You may have a child with a quite extreme temperament, as the boy in this grandparent's story has. Your child may regularly react by having a tantrum when he does not get what he wants, or even when he experiences the slightest disappointment or frustration. If you have been living with tantrums for years, you may feel as if you have tried everything. You may not believe that it is possible to achieve ninety percent cooperation the first time and without a fuss. You may assume that whatever new strategy you might practise, tantrums will still be happening. I want you to know that tantrums truly can become a thing of the past.

Everything changed in that moment

Though our three-year-old is the love of our life, up until a few days ago almost <u>everything</u> was a battle – getting dressed, stopping playing to eat dinner, and there was hitting and endless tantrums. It was stressful on so many levels as a parent and as a husband, and I felt worn out.

Then my wife and I learned about Descriptive Praise. My son was having a tantrum, and my wife called me, asking what to do. I yelled over his screams, so she could hear me, 'When he breathes and the crying stops for just a second, PRAISE HIM!!' Everything changed in that moment. He stopped crying and smiled, then played with us for the rest of the afternoon. Since that moment our son is so much more himself all the time; he listens, we listen, and it has changed our lives! So thank you, thank you, thank you!!!

Father of a 3-year-old

This family is not alone in feeling utterly worn out by a child's tantrums. From talking with thousands of parents over the years, I know how much parents dread tantrums, how stressful, and sometimes even frightening, tantrums can be. The child seems out-of-control, and parents feel helpless.

So don't throw this book away in disgust when I say that tantrums are not in fact as terrible as they seem. Yes, tantrums are upsetting and, when they happen in public, can be excruciatingly embarrassing. It's important to remember that although tantrums appear to be deliberate misbehaviour, they are usually an impulsive over-reaction, a young child's way of showing us that he is upset. But because parents pay so much attention to tantrums and will do almost anything to make them stop, the result is that some children learn to use tantrums and tears to manipulate adults. And some children learn to use physical aggression, or the threat of it, to intimidate parents. Most children, even the highly impulsive, over-reactive ones who are given to tantrums, will be having very few tantrums by now if you have been putting the core strategies into practice. The following strategies will further reduce tantrums.

Different types of tantrums

There are two main types of tantrums. There is the purely vocal tantrum, during which the child is crying, threatening, insulting or screaming. And then there is the physically aggressive tantrum, where, in addition to the vocal component, the child might be hitting, pushing, biting, kicking, scratching, spitting, throwing or destroying things, stomping around or slamming doors. These two categories of tantrums each require a different strategy.

The Calmer, Easier, Happier Parenting strategies are very effective at preventing most tantrums and also at minimising the frequency, intensity and duration of tantrums when they do happen. But we need to realise that if tantrums have worked in the past to get your child out of doing something he does not want to do or to get him more attention, he will not want to give up a strategy that has worked for him. And please remember that it will probably take longer to see significant results with these strategies if your child has a more tricky temperament. But persevere! These strategies will work!

I'll begin with how we can Prepare for Success to minimise the likelihood of both types of tantrum erupting. And then, because Preparing for Success is not an instant cure, I'll move on to some specific strategies for dealing with a tantrum when it's happening.

1 Preparing for Success

There is a lot we can do to prevent most tantrums and to minimise tantrums so that they occur less often, are shorter and
are milder.

- **Become a United Front: Agree with your partner how
  you want to tackle your child's tantrums**

Read through the suggestions I make here and see which
strategies you both want to commit to. There are a lot of strategies here, and you may not want to commit to all of them.
But most parents feel that an all-out campaign is well worth it
when they start to see their tantrum-prone child becoming
calmer and more sensible and less easily triggered to react
with aggression.

- **Decide which new rules you need to make or which
  existing rules you need to clarify with think-throughs**

Use *think-throughs* to help children visualise how they should
behave when they are feeling upset. *Think-throughs* clarify the
behaviour you expect of them, so they play a vital role in helping to prevent and minimise tantrums. You can eliminate the
majority of tantrums within a week or two using this Preparing
for Success prevention technique. Here are some ways you
can use *think-throughs* to help you succeed:

Use think-throughs to teach your child alternatives to hitting.
The kinds of questions you could ask during the *think-throughs*
are:

When you're really angry, instead of hitting, what should you do?

When you're so frustrated because you can't have what you want, instead of kicking, what's the right thing to do?

When you're so disappointed because there wasn't time for you to have a second turn on the equipment, instead of screaming, what should you do?

Don't be surprised if your child answers these questions by saying, 'I shouldn't hit,' or 'I shouldn't scream.' Children can usually tell us what they should <u>not</u> do because they have heard us talking a lot about what they should not do. But they often draw a blank when asked to imagine what they should do instead, unless they have specifically been taught a more constructive response. We can teach our children to:

- take ten deep breaths
- clench and unclench their fists
- use their words to say how upset they are
- punch a punch bag
- go to a parent for a hug
- find something else to do to calm themselves down
- do something physically active
- draw or write their feelings.

These are all useful and constructive responses to frustration, disappointment and anger. These responses have been successfully taught to children and teens who have a highly sensitive, intense and reactive temperament, the children most likely to have a tantrum when things go wrong. Teaching and training these alternative ways of responding is easier than you might think. The key is to do lots of *think-throughs* (even ten a day) at neutral times, coupled with rehearsals, and to Descriptively Praise every tiny glimmer of self-control and flexibility.

Use think-throughs to teach your child to respect you and your possessions.

Make a rule for yourself not to do things for your child that he is capable of doing for himself. Your child will not respect you if you behave like his unpaid staff!

I have found that a common characteristic of children who are given to tantrums is that they are in the habit of treating their parents' bodies and possessions with disrespect. Your child may pull on you to get your attention; he may hang on you or play with your clothes or jewellery; he may go into your handbag without asking. The problem with allowing our children to behave like this is that it sends a subtle message that the child does not need to respect us. It's almost as if he regards the parent as a plaything. This definitely does not help him take anything you say seriously. We can use *think-throughs* to clarify what the rules are about respecting you and your possessions. For example:

What should you say when you want something that's in my handbag?

Instead of pulling on my clothes when you need something, what should you do?

Who can touch Mummy's earrings?

Use think-throughs to teach and train your child to think more flexibly.

Make a rule for yourself never to promise your child anything. Children with inflexible thinking take things literally. This leads to severe disappointment and frustration. Therefore, don't say something is going to happen unless you can be one hundred percent sure that it will happen. When we say, 'We're going to the zoo on Saturday,' a child with an inflexible temperament will take this as gospel. Then when an unforeseen circumstance prevents the trip to the zoo from happening, this child feels very let down. He may even feel that his parents have lied to him. His disappointment and anger overwhelm him, and he may react by having a tantrum.

You can use *think-throughs* to help children become more flexible and to help them to imagine what might or might not prevent any event from happening. For example:

What do you think will happen about our zoo trip if it's raining on Saturday?

What do you think will happen if one of us is ill on Saturday?

How about if there's an emergency at the office?

Give your child plenty of practice at being flexible. Getting children used to minor disappointments helps them, over time, to realise that life can be enjoyable even when things do not go just the way they want. For example, when your child is making a fuss because he really wants the red cup, give him the green one instead. This may seem counter-intuitive and even harsh. We think we might as well give him the red cup because after all it's such a small thing, and it seems to matter so much to the child. Not giving him exactly what he wants might feel harsh to your child if you were angry, judgemental or blaming. But I am recommending, of course, that you stay calm and friendly and do lots of Reflective Listening. *Think-throughs* will guide a naturally inflexible child to become more flexible (but not, alas, overnight).

You might start a *think-through* by saying:

The new rule is that from now on, if you want something to be a certain way, a lot of the time Mummy and Daddy will make sure that you have it a different way, not the way you want.

Remember to Reflectively Listen to whatever feelings come up. Ask your child to tell you the new rule. Also, ask her why she thinks Mummy and Daddy have made this new rule. She probably knows. If not, she has to take a sensible guess.

You'll probably need to do several *think-throughs* a day about this new rule, coming up with relevant examples:

So if you want the blue flannel, which one will you get?

If you want to sit next to Daddy in the café, where will you have to sit instead?

- **Prepare the environment**

Improve your child's lifestyle.
The child who tends to be quite sensitive, intense, impulsive or inflexible is often very affected by circumstances that a more easy-going child would shrug off. We can reduce the frequency, the intensity and the duration of tantrums by improving what (and when) our children eat, making sure they get enough sleep and lots of exercise and by cutting way back on screen time. In Section Two of this book, I address each of these lifestyle issues in separate chapters and give recommendations, all of them practical, for how to improve each of these areas.

Find alternative ways of saying 'No'.
Every day parents find themselves replying with some version
of 'No' to many of our children's demands, pleas and complaints:

Can I have another biscuit?

Will you play with me?

Can you give me a ride to the shops?

I never get to sit there.

I want chips, not mashed potatoes.

Tie my shoes.

When we reply 'No', the child with a sensitive or intense or
inflexible temperament gets easily upset. He may fall back on
a familiar repertoire of reactions that have been effective in
the past at getting his parents to change their minds, at least
some of the time. He may whinge, badger, sulk, cry, scream,
insult or even kick and hit. It's important to deal with these
behaviours by waiting until the child has stopped before there
is <u>any</u> discussion about what the child has asked for. If we get
drawn into talking about what the child wants while she is still
misbehaving or whingeing or speaking disrespectfully, we are
unintentionally sending the message that it is acceptable for
her to react that way.

Especially with a child who is more intense, we need to
get into the habit of pausing before we speak. Stop for a
moment before you say 'No' and consider whether you really
mean 'No'. If you think that you might be tempted to change
your mind after a while, it's important not to say 'No' in the

first place. If your 'No' later turns into a 'Yes', you may manage to convince yourself that you are changing your mind because you have carefully reconsidered the evidence or because you want to show that you are being flexible or fair. But from the child's point of view, he pestered you, or he cried or threatened or sulked, and you gave in. Changing your mind makes it more likely that he will try the same tactics again . . . and again.

We can reduce the intensity of the child's negative reaction and make it easier for her to accept our 'No':

- Smile and stay friendly.
- Feel free to say, 'I haven't decided yet. I'll let you know in a few minutes.' It is very useful for impulsive, intense children to learn to be patient.
- To make sure that your child learns not to keep asking or pestering you, a good rule to establish is: 'If you talk about it any more before I say yes or no, my answer will definitely be <u>no</u>.' If you are willing to stick to this, you will find that very soon your child will start thinking before he speaks.

Rather than focusing on the 'No', you can convey the same information using a 'Yes' attitude:

- Instead of saying, 'No more biscuits, you'll ruin your appetite,' you could say, 'Yes, you can have another biscuit after dinner.' (This helps teach your child patience, impulse-control and the skill of delaying gratification.)
- Instead of, 'You're old enough to tie your own shoes,' this response would be more helpful: 'I know you can do some of it. I'll watch while you tie the first knot. Then you watch while I tie the bow. And I'll show you how I

get it really tight so it stays tied.' (Here you are Preparing for Success by teaching a life skill. Soon your child won't be asking you to tie his shoes or walking around with loose laces flopping.

- Instead of saying, 'No, how many times have I told you!' the following response is easier for your child or teen to hear and just as firm: 'My job is to take care of your health. That's why we have a rule: sweets only once a week. Three more days to go.' (This response helps the child realise why we have said 'No'. Otherwise an explosive, immature child can easily jump to the conclusion that we said no about the sweets because we are angry with him.

- Instead of, 'I don't have time to play,' this sounds friendlier: 'I'd love to play with you for ten minutes. I'll be ready as soon as the laundry is folded. Would you like to help me fold so it goes faster?' (This teaches the child how he can use problem-solving skills to get at least some of what he wants.)

- **Plan your day realistically**

Rushing children never brings out the best in them. And in particular, children who tend to be sensitive, intense, impulsive or inflexible react very badly to being hurried and chivvied along. We need to build a bit of extra time into each activity throughout the day so that we are less tempted to repeat, remind and nag. A little cushion of time will enable us to remember to use the new strategies rather than reacting in the same old way.

- **Special Time**

Parents always find that frequent, predictable and labelled Special Time reduces tantrums. Special Time helps a child feel valued, liked and appreciated. Special Time helps children want to control their impulses.

2 Descriptive Praise

When you remember to Descriptively Praise an upset child's self-control, he will try to control himself more and more. When we say, 'I could see you were upset, but you didn't hurt anybody,' that helps him to reinvent himself as someone who can stay calm and sensible even when he is upset.

We can help children learn to be more flexible by Descriptively Praising any tiny glimmers of flexibility:

You wanted to sit next to me, but your sister got there first, and you didn't try and push her away.

Your friend took the last biscuit. There's none left for you, but you're not complaining. You're being very flexible.

You didn't win, but you're not crying.

Even if your child is reacting in an unacceptable way, we can look for and Descriptively Praise small bits of OK behaviour, or even the momentary absence of the negative behaviour. This is much more motivating than telling off:

That's a friendlier voice. So now I can listen.

You're not trying to grab it away from me. Thanks.

I don't hear any swearing. You're being respectful now.

3 Reflective Listening

Reflective Listening is a very helpful way of defusing your child's upset before he even has a chance to work himself up into a tantrum. When you Reflectively Listen, you show your child that you care about how upset he is feeling. This can take the sting out of his upset. If your child is disappointed or frustrated when something goes wrong, you can say:

You really want to show me the city you built, and now you're going to have to wait because I'm not ready. That's really disappointing for you. And maybe you're worried I'll forget all about it.

I can see how angry you're feeling. That wheel keeps falling off – so frustrating. You're wishing I would fix it, even though I said I won't because it's broken and it will just fall off again.

4 Never Ask Twice

Tantrums are often sparked by our repeating and reminding and getting annoyed. For a sensitive, intense child, this nagging, and our impatience, feels unbearable. Instead, we need to use the Six Steps of the Never Ask Twice method to guide our children into the habit of first-time cooperation without a fuss ninety percent of the time. Your children will be so much happier and more relaxed.

5 Rewards and Consequences

In Chapter 8, I address rewards and consequences, which will significantly reduce future misbehaviour, including tantrums.

You will see that the focus is on rewards because rewards are so motivating. I will also introduce two types of consequences, and show you how to use them to minimise future misbehaviour.

As I've said, the Calmer, Easier, Happier Parenting strategies will work to make your child's tantrums shorter and milder and, over time, to prevent them from happening. But the strategies won't work instantly. So you still need to know what to do when your child is having a tantrum. At these times, we want to contain the damage (and embarrassment), we want to help the child feel better, and we want to show the child a more acceptable way to express his strong emotions.

Now comes the part you've been waiting for – what to do when your child is in the middle of a tantrum. Here I will give you strategies for both vocal and physical tantrums.

How to deal with a vocal tantrum (no matter how loud or how insulting)

- The first step, as always, is the hardest: make sure you stay calm (at least on the outside) so that you don't go down the path of answering, explaining, reassuring, justifying, repeating, reminding or shouting.
- Occasionally a child will calm down more quickly when left alone, but most upset children respond very well to a parental presence, as long as the parent is not lecturing, telling off or threatening. Sit near him, <u>saying very little</u>. When a child is screaming, almost anything a parent says (other than giving in!) will further inflame the situation. Instead, offer a hug.

- Let your child have his feelings, even if it's at the top of his lungs, rather than trying to reason with him or distract him or jolly him out of his upset. Usually we can just wait out a vocal tantrum. It is easier to wait out a tantrum if you deliberately allow more time for each activity. Your child will see that the crying, screaming, insulting or threatening doesn't get the desired reaction. And our calmness helps him calm down more quickly. Over time, he will learn to control his reactions better.

- There is no point in even talking to your child until she is calmer and can listen. As soon as the volume goes down or as soon as there is a slight pause in the histrionics, you can insert a bit of Descriptive Praise:

You've stopped calling me names.

You're not crying so loudly now.

You're still here. You haven't walked away.

Or you can Reflectively Listen:

You're so angry we have to leave the party now.

You had your heart set on the yellow dinosaur, and now someone else is playing with it.

That's so upsetting.

- It is amazing how calm and sensible children usually are once a tantrum has been allowed to run its course. After the child has come out on the other side of the tantrum, it's important to remember to *follow through* by insisting that your child cooperates with whatever your original instruction was. This helps rewire your child's brain in favour of calm, rational thought, rather than stubborn over-reacting.
- In the next chapter I will explain how you can use rewards and consequences in a new way to minimise tantrums in the future.

How to deal with a physically aggressive tantrum

The second category of tantrum, in which the child is physically aggressive, needs to be addressed much more directly. Children know in their bones, without having to be told, that it is absolutely wrong to hurt their parents and wrong to destroy property. So when we allow children to be aggressive or destructive it only makes them feel worse about themselves, very guilty and ashamed. These emotions are so painful that they can easily lead the child to shift the blame onto the parent – demonising the parent to justify his aggression. And having justified his actions, the child now feels free to repeat those actions, and possibly even to escalate to worse aggression. A child who acts out in aggressive or destructive ways often feels fury towards the adults whose weakness has led him to feel so bad about himself.

There is another very important reason why parents must do everything they possibly can to immediately stop a child hurting a parent, or even pretending to hurt. A child cannot respect parents who allow themselves to be mistreated.

So if a child attempts to hurt someone (including himself) or to damage property (even his own) he should be stopped immediately. Of course we will use the minimum force necessary, but we must not be afraid to take immediate, decisive action to physically restrain the child.

Once you have made sure that your child cannot cause any harm, you are still left with the vocal aspects of the tantrum, so follow the earlier guidelines about waiting, Reflectively Listening and Descriptively Praising.

Consequences for tantrums

Parents want to know what the consequences should be for a tantrum, particularly the aggressive or violent tantrum. If you have been dealing with lots of tantrums, you have probably tried everything you can think of to stop them in the moment. But you may not have thought much about how to prevent them in the future. Please read Chapter 8, 'Rewards and Consequences', to find out about two consequences that are very effective at reducing future misbehaviour.

You may be surprised that I do not recommend making a child apologise. This is because much of the time this is essentially asking the child to lie. A child who has just come out of a tantrum won't usually be feeling remorse or regret. First we need to help our child to feel remorse, and then we may need to help him feel brave enough to apologise.

An apology, even if sincere, should not be the equivalent of a get-out-of-jail-free card. The child still needs to make amends, for example picking up the chess pieces he scattered in anger or replacing (with money he has earned) something he has broken.

By the time the child finally apologises, we may want to put the tantrum behind us so we may say, 'That's all right, darling, Mummy loves you' or something else intended to be reassuring. Unfortunately that sends a mixed message. It may seem to our child as if the apology is not really important and therefore what he is apologising for is not that important.

To help him take his actions seriously, we need to make the apology very important and serious. When he is ready to apologise, he needs to say it in a full sentence; it is not enough for him just to say 'Sorry'. When our child has to say 'I'm sorry' and when he has to say what he is apologising for, that sends a much stronger message to his brain.

A really useful way to respond to a proper apology is to say, in a serious voice and with a serious face, something like, 'I'm so glad you're apologising. That shows me that you know you did something wrong, and you're wishing you hadn't done it. That's what I'm wishing too.'

All these strategies really do work to prevent and minimise tantrums. Of course your child will still get upset at times, and we know that some children's upsets feel all-consuming to them. But now he has a wider repertoire of responses available to him. So if you have a child who is verbally or physically aggressive, take heart. The more you put into place all the strategies you are learning in this book, the more your child will be able to show you his best side.

PARENTS WANT TO KNOW

Q: *If I'm making such a big effort to be positive and friendly, aren't my children going to think that they are getting away with misbehaving?*

A: As long as you *follow through*, your children cannot think that they are getting away with misbehaviour because they will not be getting away with it. *Following through* means insisting on cooperation, by using *think-throughs* and Rewards and Consequences.

We do not need to get angry in order to be firm. *Following through* is much more effective when we stay calm. As soon as a parent gets angry, the child is likely to get angry right back. And suddenly his focus shifts from wanting the parent's approval to wanting to prove that he is right and the parent is wrong. Our anger sometimes even prompts children to seek revenge.

Putting the Stopping Misbehaviour strategies into practice: Your Action Plan for the first two weeks

As you begin putting the Stopping Misbehaviour strategies into practice, you'll be combining Descriptive Praise and Reflective Listening in almost all of the steps. This will give you many opportunities to practise these effective strategies!

Here's an example of a 'stop behaviour' that shows how you could use the strategies outlined in this chapter to get your child to stop misbehaving as quickly as possible.

Let's say that your five-year-old daughter grabs her older sister's expensive violin off its stand and starts playing with it. I have shared eleven strategies you can use to stop this misbehaviour. You probably won't need all eleven! Chances are that the misbehaviour will stop after the first few, but I'll keep going with the examples to illustrate how this could work, in case you have a child who tends to be more defiant.

- **As always, start with think-throughs**

  If this kind of misbehaviour is happening a lot, the quickest way to see a change is to do *think-throughs* about it at a neutral time.

  Who can touch the violin?

  Where does the violin stay when your sister isn't playing it?

  When you want to touch the violin, what instrument can you play instead?

- **Be sure to Descriptively Praise her whenever she is in the same room with the violin and <u>doesn't</u> touch it!** 'You're looking at the violin, but you're remembering the rule. You're not touching it.'
- **Keep it friendly.** 'You really want to play with your sister's violin. Now it's time to put it back.'
- **Get close** – your child will probably respond by de-escalating the misbehaviour. That will give you something to Descriptively Praise. 'You're remembering the rule. You put the bow back where it belongs, and you're holding the violin carefully.'
- **Give clues.** 'You know the rule about who can hold your sister's instrument. You're really wishing you could play with it.'
- **Offer alternatives.** 'I can see it's hard to put it back, but you stopped carrying it around. We can't play with this instrument. Let's find a cushion to put on the piano bench so you can reach the keys. That's an instrument you <u>can</u> play with.'
- **Make it a rule for everyone.** 'None of us play with Chelsea's violin – even Dad and Mum. Only Chelsea.'

- **Empathise.** 'Maybe you wish you were older so you could play the violin. It can be hard to see your sister doing something that you can't do yet.'
- **Offer limited choices.** 'You really want to keep holding it. Would you like to hand it to me or put it back on the stand by yourself while I watch?'
- **Phrase it in the positive!** 'Put the violin down, please.'
- **Model the behaviour you want to see.** For this particular misbehaviour, modelling wouldn't be appropriate since the rule is that nobody plays with Chelsea's violin.
- **The bottom line: Always follow through.** If after you've gone through these positive steps, she is still holding it, remove the violin from her hands. If she keeps trying to grab it, remove her from the room. If you can be heard above her protests, you can Reflectively Listen: 'You're feeling so frustrated that you can't hold the violin'.

Summary

The strategies that I've described in this chapter are not what we feel like doing when faced with misbehaviour. Repeating, shouting, reprimanding and threatening are far more typical reactions. Our children are used to getting negative attention when they misbehave. Let's remember that when we get angry, it usually intensifies a negative situation. It makes them feel worse (and us too). However, if we can stay calm and friendly, our children will be much more willing to cooperate with us. When you stay calm, it will be easier to remember to Descriptively Praise any tiny steps towards stopping, and it will be easier to empathise with how they might be feeling. These strategies will help your children to stop misbehaving sooner than you can imagine. These positive strategies have worked with thousands of families around the world.

CHAPTER 8

REWARDS AND CONSEQUENCES: FOLLOWING THROUGH TO MINIMISE MISBEHAVIOUR AND MAXIMISE COOPERATION

Now let's turn our attention to Rewards and Consequences – what we can do to maximise future cooperation and minimise future misbehaviour. Parents often assume that there is only one thing that can significantly improve behaviour, namely consequences for misbehaviour. We can't rely on consequences to improve behaviour. Consequences on their own will not motivate children to <u>want</u> to behave well or to <u>remember</u> to behave well. After all, if consequences on their own were effective, our prisons would be empty.

And, in any case, we don't want our children to cooperate because they fear us or fear a consequence. We want our children to behave because they have internalised the right thing to do. Descriptive Praise and *think-throughs* are what teach and train a child to tell himself the right thing to do, and then to do it. Our children may well be motivated by rewards, however, and I will be giving you a number of ideas about how to use rewards to motivate your child.

KEY CONCEPT

If consequences on their own were effective,
our prisons would be empty.

With most of the Calmer, Easier, Happier Parenting skills, I can start giving you step-by-step examples straightaway. But Rewards and Consequences are a different matter. This topic is more complicated, and parents often have a number of misconceptions about Rewards and Consequences, so I want to address some of these typical issues. The whole area of *following through* can feel very problematic because if you are not yet focusing enough on motivation and prevention, you will find that you are dealing all day long with many tiny bits of non-cooperation. If you were to try and *follow through* consistently after each of those minor misbehaviours, all you would be doing all day long is doling out consequences. That would feel very negative, both for your children and for you. That is why we need to devote most of our time and attention to significantly reducing the amount of misbehaviour in the first place.

Following through, the fifth core strategy

Following through is all about what we do after a child does something. The reason that the *follow through* strategies are so important is that when you are willing to *follow through* consistently, your children will take what you say seriously. We know that children will test us if they think there's a chance that we might not *follow through*. The more you *follow through* and do what you say, the less energy children will put into testing. Our children are canny, and they will only continue to do what works!

KEY CONCEPT

When you *follow through*, your children will take what you say more seriously.

We tend to think of *following through* as what we do after misbehaviour, but *following through* also includes how we respond to the many little bits of good or just-OK behaviour. Rewards are the *follow through* for the behaviour you want to see more of. Rewards reinforce the values, skills and habits that you believe are right. The purpose of consequences is to reduce the amount of misbehaviour that remains.

Empty threats

The idea of 'following through' seems so obvious, but until I heard it explained at a Calmer, Easier, Happier Parenting seminar, I didn't really think about it much.

We weren't conscious of how little we were following through on the behaviour we expected. We used to threaten consequences over and over again but not take action and follow through, so our son never really felt that he had to do what we asked. When Noël explained that our kids lose respect for us when we make 'empty threats' and don't follow through on instructions, the light bulb went on.

Now we make sure we Prepare for Success by talking through what behaviour we expect. For example, if there's something our son needs to do when we get home from an outing, we go over that before we leave for the outing, doing think-throughs, and then we ask him again to tell us what he needs to do when we're in the car on the way home. If we get home and he still doesn't do it, then I just go to where he is and stand close to him and look at him. When he looks up I say, 'There's something you need to remember to do now that we're home.' Then I stand and wait until he gets up to do it, using the Never Ask Twice steps. He always does it.

Father of a 9-year-old

Giving rewards

Parents hope that warning children about the possible consequences of not doing what they're told will motivate them. In fact, threats can backfire; they frequently make an angry child even more rebellious. A more effective approach is to think and talk about rewards, rather than about consequences. Long before you give an instruction, while you are planting the seed or doing a *think-through*, you can mention the reward that can be earned. But once you have stated clearly exactly what you want your child to do, any continued talk of rewards will seem like pleading or bribing and will undermine your authority.

A reward is only a 'sweetener'; it provides a <u>bit</u> of extra motivation. We must not expect a potential reward to be a substitute for the work we need to do. A reward will not convince the child to cooperate. You will still need to put time and thought into establishing a United Front, clarifying your rules, keeping calm and smiling, arranging the environment so that it becomes easier for your child to behave well than to misbehave, etc. The point I am making is that there is a lot more to achieving cooperation than simply finding the right Rewards and Consequences.

At first, when children are just learning the habits of cooperation and self-reliance, they often become more motivated when we provide an incentive. The reward helps them to get started; it gets them over the hump of their initial resistance. Even though parents generally understand that a well-chosen reward can help to overcome a child's resistance, parents may worry that rewarding children for doing the right thing will spiral out of control and create a bigger problem: children who are only willing to cooperate if the reward is sufficiently appealing. In fact, the very opposite turns out to be true. As a new habit or behaviour becomes firmly established, the reward can easily be reduced and then phased out, or it can be transferred to the next good habit that you want to reinforce.

Parents assume that the kinds of rewards that they will need to offer to motivate children are big things like a new bicycle, a trip to Disneyland or new toys. One problem with a big reward like this is that a child may be desperate for the reward and yet still be too immature and impulsive to control his behaviour day after day in order to achieve a reward that is a few months or even a few weeks, in the future. Effective rewards are <u>daily</u> rewards.

Approval and appreciation are rewards

The best rewards are those that are easy and quick and cost nothing. That way you will be willing and able to dole out many little rewards every day, not just for amazingly wonderful behaviour (which you will not see every day), but for small improvements, even when the results are still not quite what you were hoping for. The very easiest, quickest and most effective rewards are our positive reactions to every little step in the right direction: our frequent use of Descriptive Praise.

Descriptive Praise is the most powerful motivator there is. It shows our children exactly which behaviour we are pleased about, and it gives them very useful information about how they can get more of our positive attention. We need to reward with Descriptive Praise all the tiny bits of sensible behaviour that would ordinarily go unnoticed when we are in a hurry or when our attention is focused on the next item on our to-do list.

Another easy, quick reward that reinforces the values and skills that we want our children to develop is smiling. When we are focused on getting things done, our children's minor misbehaviour feels <u>major</u> to us because it slows us down and interferes with our plans. So we become irritable and impatient. We forget to smile. Duty takes over, and we forget to relax and enjoy our children. Family life can become rather grim.

It's important to smile at our children a lot, even if occasionally it is through gritted teeth! The more we smile when our children are following our rules and routines and doing what we ask, the more they will want to be cooperative. The same holds true for hugs. Physical affection shows children that we appreciate them. These tiny rewards of Descriptive Praise, smiles and hugs will take you a long way towards improved behaviour. These rewards are food for our children's souls, just as vital for them to have every day as the food for their bodies that we give them daily.

Rewarding instead of indulging

Many children have too much stuff and too many treats that come too easily. Parents willingly sacrifice their own needs to give their children what the children think they need – toys, electronic gadgets, designer labels, sports equipment, etc.

Our children are usually given these things with no strings attached. But every so often, when they keep misbehaving or breaking the rules, we get furious and try to claw back some of these things. By taking things away from our child, or by threatening to, we are hoping that our child will realise the seriousness of her misbehaviours and will be motivated to improve her ways. In fact, what usually happens is that she is outraged because she was not told in the first place that these goodies were conditional on a certain standard of behaviour or academic performance. As far as she is concerned, we have changed the rules in the middle of the game, which feels grossly unfair.

So, instead of handing your children all these goodies on a plate, which often results in their having a careless, unappreciative attitude, I suggest that you have your children earn most of what they currently take for granted. This will help them to appreciate their treats, the cost as well as the time and effort that you put into providing them.

If we shift our focus from indulging to rewarding, a very effective consequence for misbehaviour will simply be that the child has not yet earned a reward. For example, the rule in your home might be that your child or teen can earn an hour of screen time every evening by completing his homework and his chores to your satisfaction within the allotted period of time. If he wastes time and therefore does not complete the homework and chores within that time, then he has not earned his screen time for the day. For your child, this is not the same as a withdrawal of his entitlement to screen time. With the new rule about earning, he cannot take it for granted that he will be able to go on the computer every evening. He knows that he must earn it daily. This will help him to keep his focus on following the family's rules and expectations.

This is a big shift in how we think about rights, privileges and responsibilities. Of course our children are entitled to the basics in life – food, clothing, shelter and love. And most children in the industrialised world can count on having these basics. I am suggesting that you require your children to earn the upgrades and the extras! When I work with parents I coach them to shift their focus from taking things away as a punishment to having their children earn things as a reward. This always results in tremendous improvements in cooperation! If your child values his screen time, this is the perfect motivator to use first.

From punishing to rewarding

Our son was so easy-going, and then our fiery daughter came along. I swear she came out of the womb fighting! By the time she turned six, it seemed like all she did was test us and do things she wasn't supposed to do. Whenever she did something wrong, our usual reaction was to punish her by taking things away that were important to her, at which point she'd become more frustrated and explode. Pretty soon we had nothing left to motivate her to behave because we'd taken everything away!

After learning Noël's strategy about 'earning', we no longer use punishment to motivate her. We now give her opportunities to earn everything that she wants. We use those things to motivate her. So on the weekends, if she wants to watch cartoons, she has a number of chores she has to do before she can do that. She has to make her bed, take out the rubbish, feed the pets, wipe down the sink and read for ten minutes. She is so motivated to earn her telly time that she quickly got into the habit of doing all these chores without complaining. Now it's just a routine she's in, and we never have to remind her.

This shift from punishing to rewarding has made a big difference in our relationship with our daughter, and it feels great to be able to reward her for all the positive things she does. We're calmer, she's calmer, and we're all happier.

Father of two, aged 10 and 7

Small daily rewards

Your children can earn many small rewards each day for little steps in the right direction. Of course, different rewards will be motivating for different children. You can get creative with these rewards. Just imagine what your child might enjoy. These rewards need to be easy to arrange, easy to do and either free or very inexpensive. They are often enjoyable for you as well! Here are ten examples of small rewards that families have told me worked well to motivate children to improve all aspects of their behaviour and schoolwork.

- An extra story or song at bedtime
- An extra five minutes of rough-and-tumble with a parent
- An outing with a parent without the siblings
- Playing a board game with a parent
- An extra fifteen minutes of screen time
- Choosing the menu for a meal
- Trying on Mum's jewellery or Dad's ties
- An adult activity with a parent, such as baking
- Camping out or having a picnic in the garden
- Sleeping in the sitting room.

It helps to focus on small, immediate rewards:

As soon as you put your clean laundry away, you'll have earned your computer time.

As long as you put the tops back on the markers, you can keep playing with them.

Once your child realises that cooperation is worth her while, you will find that she automatically does more and more of the right things. And she also starts making an <u>effort</u> to stop doing the things that annoy you. She may still be impulsive and immature, but she is now motivated to practise self-control. And with practice, her self-control <u>will</u> improve. But do not expect a child, or even a teenager, to be motivated to work for, or to keep her behaviour together for, a reward that is more than a week away. Big, long-term rewards are rarely motivating enough by themselves. Most children and young people do not have that much self-control.

Money as a reward

You can definitely use money to reward good behaviour and good work habits. Some parents believe that a child's pocket money should be earned; other parents believe that pocket money is a child's right. Some favour a combination of the two approaches. My experience has taught me that children and teenagers who have to earn most of the extras in their life become more motivated, more appreciative and more responsible. So if you are eager to improve some aspects of your child's behaviour, and if money happens to be important to your child, it seems a waste of a resource <u>not</u> to use money as a motivator. My recommendation is that children need to earn all or most of their pocket money.

If you choose to use pocket money as an incentive, I advise that you symbolically give the reward daily by marking on a chart each day the amount of money that has been earned, even if you only hand over the money once a week. Be willing to start by rewarding very small improvements. For example, achievements such as bringing home the right books from school or sitting down at the agreed time to do his homework could earn your child or teenager a small amount of money each day, even if he still makes a fuss about actually starting his homework or in the end produces much less than you think he should. A child who tends to be aggressive could earn a bit of money for each day, or even each hour, that he does not hit a sibling, even though he may still be grabbing or calling his brother names.

Be warned that money will probably not be an effective motivator if your child has a stash of cash in his bedroom or if he has a bank card and an account full of birthday money that he can spend however he wants.

As an aside, please remember that even when children are given money, by relatives for example, it is still up to the parents to decide the guidelines for when and how the money can be spent. In many Calmer, Easier, Happier families, a certain percentage of all the money a child is given or earns is automatically set aside for university or is donated to a charity. A teen or preteen may be required to pay a share of large expenses such as a new guitar or the latest electronic gadget.

One of the habits you probably want to teach your child is how to be responsible and careful about money. Another important habit is taking good care of his belongings. Children and teens will take better care of their possessions and will appreciate them more when they have to do something to earn them.

When we are arranging for our child to earn a reward, at first we need to make the task easy enough that he will be able to earn the reward with only a bit more effort than usual, rather than having to be really, really 'good'. Your child probably cannot manage a huge improvement all at once, but with practice, rewards, Descriptive Praise and a healthy lifestyle, your child will surprise you. You will see that he is becoming more and more willing and able to monitor himself.

With consistent rewards for small bits of good behaviour, your child will soon see that it is to her advantage to cooperate. She will come to realise, although she may not be able to articulate it, that the more sensibly she behaves, the more access she has to the goodies in life. As soon as children realise this vital fact of life, they become very motivated to cooperate. Once you start consistently rewarding lots of tiny steps in the right direction, it might take your child a few days or a few weeks to realise that cooperation pays off. Of course, this delightful realisation is likely to happen sooner if your child has a relatively easy-going temperament to begin with. It will also happen sooner if her self-esteem is already quite solid, thanks to plenty of Descriptive Praise, Reflective Listening and Special Time. And it will definitely happen sooner if you stay calm and friendly when your child is being uncooperative or argumentative, rather than resorting to the old strategies that do not work: lecturing, arguing back and shouting. If you skimp on the motivation and prevention strategies, your child may never make this important link between cooperation and rewards.

Tips for effective Rewards and Consequences

Here are some important guidelines that can help you to use rewards most successfully:

- Once your child has earned a reward, it's hers and can't be taken away. It's important that we never even threaten to take it away, no matter how angry we may become over later misbehaviour. Otherwise, a child with poor impulse-control will soon forfeit her hard-earned rewards, and she will give up trying to improve.

- It's important not to let your child choose a reward that requires you to do something for him that is his responsibility, such as setting the table or feeding the cat.

- Similarly, a reward shouldn't let a child get out of doing something you think is important but that she finds uncomfortable, such as music practice or sharing.

- Do not expect rewards <u>by themselves</u> to motivate a child who is quite reluctant, impulsive or angry. A reward is just one tool, something that makes it somewhat easier for your child to develop the habits of cooperation and self-reliance. Rewards are not a substitute for motivating with Descriptive Praise and Special Time or for minimising and preventing problems by Preparing for Success and Reflective Listening.

- When your child does not manage to earn the rewards, make a point of sounding disappointed, rather than angry or blaming. You could say, 'Oh, what a shame. I was hoping we could have that extra story tonight.' This is empathetic, not adversarial. It shows you're on their side, and it's far more motivating than if you were to say, 'It's your own fault, you know, for wasting time by arguing when you should have been getting on with your homework.'

- In addition to the rewards that your child knows in advance are available, it is also very motivating for her occasionally to be surprised by rewards that she was not expecting. This achieves two purposes. First, it helps her to see herself in a new light, as a person who can delight and impress the parent. It also models a very generous, giving attitude, which she will, over time, absorb and imitate. You could say:

You two were so sensible and calm at dinner. There was no teasing. Your reward is an extra ten minutes of computer time tonight.

- And my final piece of advice: it's very important not to use food as a reward. Food is too emotive an issue, too linked with love and acceptance. It's much better not to tie food to anything that has to do with approval or disapproval.

To summarise, when we use Descriptive Praise and other rewards to motivate, at first a child cooperates because receiving the Descriptive Praise and the rewards feels good. If we are consistent with our praise and rewards, cooperation starts to become a habit. Eventually your child chooses to do the right thing because he feels better about himself when he does the right thing. This is the birth of conscience.

Consequences that do work!

Now it's time to talk about what we can do after misbehaviour has happened to minimise the chances of it happening again. This is where consequences can be very useful.

Action replays

The purpose of consequences is to improve future behaviour. The most useful consequence I know is what I call an *action replay*. It is a small consequence and takes less than a minute, but it is extremely effective. An *action replay* consists of you and your child replaying the scenario, but this time he does the right thing straightaway, without any misbehaviour or fuss.

Do *action replays* after any misbehaviour, large or small, in order to give your child practice at doing the right thing, for example talking politely, doing for himself something that he can do himself, cooperating the first time without a fuss, etc.

The *action replay* will influence his future behaviour far more effectively than a scolding or a lecture will. *Think-throughs* at a neutral time about how to behave and *action replays* after misbehaviour are a highly effective combination. And *action replays* always end discipline on a positive note! They wipe the slate clean because the incident ends with the child behaving appropriately. What gets stored in his long-term memory is the last thing that happened: he did the right thing, and you were pleased with him.

KEY CONCEPT

You can do *action replays* for any type of misbehaviour, major or minor.

The best time to do an *action replay* is as soon as possible after the misbehaviour. But you need to wait until everyone is calm. Do the *action replay* before talking about anything else, before answering any questions, before giving him permission to do anything, before doing anything for him.

Let's imagine that you said, 'It's homework time' (after having eased him into the transition with a *countdown*), and at first your child argued or ignored you, but you stayed calm and firm, and eventually he complied. As soon as he has stopped being upset, you can say to him: 'Now we'll do an *action replay*. I'm going to say, "It's homework time," and this time you won't argue. What will you do instead?' Because your child is now calm, he will probably respond with, 'I'll just go and sit down,' or 'I'll get my books out,' or 'I'll say OK.' As a result of this exchange, which is really a mini-*think-through* during which you asked the questions and your child answered, you will be sure he knows the appropriate response. At that point, you both act it out. You say,

'It's homework time,' and your child says something like, 'All right,' and then he heads to the homework table.

KEY CONCEPT

Action replays end all discipline on a positive note.

Here is another example of an *action replay*. Let's say your child speaks to you rudely. Disrespectful behaviour, language or tone of voice is almost always triggered by a strong, uncomfortable feeling, usually anger, sometimes anxiety. Don't bother correcting him or saying something pointless like, 'That's not how you speak to me.' He just did – for now, that is how he speaks to you! Almost any parental response to rudeness gives the child or teen the satisfaction of seeing he can provoke you.

Instead, wait a few seconds and Descriptively Praise when he stops. Then wait a bit more and ask if he is ready to do an *action replay*. In the *action replay*, he will need to say how he feels, just as strongly, but using polite words. If you have been doing plenty of *think-throughs* about how to speak one's mind and express strong feelings politely, he will know how to. So he will probably be willing to do the *action replay*.

If he is not yet ready to do the *action replay*, don't despair. Quite soon he will want something from you. At that point, you can say, 'I'll be glad to talk about that, after we do the *action replay*.' If you stay firm, children and teenagers will soon see that you mean it. And because you are staying calm and friendly, their natural urge to please you will bubble up to the surface and motivate them to cooperate.

On rare occasions, a child will show that he is still angry, either by refusing outright to do the *action replay* or by being silly and not doing the *action replay* properly. Don't keep trying to get him to do it. That would be rewarding his negative behaviour with your attention. Remember my earlier advice about not giving a direct instruction until we are almost certain that the child will cooperate. Instead, you can say something like, 'I can see you're not ready to do the *action replay*. I'll ask you again in a few minutes.' Part of what will motivate your child to do the *action replay* properly is that in the meantime nothing fun or interesting happens, not even a brief conversation. Descriptive Praise and Reflective Listening, however, are always appropriate.

Action replays can prevent tantrums

Children's misbehaviour does not usually go from zero to sixty in five seconds. There is usually a gradual build-up. We can see that the child is becoming irritable or overexcited; we may even say he is 'looking for a fight'. It can be tempting to ignore or excuse the small warning signs of increased resistance, wild play, rude words or showing off. We are desperately hoping that the bad mood will blow over, partly because we've got lots to get done, we're on a tight schedule, and we just don't have time for a tantrum. We may choose to look the other way, rather than risk tipping the child over the edge into a tantrum. But what usually happens is that the misbehaviour escalates, little by little, until it erupts into a full-blown tantrum.

I know the following advice is quite counter-intuitive. Be willing to do *action replays* for every bit of misbehaviour; this can often prevent a tantrum. It shows your child that you are in charge, and this is likely to help him calm down.

But here's what can happen in the first few weeks of using the new strategies. Don't be surprised if on occasion (but far less frequently than parents anticipate) your firmness and consistency infuriate a child who has learned to use tantrums to get his way or to get attention. Your firmness may actually trigger a tantrum. Of course this is frustrating when it happens, but this phase won't last long. Week by week, you will soon notice that *action replays* and the other strategies are helping your child respond more calmly and maturely to life's ups and downs.

It's never too late to do an *action replay*. You can do it the next day or even weeks after the event. It will still be effective at influencing future behaviour, as long as you combine it with the other Calmer, Easier, Happier Parenting strategies. It's also a strategy that's equally effective whether you have a younger child or a teenager, as is demonstrated in this next family's story.

Positive, not punitive

We've been using action replays for ten years now. When Henry was three, like most kids his age, he sometimes threw sand when he was playing in the sandbox. We would then ask him where the sand needed to stay, and he'd say, 'Low.' We would praise him for remembering but also have him do an action replay and pick up the shovel again and show us how he could dig and keep the sand low. When he did it right, we had more to Descriptively Praise.

Now that he's thirteen, we tend to do action replays more for things like being disrespectful. The other day I asked Henry to pick up the clothes that he left on the floor, and he rolled his eyes and said, 'Whatever' and walked to his room. I started to walk away, thinking, OK, at least he's going to do what I asked. Then I realised I was letting him get away with being disrespectful, and that wasn't something I wanted to encourage! I went into his room and acknowledged that he was doing what I asked, but I asked him to say it again and this time answer me politely and without eye-rolling. We find action replays such a quick and effective consequence, and we really like that they're positive, not punitive.

Father of two, aged 13 and 11

PARENTS WANT TO KNOW

Q: *My six-year-old has started acting like a teenager! She'll do what I ask eventually but with such a bad attitude, rolling her eyes and slamming the doors on her way up to bed. What's the best consequence for rudeness?*

A: Cooperating with bad grace is definitely a step in the right direction towards cooperating with good grace! Descriptively Praise that she's doing the right thing. Also acknowledge her anger or resentment by Reflectively Listening. And as soon as she is calm, have her do an *action replay*.

Here is how you can minimise rudeness and disrespect in the future:

*   Do a few *think-throughs* every day, asking her questions about how she needs to talk to you so that she is visualising herself cooperating politely and expressing her upset more appropriately.
*   Make sure she has the best possible lifestyle, with plenty of sleep, daily vigorous exercise, excellent nutrition and very little screen time. It's amazing how quickly behaviour improves when children are well rested, get plenty of exercise, have a healthy diet and aren't glued to a screen.
*   Be sure she is doing everything for herself that she is capable of doing. The less you do things for her, the more she will respect you, and the more polite and friendly she will be.
*   Spend some Special Time with her every day so that she is less and less tempted to misbehave as a way to get your attention.

Q: *I'm wondering how to get the balance right with my thirteen-year-old daughter. I'm fine about Reflectively Listening when her anger comes out in a casual, rude comment or a slammed door. But what about when she breaks a rule? Shouldn't she have a consequence?*

A.   For misbehaviour that hasn't been tied to a stated consequence, just Reflectively Listen and then have your daughter do an *action replay* once she is calm.

   For misbehaviour that is covered by an existing rule and has a stated consequence, the steps will be similar, but you will *follow through* with the consequence. Start with Reflective Listening at the time of the upset and then, when she's calm, do an *action replay*. And if there seems to be any doubt in her mind about the consequence, make sure she knows it will happen.

   Of course, if this is happening a lot, daily *think-throughs* should be happening. That way the consequence won't come as a surprise to your daughter. And the *think-throughs* will greatly reduce the amount of annoying behaviour.

Sitting apart instead of time-outs

Another effective consequence is what I call *sitting apart*. This technique is very useful when a particular misbehaviour keeps recurring in spite of the fact that you have been doing <u>lots</u> of Descriptive Praise, Preparing for Success, Reflective Listening, Special Time, Never Ask Twice, and *action replays*. These strategies and techniques improve behaviour significantly so you will very, very rarely need to use *sitting apart*. It is an excellent consequence for physical aggression or for any recurring impulsive misbehaviour, even actions that you think are beyond your child's conscious control.

Sitting apart is similar in some ways to a time-out, but is much more manageable. Many children hate time-outs and have huge tantrums during them, so parents tend to threaten time-outs, rather than actually *following through* with them. For example, we may say, 'Do you want a time-out?' What child will say, 'Yes please, Dad. I know I've been misbehaving. Please give me a time-out because I know I deserve it'?

What is the <u>same</u> about *sitting apart* and a time-out is that your child has to stay sitting in one place. His freedom of movement is temporarily curtailed. What is different between *sitting apart* and a time-out is that the *sitting apart* happens in the same room where you are. He will not be nearly so upset because he isn't being banished to the farthest corner of the house. Plus, you can monitor what he is doing. He will not be able to trash his room in fury or sneak off and play, as can often happen with time-outs.

Sitting apart is an effective consequence because children do not want to have to stay in one place. They want the freedom to move around and go where <u>they</u> want to go, and they are therefore motivated to improve their behaviour so that they do not end up *sitting apart*. Even very impulsive children, who seem as if they simply cannot remember or follow rules, will quite soon start to remember the rules and follow them when *sitting apart* happens consistently.

During the *sitting apart* you are right there teaching and training. You can Descriptively Praise and Reflectively Listen to help him behave and to help him calm down. This is very different from a time-out, where not much learning takes place. During the *sitting apart*, refrain from answering questions, chatting, reminding, reassuring, warning or scolding.

You may be wondering how long a child should stay in

the *sitting apart* place. The usual guideline, just as with time-outs, is a minute for each year of the child's age. Use a timer so that you do not give yourself another thing to have to keep track of. Timers also help to depersonalise the consequence, which often makes it easier for the child to cope with emotionally. Set the timer only after your child has stopped screaming, stopped whingeing, stopped throwing the cushions off the sofa, stopped sliding off the chair, etc. And be prepared to reset the timer to the very beginning if your child gets up from the *sitting apart* place or misbehaves at all. The first few times you require your child to *sit apart*, it could take up to half an hour of crying and whingeing and testing and trying to provoke you before your child is still and silent for the right number of minutes. It's just a test! Persevere and *follow through* so there is less and less testing in the future.

How to do a sitting apart if your child misbehaves in a public place

If the misbehaviour for which you want to do a *sitting apart* happens in public, you can wait and do the *sitting apart* as soon as you get home. It will still be effective as long as you make sure that *sitting apart* always happens after that misbehaviour. Or you can take your child to some place more private or back to the car temporarily, and do the *sitting apart* right there. I have even known very committed parents to handle misbehaviour at a party or playdate by doing a *sitting apart* in the host's bathroom!

What to do if your child keeps leaving the sitting apart place

If your young child keeps getting up from whichever part of the room you have designated as the *sitting apart* place, keep putting her back immediately and Descriptively Praise her a lot whenever she stays there, even for just a few seconds. Don't try to physically hold her in the *sitting apart* place. Each time you put her back, move away, but only a few steps away. This gives her the chance to learn that she has to stay there of her own accord. You are right there, ready to intercept her and put her back in the *sitting apart* place as many times as necessary, until she finally realises that you are not going away and you are not going to change your mind. After a while she will take you seriously and stay in the *sitting apart* place until the timer goes ding. This <u>will</u> happen, although the first few times you give this consequence it probably will not happen as quickly as you would like! Of course, remember to Reflectively Listen throughout about how upset or angry your child may be.

If an older child leaves the *sitting apart* area or refuses to go there in the first place, you will not be able to physically put her there, so do not even try. What you can do is make it clear that nothing will happen until the *sitting apart* happens. If you have been doing plenty of Descriptive Praise, Reflective Listening, Special Time and Preparing for Success, your child will be respecting you more and wanting to please you more, with the result that she will do the *sitting apart* – eventually!

If your child tests you a lot, you may find your blood beginning to boil. You may think to yourself, 'How dare he be so disobedient or disrespectful?' Here is the answer. He dares because misbehaviour and disrespect feed on inconsistency. Your child does not yet know <u>for sure</u> what you will do if he misbehaves. So he is internally driven to test your reaction so that he can find out for himself where the boundaries really are.

Keep reminding yourself that a misbehaving child is simply a child who has not yet been taught and trained in the <u>habit</u> of cooperation. Remembering this will make it much easier for you to stay calm and friendly, which will make your *follow-through* much more effective. It is much, much easier to remember that our children are not supposed to be perfect and that our job is to teach and train, which includes staying calm and friendly, when we are planning our day realistically. This means that we should not be rushing, and it means that we should be taking care of our own needs so that we are not running on empty.

Sitting apart is not intended to be a punishment (although your child may perceive it that way at first). *Sitting apart* is not a matter of simply serving one's time and walking away without a backward glance, having paid one's debt to society. *Sitting apart* is a slightly unpleasant, but not horrible, consequence that helps teach and train more sensible habits.

When the timer goes ding at the end of the *sitting apart*, your child is not yet free to simply walk away and forget it ever happened. The learning is not yet finished.

Once your child has completed the *sitting apart* by sitting quietly until the timer goes ding, he has to tell you in his own words and in a full sentence why you gave him a *sitting apart*. Don't accept, 'I don't know,' or 'I don't remember.' Kids have much better memories than we give them credit for! And in the unlikely event that he really has forgotten what happened less than half an hour ago, he can always take a sensible guess.

Remember to Descriptively Praise something about his reply. You might say:

That's right. You had a sitting apart because you took the inside toys out into the garden.

I can see you're cooperating now.

It's brave of you to tell the truth about what you did wrong.

Next he needs to do an *action replay*, first telling you what he should have done differently and then acting out doing it right, so that the last image that gets stored in his long-term memory is of himself doing the right thing. And the contents of his long-term memory are what will influence his future behaviour.

If after the timer goes ding, your child is still so angry that he is not yet willing to speak sensibly or to do the *action replay* properly, just set the timer for another minute or two of *sitting apart*. That is usually enough to show him that the only way he can earn his way out of the *sitting apart* is to tell you why he had the *sitting apart* and then do the *action replay*.

PARENTS WANT TO KNOW

Q: *What about when my child does something morally wrong, like lying? Should there be a consequence?*

A: First of all, let's acknowledge that all of us lie every day. We tell little white lies to avoid giving offence, or we say we have nearly finished a report, when we have barely started it, to keep our boss from being annoyed with us. The difference between our lying and children's lying is that children have not yet learned what kind of lying is socially acceptable in this culture. So let's not think of children's lying as a moral defect. Often the child has not yet learned when it is considered right in this culture to lie and when it is considered wrong. It is our job as parents to teach and train this rather tricky skill. Generally, we want children to lie when honesty would hurt someone's feelings, but we don't want them to lie to try to get out of trouble, to get someone else in trouble or to try to impress.

Parents often make the mistake of asking a child if something is true when they already know it is not true. This just gives your child the chance to dig herself deeper into the lie.

So let's not tempt our children to lie. When we know a child is lying, we need, in a very friendly manner, to just say so. Don't beat about the bush. Don't say, 'Are you sure?' You can say, 'I know what the truth is. You'll have to practise being brave and telling me the truth.' This may be emotionally difficult for your child. Be willing to Descriptively Praise each tiny step in the right direction.

If you suspect that your child is lying but are not sure, check up in some other way, such as by asking the teacher, rather than by asking your child, who is likely to keep lying. If you ask, 'Do you have any homework?' do not be surprised if your child looks at you with wide-eyed innocence and says 'No' emphatically. In that moment, she may even have convinced herself that she has no homework. Instead, you could say, 'Sit here and show me all your homework.' That way you are making it easier for your child to tell you the truth.

If you think your child is lying and if there is no way to find out for sure, your child still needs to know that you seriously doubt that what she is saying is true. You can say something like, 'I really wish I could believe you, but what you're saying just does not sound likely.'

If you find that your child or teen lies to avoid blame or responsibility, you can help her become more willing to own up to her mistakes and misbehaviour by Descriptively Praising her a lot, especially when she says or does anything that is difficult or uncomfortable or requires courage. If, when our children tell us the truth, we are pleased that they have been brave enough to tell us, then they will want to please us by being truthful, and they will become more and more truthful.

If we react with anger or give consequences when our children do something wrong, it is completely understandable that they will do whatever they can to avoid our reaction or the consequences. That can lead them to lie and to try and pin the blame on someone else. So we need to practise disciplining our children calmly. The calmer and more positive we are when dealing with misbehaviour, the more honest with us our children will become.

When consequences don't seem to work

Parents frequently tell me that consequences just don't work with their child. When consequences haven't been working it is usually because parents have used them inconsistently, and therefore the child does not really take the parents or the consequences seriously. Instead, he is continually testing to see what will happen this time because he does not really know for sure. Inconsistency about consequences means that at different times a parent responds differently to the same type or level of misbehaviour, depending on the parent's mood, stress level or what may seem to be extenuating circumstances.

Why parents may avoid consequences

Most of us don't really want to have to give consequences, so even if we have a rule with a stated consequence, we often try to avoid giving consequences. There are a number of reasons why. We may not want to seem like the bad guy, and we also might worry that our child would react negatively to the consequence, possibly refusing to accept our authority or becoming verbally or even physically aggressive. We may make excuses for the misbehaviour, blaming circumstances or outside forces. We may start to believe that our child cannot help himself because he is hungry, tired, jealous of the new baby, starting a new school, etc. Of course we need to empathise when our children have difficult experiences. Nevertheless, we're not doing them any favours when we teach them to make excuses for their behaviour. Our children may even start believing that they cannot control themselves.

We might tell ourselves that our child will eventually grow out of the annoying behaviour. He may, in time, but meanwhile he is annoying people on a regular basis! And he might not grow out of it. The opposite may happen: the habit may become more firmly entrenched. If we have a child with a more extreme temperament, we might also believe that our child's temperament or innate stubbornness prevents him from improving his behaviour.

When we avoid giving consequences, we may instead react to misbehaviour with nagging, shouting, arguing, bribing, negotiating and the other counter-productive responses we have already discussed. By the time we are exasperated enough to finally *follow through* with a consequence, we are likely to be furious and so may over-react, impulsively blurting out a dire consequence. On reflection, we may worry that the consequence seems too harsh, or maybe we realise that the consequence would inconvenience ourselves or someone else. Or maybe our child cries or pleads for one more chance or manages to convince us that the consequence is not deserved. At this point the consequence may be delayed or shortened or forgotten altogether. What children are learning when this happens is that they can risk ignoring or defying rules and probably nothing very serious will happen. This is not good preparation for real life!

Taking away privileges

One of the main reasons that consequences may not seem to work in families is that we may be trying to take away things and activities that our child has been led to believe are her birthright.

This is likely to confuse and infuriate any child, but particularly one who is relatively sensitive and intense. She may react with anger and defensiveness, possibly with anxiety. In that emotional state, she will learn nothing useful from any consequence.

KEY CONCEPT

Earning rewards vs Losing privileges
Taking away a privilege for misbehaviour, while an understandable reaction, seems unfair to children and generates resentment. On the other hand, allowing your child to earn a privilege through good behaviour is positive and far more motivating. You'll see behaviour improve sooner than you can imagine.

A mother told me a story about a consequence that backfired when her feisty daughter, Susanna, was five. It was Hanukkah. As is the custom, on each of the eight days of this holiday, Susanna would receive a gift. On day four, when the mother picked Susanna up from kindergarten, Susanna had a tantrum, screaming that she wanted a playdate that afternoon. Her mother explained that it wasn't possible, and Susanna got more and more angry, kicking the back of her mother's seat in the car. The mother finally lost her temper and told Susanna that she would not get her Hanukkah present that night. She followed through and didn't give her the present, and Susanna was furious. The mother thought Susanna would be motivated to behave better so she could get her present the next day, but Susanna only became angrier and misbehaved even more.

This same type of scenario is played out in many families. When we get angry enough, we may look for some privilege we can take away from our kids. In this story, the problem was that Susanna had never been told that her Hanukkah gifts were in any way linked to her behaviour. The gifts had not been set up as something she had to earn, so she believed she had a right to the gifts. So really, her fury was justifiable. When we take away treats or privileges that our kids didn't know could be taken away, it makes our children very resentful.

PARENTS WANT TO KNOW

Q: *What if these Rewards and Consequences don't work?*

A: I sometimes hear this question from parents who haven't yet begun practising the motivation and prevention strategies, so they haven't experienced how much these other strategies can reduce misbehaviour. I have never seen Rewards and Consequences fail when used in combination with the other Calmer, Easier, Happier Parenting strategies, but consequences will probably not be effective if used in isolation.

There is a very honest parent story at the beginning of Chapter 7. It explains that shifting from giving negative attention to giving positive attention is a process, and when we change and use these proactive strategies, misbehaviour will be reduced <u>over time</u>. If you have a child with a more challenging temperament, with more behaviour issues, as this family did, it may take longer to see significant results. There's no such thing as an instant fix, but these Calmer, Easier, Happier Parenting strategies will always work to improve habits because children and teens are motivated to please their parents, as long as parents are staying friendly and calm.

With practice and dedication you will get a wonderful result: family life that's calmer, easier and happier. You have nothing to lose and everything to gain.

Putting Rewards and Consequences into practice: Your Action Plan for the first two weeks

Now I will show you an example of how we can use rewards to help us get more of a behaviour we want and consequences to minimise the chances of that misbehaviour happening again in the future.

Think of a misbehaviour that's happening a lot – even after you've been doing the motivation and prevention strategies.

Let's say that your child's cooperation and motivation have improved a lot, but he is still disrespectful to you more often than you would like. When he's annoyed, he is sarcastic, he rolls his eyes and he walks away when you're talking to him.

Start with Preparing for Success and Descriptive Praise

As always, make sure that you are continuing to do *think-throughs* at a neutral time about how your child needs to speak to you:

When I'm talking, where do your eyes need to be?

What kind of voice do you need to use when you respond to me?

You might want to walk away when I'm asking you questions. What should you do instead?

What will happen if you ask me for something in an unfriendly way?

And remember to Descriptively Praise <u>whenever</u> your child talks to you in a friendly, respectful voice. You've got to catch him doing it right.

Rewards you could put in place

- Keep Descriptively Praising, even if at first your child acts as if he doesn't like it. He may be used to getting a big reaction from you, and even though a calm parent is a positive change, he may not like the fact that you're getting back in charge!
- You could arrange for him to earn his daily screen time by talking to you in a friendly voice. If he forgets, then he just hasn't earned his screen time that day, and you don't need to tell him off.
- Think of some other small rewards that could be given throughout the day for small steps in the right direction.

Consequences you will need to use

- The best consequence is an *action replay*. When he speaks to you disrespectfully, stay calm, praise him when he stops, and have him say it over again in a polite way. Then Descriptively Praise and also Reflectively Listen: 'You were probably feeling so irritated; you didn't want to say that over in a nice way, but you did the right thing. We're all practising speaking to each other in a friendly way.'
- You could decide that the consequence for rudeness is *sitting apart*. If so, you will need to *follow through* every time! After the *sitting apart*, have him tell you why he was there. Then do an *action replay* and *follow through* with more Descriptive Praise and Reflective Listening.

Summary

If you have started practising this proactive parenting approach, you are now motivating your children to cooperate by noticing and mentioning the many little things they are doing right every day. You have clarified your rules and expectations. Your children are cooperating more and more because of the Preparing for Success techniques. You are acknowledging your children's strong emotions, which helps defuse rather than inflame them. You are using the Never Ask Twice steps to get your children into the habit of cooperating the first time.

As a result of the changes you have been making in how you communicate with your children, you will be vastly reducing the amount of misbehaviour you have to deal with, and consequences will hardly be necessary. You will notice that you are no longer thinking about consequences as much as you might have in the past because your children are now taking you more seriously. That means they are listening more carefully, cooperating more quickly, responding to your friendly but firm tone of voice and to that friendly but serious look in your eye that says, even without words, 'I mean what I say.' With your new tools you will find that you are nipping in the bud many misbehaviours that in the past would have escalated to the point where it seemed like a consequence was necessary just to get your child to come to his senses. The *action replay* will become the one consequence you will use on a regular basis.

This may be hard to believe, I know. But as I've said before, just start practising these techniques, and you'll experience the positive results.

SECTION TWO

• •

TRANSFORMING FAMILY FLASHPOINTS: USING THE CORE STRATEGIES TO IMPROVE BEHAVIOUR ALL DAY LONG

What is the worst time of day for you? Do you dread mornings? Are mealtimes miserable? Or are bedtimes a battle? In most families there are certain times of day, and certain issues, that families find particularly difficult. These are the times when tension can quickly flare between parents and children, resulting in anger, frustration and stress. We come to dread a certain time of day, or we dread having to deal with a certain issue. These are what I call the 'family flashpoints'.

One of the many benefits of the Calmer, Easier, Happier Parenting strategies is that they work across all behaviour issues. So now I want to show you how to combine all the skills and strategies you've been learning and apply them to these typical flashpoints so that you can minimise misbehaviour and maximise cooperation and self-reliance. After practising the Calmer, Easier, Happier Parenting techniques, you and your children will no longer dread these times of day. You may even look forward to them!

Below is a list of the most common family flashpoints and the chapter that addresses each one. How many of these are an issue for your family? It's quite common to have several flashpoints that are problematic. Parents frequently come to me for help because they are having big issues with one particular flashpoint, for example with their child resisting going to bed. When I ask if bedtimes are the only time of day when they have trouble getting their child to do what they ask, ninety-nine percent of the time their answer is 'No'. It's just that bedtimes can <u>feel</u> the most problematic. As much as we love our children, we're exhausted at the end of the day and are ready to relax and be done with them!

If a number of flashpoints are causing stress, it probably means that the underlying problem is a lack of cooperation throughout the day. Once you focus on the five core strategies and put those in place, you'll find that you have fewer and fewer flashpoints that feel problematic.

- Getting ready in the mornings: Starting the day calmly – Chapter 9
- Mealtimes: Transforming fussy eating and improving table manners – Chapter 10
- Sibling relationships: Reducing squabbles, helping children get along – Chapter 11
- Screen time: Getting back in charge of the electronics in your home – Chapter 12
- Homework: Making it hassle-free – Chapter 13
- Tidying up and looking after belongings: Fostering responsibility, reducing resistance – Chapter 14
- Household chores: Improving willingness, teaching teamwork – Chapter 15
- Playing independently: Training self-reliance and problem-solving – Chapter 16
- Bedtimes and sleep: Ending the day peacefully – Chapter 17.

Here's what to do

1 Choose two flashpoints that are particular problems in your family.

It's important to set aside some time to sit down with your partner – or with a friend, if you don't have a partner – to discuss what the problems are in your family and to plan together what you want to be different. Even if quite a few of the flashpoints are an issue in your family, don't tackle them all at once. You'll find it overwhelming if you're trying to focus on too many things at the same time. I suggest that you concentrate on two flashpoints in the first week. The core strategies will lead to improved behaviour sooner than you can imagine. When you have had some success dealing with the first two flashpoints, then you can add two more flashpoints the following week.

2 Fill in the questionnaire before you begin.

At the start of each chapter in this section I have included a questionnaire that lists some of the common problems for that flashpoint. Mark which are issues in your family. This will help clarify which problems you want to work on. You may be experiencing other problems that are not on the list, so feel free to add to the list whatever behaviour is troubling you.

3 Decide when you want to begin putting the new strategies into practice.

You want to find a time when you are not under too much pressure. Don't start this when work is very demanding, or when the in-laws are due to come and stay! You want to be able to focus on making this a concerted campaign, knowing that you have the time and energy to support each other.

4 Spend two weeks practising the techniques, and then fill in the questionnaire again.
I promise you that the results will help motivate you to keep on practising!

Trouble-shooting checklist

You can use the following checklist for all of the flashpoints and for any burning parenting issues you want to address. You might be surprised to see that the Preparing for Success strategies are first. As I mentioned earlier, the two strategies of Preparing for Success and Descriptive Praise are inextricably linked. By practising the Preparing for Success techniques, you're helping your child do more and more things right the first time, so there will be even more that you can Descriptively Praise! I hope that by now you are Descriptively Praising many times throughout the day. This will continue to motivate your children to want to listen to you, to do their best and be their best.

1 Preparing for Success

- Have you established a United Front and agreed on the rules and routines with all the adults involved?

- What think-throughs do you need to do?
Do you need to establish some new rules and routines? Or do you already have a useful rule, but you haven't been sticking to it?

- How can you prepare the environment?
What can you arrange that would make it easier for your child to do the right thing?

- How can you plan your day realistically?

How can you build in more time? What could help you do this?

- Are you (and your partner if you have one) remembering to have Special Time with each child?

2 What can you Descriptively Praise?

Remember to Descriptively Praise every tiny step towards the behaviour you want to see. When will you praise? Which phrases can you use?

3 How can you use Reflective Listening to deal more constructively with your child's upset?

What uncomfortable emotions might your child be experiencing regarding this issue?

4 Are you remembering to use the Six Steps of the Never Ask Twice method, rather than repeating and reminding?

5 Do you think a reward would help reduce your child's resistance to the new rule or routine? Are you doing action replays to end misbehaviour on a positive note?

Again and again, parents tell me that whenever behaviour starts to become a problem, it's because they've forgotten to use one of these core strategies. Whatever the behavioural challenge is that you'd like to overcome, go through the questions on this checklist, put the strategies into practice, and you'll start ticking flashpoints off your list! When we communicate in positive, constructive ways, our children will respond, and we can head off or resolve most behaviour problems.

CHAPTER 9

GETTING READY IN THE MORNINGS: STARTING THE DAY CALMLY

How we reclaimed the mornings

Mornings were stressful, with lots of drama, crying and misery. After we learned Noël's techniques, the first thing we did was to figure out what wasn't working, agree on what we wanted to change and make a plan. We decided the two culprits that stalled our mornings were having our three-year-old pick out her clothes in the morning and having her eat breakfast before getting dressed.

Our solution was to move picking out her school clothes to the night before, during the bedtime routine, and have her eat breakfast after she got dressed. Being hungry was a great way to motivate her to get dressed! We started with a family meeting and told her the new routine. We said, 'Anya, we're going to change our morning routine. You're going to pick out your clothes at night, and in the morning you'll put your clothes on first, before you eat breakfast.' Then we did a think-through, asking her to tell us what the new routine would be. To make sure she was prepared, we did several think-throughs for two days before we started the new routine.

The first night we started, she took out her clothes and put them on her chair. In the morning, she woke up, got dressed straightaway and then ate breakfast. Then she went in her room and looked at the morning checklist we had made for her. I said, 'What's the next thing on your list?' and she said, 'Make my bed,' and she liked checking that off the list. We went through the list, and the morning was a breeze, plus we had so many things we could Descriptively Praise! I think we had one morning when she resisted the list, but I stayed determined and just Descriptively Praised every little glimmer of cooperation, and eventually she did everything on the list.

> *This has been a great change for us – we've reclaimed our mornings.*
>
> Mother of a 3-year-old

Like this mother, lots of parents find that mornings are the most stressful time of day, with the most rushing and repeating and reminding. The children are moaning and complaining, maybe bickering over who gets the Mickey Mouse cup or dawdling maddeningly, then suddenly panicking over a mislaid exercise book. Parents are reacting with nagging and shouting. Rush! Rush! Stress! Stress! It's a horrible start to the day for everyone.

If you have been living with a daily dose of morning stress for a long time, this state of affairs may seem inevitable, and even normal. But mornings don't have to be mayhem. By using the Calmer, Easier, Happier Parenting strategies and making just a few changes to your usual morning routine, like this mother did, you really can transform your mornings. You'll be able to drop your children off at the school gates confident that you've done everything you can to help them succeed at school, instead of worrying that they'll face a heavy day of learning with your impatient criticism ringing in their ears. A calm, relaxed morning helps everyone to enjoy the rest of the day.

The questionnaire

I have listed below some common problems that families have with mornings. In the top triangle, mark how often this behaviour occurs now. Revisit the questionnaire in two to four weeks and mark a bottom triangle. You will see progress!

Your child	Hardly ever	Sometimes	Too often
Has difficulty getting out of bed			
Dawdles			
Is fussy about choosing clothes			
Is slow to get dressed			
Resists brushing teeth, combing hair, making bed, tidying room, etc.			
Is in an irritable or uncooperative mood			
Is fussy about breakfast or not hungry			
Is disorganised, distractible			

Action Plan for Calmer, Easier, Happier mornings

I'm now going to show you how to use each of the Calmer, Easier, Happier Parenting strategies to help make mornings calmer and more pleasant.

1 Preparing for Success

• Be a United Front

With your partner, identify one or two problematic behaviours that are making mornings more stressful than necessary. Agree to tackle them together. You may need to compromise at this point.

Here are some rules that parents have brought in to make mornings easier:

If your child frequently makes a fuss about what to wear, have a rule that clothes need to be chosen and laid out the night before. That is what they need to put on the next morning, and they are not allowed to change their minds. Once your children are used to the new rule, which may take a few days, this rule will save time and avoid arguments.

Children who are able to dress themselves need to dress themselves, every single day, even when you are in a hurry and even when they are whingeing about it.
If, for a 'quiet life' or for a quicker start to the day, you sometimes do for your children some of the bits that they are able to do for themselves, you will be sending mixed messages, which will reinforce the dawdling or moaning.

Be warned that a child who has been used to having you perform this service for him may feel at first that he is being deprived of your love, care and attention when you tell him that it is now his job to dress himself. To ease him through this understandable reaction, stay with him while he dresses himself, and be willing to Descriptively Praise all of his efforts, however feeble. Requiring your child to dress himself will, of course, take longer than if you were to help him, but it is an investment that will pay off rapidly. Soon your child will be proud of his new competence. This self-reliance and self-confidence will gradually spread to other areas of his life as well, as long as you don't jump in and do things for him that he can do for himself. As a bonus, you will feel less annoyed, and you will soon have more time to get on with doing other things.

Everyone has to be completely dressed, hair brushed, beds made, pets fed, pyjamas put away and school bags near the door before breakfast is served.
This rule motivates children to stay focused on what they have to get done. It eliminates most of the dawdling and staring into space or the sudden urge to build a fort or practise a magic trick. It also eliminates most of our nagging!

No screen time before school.
Time in front of a screen makes dawdling worse, and it also tends to switch off the types of brain function that children need in order to get the most from school and develop more mature social skills.

* Do think-throughs to establish new rules or clarify existing rules

Examples of think-throughs
You may need to do quite a lot of *think-throughs*, especially if the rule you want to establish is in any way complicated

or has several parts to it. In the following example you will
see that it takes three separate *think-throughs*, each a
maximum of sixty seconds, just to make sure the child
knows the new rule.

The new rule that is being introduced here is: Starting
Monday, on school days, everyone in the family gets ready,
and then we sit down for breakfast.

First think-through: At a neutral time

Parent: *I'm going to tell you a new rule.*
Child: (Looks at the parent, saying nothing)
Parent: (Smiling, Descriptively Praises) *You're looking at me,
    and you're not making a face, even though you might not want
    to be hearing about a new rule.* (Pause) *The new rule is that
    starting Monday we'll have breakfast after we are completely
    ready to leave the house, except for cleaning teeth because we
    have to do that after we eat.*
Child: *Huh? Why?*
Parent: (Reflectively Listening) *You might not like this new rule.
    You might be feeling there are too many rules already.*
Child: *What do you mean – do everything before breakfast?*
Parent: *That's a sensible question. I'm glad you're thinking about
    what I said. What are some of the things you'll need to do in
    the morning before breakfast?*
Child: *I know what I have to do. Why do I have to tell you?*
Parent: *I'm glad you know what you have to do. So why do you
    think I'm asking you to tell me?*
Child: *Because I don't always do it?*
Parent: *That's right. You thought about it, and you came up with
    the answer to your own question.* (Pause) *So what's the new
    rule?*

Child: *I have to get ready in the morning before breakfast.*

Parent: *You remembered the new rule. A minute's up, so the next time I ask you about the new morning rule, I'll ask you to tell me four things you have to do in the morning before breakfast.*

Second think-through: At another neutral time

Parent: *I've got some questions for you about mornings.*

Child: (Groans and makes a face)

Parent: (Reflectively Listening) *Maybe you don't feel like talking about mornings right now.* (Descriptively Praising) *Now your face is looking polite again. Here's my first question: What do you have to do in the morning before breakfast?*

Child: *Get dressed, that's all I have to do.*

Parent: *That's one of the things you have to do. And what will you do with your pyjamas?*

Child: *Oh yeah, under my pillow.*

Parent: *That's where they go. So you've already remembered two things you have to do before breakfast. And what about your bed?*

Child: *Make it?*

Parent: *Yes, you remembered that you have to make your bed.*

Child: *But I don't have time in the morning. It's too hard! You have to help me.*

Parent: *I know that's been a problem for you. I have a solution to that problem. My job will be to wake you up in plenty of time to do everything you need to do.*

Child: (Groans)

Parent: (Waits a few seconds and then Descriptively Praising) *I can hear that you've stopped complaining. So you've already said: getting dressed, putting your pyjamas under the pillow and making your bed. There's just one more thing you need to do before breakfast. But our minute is up, so I'll ask you next time we do a think-through about the mornings.*

Third think-through: At another neutral time

Parent: *I'm going to ask you about our new morning rule. You already told me three things you have to do before breakfast on a school day. And even though you've already told me, I want you to tell me again. And I think that might be really annoying.*

Child: *I have to get dressed, put my pyjamas under the pillow and make my bed. That's everything.*

Parent: *That's everything you've already told me. And number four is about your hair.*

Child: *Of course I'm going to brush my hair. I don't even have to tell you that.*

Parent: (Reflectively Listening and Descriptively Praising) *You didn't want to tell me, but you did tell me. You did what I asked. So now, you need to tell me all four things that you have to do before breakfast.*

Child: (Groans) *I have to get dressed. I have to brush my hair. I have to make my bed.*

Parent: (Waits silently, smiling)

Child: *And I have to put my pyjamas under the pillow.*

Parent: *You've told me everything! And when you've done all those four things, what do you think will happen?*

Child: *Breakfast!*

Parent: *That's right! You know the new rule. And this isn't just a new rule for you. This is a new rule for everybody in the family, even Mum and Dad. And we won't always like this new rule. You answered all my questions, and the minute is up so you can go play now.*

- **Preparing the environment**

How a chart helped me become a morning person

I was in denial about how awful the morning rushing and nagging was in our family and just assumed it was normal. It was only after hearing the Preparing for Success techniques at a seminar that reality struck, and I got motivated to turn our mornings around.

I started by making a chart. I sat down with my three kids, ages seven, five and two, and we made a list of all the things that they needed to do each morning before school. We drew pictures of each thing on a poster board, the kids coloured them in and then wrote descriptions underneath the pictures.

Before we made the chart, I spent my mornings rushing around, reminding my kids of everything they needed to do in order to get out the door on time for school. After we had the chart, I was amazed at how such a simple tool like that could change our routine. All I have to do is point to the chart, the children run to check it, and they're immediately right back on track. They love to check the chart because it's something they made, and they're very proud of it. The chart took the place of my repeating and reminding, and our mornings are so much smoother and calmer! I'm happier, and my kids are happier.

Mother of three, aged 7, 5 and 2

Charts make rules easy to remember.

Many parents, like the mother in this story, find that having a chart or checklist is a much calmer way of refocusing children than endlessly repeating and reminding. Sitting down with your children and asking for their suggestions of what to include on the chart is a good way of getting them involved.

The following morning chart has eased tempers and improved cooperation in many households:

Get out of bed
Get dressed
Put your pyjamas away
Brush your hair
Make your bed
Eat your breakfast
Put your bowl and cup in the sink or dishwasher
Clean your teeth
Play if there is time

You can give ticks, stickers or stars when children do the things on the chart the first time they are asked and without a fuss. Most children find this very motivating, as long as Descriptive Praise accompanies the tick or star.

Children's breakfasts need to be healthy.

This sounds obvious, but many parents buy sugar-laden, high-salt or high-fat breakfast foods because that is all their children will eat in the mornings, and the parents, under-standably, do not want their children going off to school on an empty stomach. But remember who is in charge. We know what is good for children, whereas they mostly know, and care about, what they like and don't like. In the next chapter I explain a fool-proof method for expanding the range of foods that children will eat – and eventually even like.

- **Plan your day realistically**

For most families, not having enough time to get everything done in the morning is one of the main reasons why mornings are so stressful. Parents are rushing around trying to get everything done, trying to hurry their children along, while the children – feeling annoyed at being rushed – perversely decide to move even more slowly. Giving ourselves more time by planning our day differently can transform your mornings. Here are some suggestions:

Together, do everything you possibly can the evening before.
This may include signing the homework diary, making packed lunches and laying out the next day's clothes. Make sure your children check that they have everything they need in their schoolbags and that the schoolbags are placed by the front door. After a few days of whingeing or tantrums, they will get used to the new rules, and mornings will be much calmer.

Give everyone more time in the morning by waking the family up ten to twenty minutes earlier.
The increased peace of mind that comes from not having to rush around will more than make up for getting a bit less sleep. Think of this extra ten or twenty minutes as a cushion. You're building in time for your children to do what they need to do at their own tempo, to dawdle or search for a vital slip of paper or have a tantrum without your having to be concerned that it might make you late. When you allow more time, you will be less stressed, and that translates into your being less irritable and annoyed. And when you are feeling calmer, you can remember to Descriptively Praise every tiny step in the right direction. And if everything goes smoothly, you may even have some extra time to play a short game with the children before leaving for school.

• **Special Time**

Children often mess about in the morning to get our attention. Frequent Special Time fills a child's need for positive attention, making it easier for her to cooperate.

2 Descriptively Praise tiny steps in the right direction

Here are some examples of what you could say in the morning to highlight the tiny OK things that your children are already doing right. The more you say these kinds of Descriptive Praises, the more smoothly your mornings will go:

Your eyes are open, and you're not complaining, even though I know you probably don't want to get out of your warm, cosy bed just yet.

For the past three days, you've jumped out of bed the moment your alarm rang. That gives you more time in the morning to get ready. And it makes our morning together so much nicer because nobody's rushing.

Thanks for not throwing your clothes around the room, even though you don't want to get dressed. This way the room stays neat.

You're not playing now because you know it's time to get dressed. You remembered that getting dressed comes before playing, so I didn't have to remind you.

You remembered the new rule, and you got completely dressed before you sat down for breakfast. You even remembered your shoes.

You remembered to put your homework in your backpack last night. That's a sensible way to make sure you have everything you need for school.

I'm glad you picked up your books from the floor and put them on your bed. I didn't have to say a word. That shows self-reliance.

Just now, when your sister spilled her juice, you didn't laugh. You didn't even make a silly face. You're being tolerant.

3 Reflective Listening

Here are some examples of how you can use the skill of Reflective Listening to address and defuse many of the problems that happen in the morning.

It can be really annoying when you can't find two matching socks.

I bet you're wishing you could spend ten more minutes in bed. It's so cosy under the duvet.

Maybe you're feeling nervous about the science test today.

You were looking forward to your banana, and your brother's eaten the last one. How disappointing! But you didn't scream at him. You're controlling yourself.

(This is an example of how you can combine Reflective Listening and Descriptive Praise. This is a very powerful combination.)

Teaching Sarah to dress herself in the mornings

One of the things I decided I had to change about our mornings was teaching and training my four-year-old daughter, Sarah, to get dressed by herself. In the past I always helped her because it was so much quicker and easier. It felt like I didn't have time to wait for her to do it. But I realised I was doing this for me, and it wasn't helping Sarah to be self-reliant.

To give ourselves more time for this we'd have to get up earlier. Once my partner and I agreed on the rule, we started by doing a think-through with Sarah to explain the new rule. We told her that after the weekend we were all going to get up ten minutes earlier, and she would have to dress herself before breakfast every day. She seemed happy with this, and we spent the weekend practising doing up buttons and the other things she found difficult. So I knew she could do it. On the first day, Monday morning, I couldn't believe how well it went. I Descriptively Praised everything she did right and she was so proud of herself, she couldn't wait to tell her teacher at school – we even got to school early! But a few mornings later, it seemed like the novelty of dressing herself had worn off. She complained about putting her clothes on and held out her dress for me to help her. I waited a minute, trying to think what the problem was before reacting, and then tried Reflectively Listening. I said, 'Maybe you think I'm not helping you because you think I don't care?' She nodded, and I gave her a great big hug. After that she put her dress on all by herself, and since then she has done it every day without any fuss. Being more self-reliant has boosted her confidence to try other new things by herself. And I no longer need to stay with her while she gets dressed, so it's saved time too.

Mother of a 4-year-old

4 Never Ask Twice

At first you may need to use the Six Steps for each morning task you want your children to do, first for getting out of bed, then for getting dressed, then for brushing their hair, etc. Be sure to build in extra time to *follow through* with all six steps, if necessary. If you are willing to use the Never Ask Twice method consistently, soon you won't have to go beyond Step Three most of the time.

5 Rewards and Consequences

The reward for not wasting time could be a game with Mum and Dad before leaving for school.

Summary

When you start using these strategies, mornings can quickly shift from being stressful to being relaxed. Your children will leave for school feeling better about themselves, more confident that they can tackle the challenges of the day. And it will be a calmer start to the day for you too. The more of these strategies you incorporate into your mornings, the faster you'll see improvements!

CHAPTER 10

MEALTIMES: TRANSFORMING FUSSY EATING AND IMPROVING TABLE MANNERS

The day the grandparents came to dinner

Calm and dinner time were words that did not go together in our house! I really wanted to sit down and share an enjoyable, relaxed meal with the children, but until we started practising the Calmer, Easier, Happier Parenting techniques, I didn't know how to make this happen. The only 'conversation' at the table was along the lines of 'Just take one more bite, and then you can get down,' or 'No pudding until you've finished your peas,' or 'Elbows off the table, please,' or 'Stop kicking your brother.' It was anything but relaxing! In fact, it was so stressful and the kids were such fussy eaters that I'd got into the habit of cooking separate meals for each one – at least that way they'd eat something.

And this had started to seem normal until the grandparents came to dinner! I saw the children's table manners through their eyes, and I was so embarrassed I became determined to change things.

We started learning Noël's strategies, and the first thing we did as a family was to make a list of how we wanted our mealtimes to be. Top of my list was that we were all going to eat the same meal so I could stop being a restaurant chef. We also included rules about table manners. To begin with the kids weren't too happy about some of the rules, but we did lots of Descriptive Praise, think-throughs and Reflective Listening. We also used The First Plate Plan to teach our children to be more adventurous about food. About a month later the grandparents came again for lunch, and they could hardly believe the change. We actually did have a relaxing meal, and I was so proud of the kids.

Mother of three, aged 10, 8 and 5

Don't wait for the grandparents to come if mealtimes are a problem in your family! You can use the Calmer, Easier, Happier Parenting strategies to improve your family mealtimes, whether you're having problems with what and how much your children are eating or with how they are behaving at the table. Mealtimes are such an important part of family life, and providing our children with healthy food is so vital to their wellbeing and success that the sooner you can start solving mealtime problems, the more relaxed everyone will be.

KEY CONCEPT

It's never too late to guide our children into better mealtime habits.

The parents I talk to want meals to be calmer and more relaxed, a time when the family enjoys coming together to share good, healthy food and exchange news of their day. Parents want children to eat what is put in front of them without a fuss; they want pleasant conversation instead of complaining and interrupting. And of course they want good table manners.

What you want for your family meals may be different from this. It is not my job to tell you what mealtimes should be like in your home. In this chapter, I want to share with you some tools that will help you transmit your values in a positive, loving and respectful way, so that mealtimes stop being stressful and problematic and start being a relaxing, enjoyable experience. The Calmer, Easier, Happier Parenting strategies that you have been learning will help you achieve this. In this chapter I will also share with you some additional strategies that target particular mealtime problems.

The questionnaire

The first step to achieving Calmer, Easier, Happier mealtimes is to identify what the problem areas are in your family, what habits you want your children to develop and how you want mealtimes to be. This questionnaire lists some typical mealtime problems. Filling it in will help you to focus on what changes you want to make.

After you have been putting the strategies into practice for two to four weeks, you will see a big difference.

Your child	Hardly ever	Sometimes	Too often
Complains about the food			
Is fussy about what foods he will eat			
Is fussy about foods touching on her plate			
Resists trying new foods			
Teases or argues with siblings at the table			
Has poor table manners			

Your child	Hardly ever	Sometimes	Too often
Gets down from the table before he is excused			
Chews with his mouth open or talks with his mouth full			
Doesn't hold his cutlery correctly			
Is a messy eater			
Is silly or too noisy at the table			
Dawdles over the meal			
Eats too quickly			
Wants to snack all day long but is not hungry at mealtimes			

Action Plan for Calmer, Easier, Happier mealtimes

1 Preparing for Success

- ### Getting united on family rules and expectations

To make it easier for children to remember to do the right thing at mealtimes, you need to be clear yourself about what behaviour you want and what your expectations are. Make sure that all the adults in the family agree to the same rules and routines. It helps to write down your rules. If your children are old enough, the whole family could sit down together and draw up a list of mealtime rules. You'll find that your children will be keener to comply if you make it clear that most of the rules apply to the parents as well as to the children.

In case you're not sure which rules would help achieve your mealtime goals, here are some rules that parents have successfully used to make mealtimes calmer, easier and happier. It's a long list of suggestions, so you can just choose the ones that are relevant to you and are consistent with your values.

Everyone helps before and after meals.
Setting the table and clearing away at the end of the meal are obvious ways children can contribute. But you can also include your children in helping to prepare the meals. Even young children can help find ingredients, and will enjoy weighing, measuring and pouring. Older children can be taught how to cook parts of a meal, and eventually a whole meal.

All family members who are at home sit together for the meal, even if they are not hungry.

In many families, children eat on their own while the parent is busy in the kitchen. This causes a number of problems. When you are acting like a servant, you are likely to be treated like a servant. And the way that children learn good table manners and more mature conversational skills is by imitation, so you need to be with them at the table so that they can imitate you. Even if you are intending to eat your own dinner later, after the children are in bed, put a small amount of food on your plate when you are sitting with the children so that all of you are eating together.

All the family comes to the table as soon as they are called.

Start the meal with a short ritual, maybe giving thanks.

This helps everyone to slow down and focus on the experience of coming together to enjoy the meal.

Everyone waits to start eating until the whole family is at the table and until a parent has said everyone may begin.

This helps children learn to curb their impulsivity, and it prepares them for what will be expected of them outside the home.

No screens on, no toys or books or mobile phones or earphones at the table.

Mealtimes are for eating and for pleasant conversation.

Everyone is served the same meal.

If you don't like something, leave it and say nothing. But if you do like the food, then say so. This teaches children to be considerate.

Wipe your fingers and your mouth on your napkin.

Only ask for seconds when you've finished everything on your plate.

Ask for something to be passed to you, instead of reaching across someone.

Sit up straight with your legs down, and elbows off the table.

Children stay at the table until excused by an adult.
This helps children focus on the meal, and it teaches patience and politeness.

One rule I recommend you <u>don't</u> have is a rule about children finishing everything on their plate. This rule almost always leads to children complaining and to parents cajoling, nagging and negotiating. This rule definitely doesn't help to make mealtimes calmer, easier and happier. You may be wondering how you can get your children to eat anything green without this rule! Later in this chapter I will explain a specific strategy, called The First Plate Plan, which successfully addresses this issue, resulting in children eating a wide variety of foods without a fuss.

Examples of think-throughs to help children remember rules and expectations and take them seriously
Here are some examples of *think-through* questions you can ask to help focus your child's mind on what she should do at mealtimes. Remember to do *think-throughs* at a neutral time and only for one minute.

How does every meal start?

What does good table manners mean in our house?

What's the rule about your napkin?

What should you do if you want seconds?

How long is dinner going to last?

What can we talk about at mealtimes?

When can you ask for seconds?

Who decides when you can get down from the table?

Why is it important to say please and thank you?

What can you do if you don't like the food on your plate?

Here's an example of a *think-through* used by a parent to re-establish the rule that the child needs to ask to be excused, rather than leaving the table whenever he feels like it. It takes just sixty seconds.

Think-through: At a neutral time
Parent: *I've got three questions for you to answer.*
Child: *Oh, do I have to?*
Parent: (Waits a few seconds, then Reflectively Listens and Descriptively Praises) *Maybe you don't feel like answering*

questions right now, but you've stopped complaining. Here's my first question. At dinner time, when you're all finished and you want to get down, what do you have to say?

Child: *I have to ask if I can get down.*

Parent: *You answered my first question straightaway. Here's my second question. How will you say it?*

Child: *Can I get down?*

Parent: *That's most of what you have to say. Just one more word.*

Child: *Please.*

Parent: *That's the extra word! You remembered it. Now tell me everything you have to say, including that important word.*

Child: *Please, can I get down?*

Parent: *That's exactly what you have to say; that sounds so polite. And most of the time we'll say yes. Now here's my third question. It's the last question you have to answer for now. Where will you have to be when you ask if you can get down?*

Child: *Huh?*

Parent: (Waits silently, smiling)

Child: *I have to be sitting down properly.*

Parent: *That's right, you have to be sitting down properly. And I won't even ask you what properly means, because you've already answered all three questions, and without a fuss!*

- Preparing the environment

Here are some suggestions to make it easier for kids to do things right:

Offer children a healthy snack between breakfast and lunch and another between lunch and dinner.

When children are allowed to get too hungry, they become irritable, more easily frustrated, harder to comfort, less willing to cooperate. Most children need to eat some healthy food every few hours. After that length of time, you can expect subtle misbehaviour to creep in.

To help children eat more healthily, do not even keep in the house the foods that are not good for them.
If you choose to give some of these foods to your family, only buy the amount you will need for a particular meal or treat, and throw out any leftovers. This will automatically reduce the amount of these foods that you and your children eat.

Make sure there is always a napkin at each table setting to train children not to wipe their mouths on their sleeves.

Serve children small portions.
That way they are likely to finish what's on their plate without a fuss and may even ask for more. You will be less tempted to urge them to eat up, and your children will soon start to think of themselves as 'good eaters' who regularly finish their food without reminders.

Give children cutlery that is the right size for them so it is easy to use.
Once your child can feed herself (usually between one and two years old), no longer spoon-feed her, even when she is tired, even when she is not feeling well, even when you are in a hurry. Self-reliance leads to self-confidence. And if you act like her unpaid staff, that's how you will be treated!

Provide children with chairs that are the right size and the right height.

Children tend to fidget more and to slouch when their feet are dangling. They will sit up straighter and behave more sensibly if their feet are firmly planted on the floor. Smaller children might need a lower table or a chair with a foot rest.

The First Plate Plan: A strategy that transforms fussy eaters into adventurous eaters

How my children went from eating three things to thirty

I have two kids, now aged twelve and ten. Two years ago, our big problem was food. There was hardly anything they would eat except for macaroni cheese or pasta with butter. If we gave them sauce with their pasta, it had to be separate or they wouldn't touch it. It seemed like we'd tried everything to get them to eat a wider range of foods. We tried forcing them to eat, which made them just hate those foods even more. We tried bribing them with dessert, but that didn't work either. Nothing was working, so we ended up just making them separate meals of the few foods we knew they would eat.

So it made sense to us to try Noël's First Plate Plan. We started off giving them a First Plate of microscopic amounts of food they thought they didn't like. The amounts were so small it was almost comical. They had to eat this if they wanted a second plate of the foods they did like. And it worked! After gradually increasing the portion sizes of food on their First Plate, foods they had previously hated, like fish or ethnic food, became their favourites. Now we can put food on the table that they've never eaten before, and they'll try it. They might not like it, but they're willing to give it a try. From eating only a couple of different foods, the kids will now eat more than thirty different foods. Using Noël's First Plate Plan ended our mealtime battles.

Father of two, aged 12 and 10

Fussy eating is one of the most common problems parents are dealing with at mealtimes. Many children have a history of being faddy, fussy eaters who are willing to eat only a relatively narrow range of foods. Often entire food groups are rejected, usually vegetables and fruits. These children are easily turned off, sometimes even to the point of gagging, by the taste, smell, texture or appearance of certain foods. We can guide children to become healthier, more adventurous eaters by using a strategy called The First Plate Plan. Here's how:

Start each meal for <u>all</u> family members with a First Plate, on which you will put <u>tiny</u> amounts of five to eight different foods that your child has been known to eat on occasion but does not like. The amount of each food needs to be so tiny (for example a quarter of a pea) that it has no discernible taste!

Only after your child has eaten everything on his First Plate will you then give him his second plate, which is a smallish amount of whatever you have made for dinner that your child does like.

If you use The First Plate Plan consistently, over time your child will become used to eating little bits of many foods that he previously thought he couldn't possibly eat. Soon he will grow to tolerate these foods, and after a while he will even come to like most of them. But this transformation will only happen if you resist the temptation to urge, repeat and remind. Let your children's hunger, and their natural desire to please you, be the motivators.

You may worry that a stubborn child would continue to refuse to eat the tiny bits of food on her First Plate and would therefore never get her second plate so she would starve to death. This has never happened! Sometimes a child with a more inflexible temperament will miss a meal or two at first, but pretty soon her growing hunger will prompt her to eat the tiny bits of food on her First Plate in order to get her second plate. Remember to Reflectively Listen and Descriptively Praise. This will help children become accustomed, over time, to the new rules and routines.

If your child refuses at first to eat the tiny bits of food on his First Plate, you may worry that he will become too hungry before the next mealtime. Rather than giving him a snack, you can give him his next meal, complete with a First Plate, earlier than usual.

As your child gradually learns to tolerate the First Plate foods, you will be able to slowly, very slowly, increase the amounts. You can also graduate to putting on the First Plate some foods that he thinks he cannot stand. Eventually he will grow to like a lot of these foods, and they can then become second plate foods. I have known many children for whom the First Plate started out as one tiny bit of carrot, one tiny bit of celery, one tiny bit of green pepper, one tiny bit of lettuce, etc. Within a few months these children were eating big salads and relishing every bite.

There will probably always be some foods that you wish your children would eat more of or that you wish they would eat with more enthusiasm, so keep The First Plate Plan going indefinitely. I know families who have been using The First Plate Plan for years, long after the fussy eater in the family is no longer a fussy eater. For example, you may have a child who tends to leave his vegetables until last. You may be tempted to remind him to eat up. Instead, serve a small portion of the vegetable as the First Plate for the whole family. Hunger will motivate your child to eat up.

- Planning your day realistically so the family has enough time to enjoy each meal without feeling rushed

Mealtimes will be much more relaxing if you're not hurrying. Give yourself plenty of time to allow children to help set the table and to clear away afterwards. A common problem, however, is that some children take a long time to finish their meal. Here is what I suggest:

Any child who is hungry will eat her fill in fifteen minutes, so do not drag out mealtimes.
If your child habitually dawdles over meals, set a timer (for twenty minutes, to give a bit of leeway). When the timer goes ding, the meal is over, with no threats, lectures, cajoling or second chances. Just smile and Reflectively Listen. Within a few days your child will no longer be dawdling. Of course you will need to do several *think-throughs* before this new rule comes into effect. That way your child will be prepared.

No more dawdling or rushing at breakfast

One of our sons tends to take a long time to eat his breakfast – mostly because he gets so interested in the conversation that he forgets to keep eating! With the typical time crunch on school mornings, we were always worried about running out of time, so we nagged him endlessly. 'Hurry up! You're going to be late,' we'd urge our son. We would say, 'Tell us the story after you take another bite,' or 'Keep eating.' We had an extensive repertoire of nags. He started to tell us that he wasn't hungry.

My husband and I knew that constantly rushing and reprimanding him for being too slow wasn't good, and we remembered hearing Noël say that nagging at mealtimes can actually take a child's appetite away. This was a wake-up call for us. We sat down together and decided that we needed to designate a time that breakfast had to be finished by. Our son was old enough to tell the time so we had a meeting and started with Reflective Listening. We said something like, 'We've made mistakes, and it must be so

annoying that we're always rushing you. We're so annoyed with
ourselves for criticising you. It can't be nice for you.' We explained
to him what the new rule was going to be, that breakfast had to be
finished by a certain time and that it was up to him to pay
attention to the clock and to make sure he was finished. We
wouldn't nag or tell him to hurry up any more. He was happy with
the new rule.

The result? We stopped nagging, he finishes on time most
mornings, and his appetite soon returned.

Mother of two, aged 10 and 8

• Special Time

Negative attention-seeking is often the reason children play
up at mealtimes. Special Time is not a magic wand that automatically eliminates all annoying misbehaviour. But you will
be very pleased to find that consistent Special Time motivates
children to want to get positive attention.

2 Descriptively Praising small steps in the right direction
motivates children to want to behave well at mealtimes

Remembering to Descriptively Praise all the OK things your
children are already doing is the best way to help them want to
cooperate and to do the right thing more and more. As long as
your children are eating or behaving the way you want, smile
often and give some Descriptive Praise every few minutes.
Here are some examples of Descriptive Praises you can adapt
for mealtimes with your family:

I asked you to put your toy away before coming to the table, and you did what I said.

I can see you're holding your spoon the right way, like a pencil.

What a nice, straight back. You're not slouching.

Even though you both want me to listen, you're not interrupting. You're waiting patiently for your turn.

It's nice to sit and have dinner with you all when no one's playing with their food.

Thanks for not complaining about the food. You're just eating what you want and leaving what you don't want, without even talking about it. That takes self-control.

You took a bit of broccoli. Very brave. And you didn't say 'Yuk!'

When I asked you if you wanted another helping you remembered to say, 'Yes please,' instead of, 'Uh, huh.' That's very grown-up table manners.

When you wanted more milk, you just got it for yourself. You didn't even expect me to get it for you. You're really becoming self-reliant.

I can see you're remembering to use your napkin. Your face looks nice and clean. I can hardly tell you've been eating.

When I look around, I see that everyone's chewing with their mouths closed. That's the polite way to eat.

Three children eating breakfast, and nobody's kicking under the table. It's so pleasant to sit here with you.

Thank you for staying at the table, even though you're not hungry. You're remembering the rule about staying at the table until a grown-up says you can get down.

Even when your child is not quite doing what he should be doing, find something good, or even just OK, to Descriptively Praise. This often helps your child want to behave better and is much more effective than nagging or scolding:

Even though you're complaining, you were brave and you tasted the new food.

You're not interrupting. (Even though your child may be doing something else you don't like, such as picking up the food with his fingers)

Thanks for not grabbing. (Even though your child may be banging his cup on the table)

3 Reflective Listening

When we make new rules or re-establish old rules, our children won't always be delighted! Reflectively Listening to how your children may be feeling about the mealtime rules and routines will help them to move through their upset more quickly:

I can see you don't want to wait for everyone to sit down. You're so hungry!

You're probably wishing it was pizza tonight instead of casserole. But you only said 'Yuk' once. Now you're being polite.

(This is an example of combining Reflective Listening and Descriptive Praise. Because Reflective Listening usually improves behaviour quite rapidly, very soon you will have something to praise.)

It sounds like you're disappointed there's no pudding tonight.

Wouldn't it be fun if sweets were good for you but broccoli gave you cavities!

Dad and I used to feed you sometimes when you were tired. Now we're telling you to feed yourself. Maybe you think we don't care about how you feel.

4 Never Ask Twice

Remember to use the Six-Step method whenever you want your children to stop playing and set the table or wash their hands or come and sit down to eat.

5 Rewards and Consequences

The easiest, quickest and most effective reward is Descriptive Praise. The easiest, quickest and most effective consequence is an *action replay*. This time your child does it right.

- So if your child is misbehaving at the table, do not remind, warn, lecture or plead. Instead, wait a few moments and Descriptively Praise him when he stops.

- If the misbehaviour is continuous, temporarily remove his plate, but have him stay at the table until mealtime is over. As soon as his behaviour improves, Descriptively Praise him and return his plate to him.
- Then do an *action replay*.
- If misbehaviour at meals is an ongoing problem, remember to do plenty of *think-throughs* at neutral times throughout the day. This will help improve mealtime habits, whether your child has simply forgotten a rule or whether the misbehaviour was deliberate.

Here's an example of how to do an action replay when your child complains about the food

If your child takes one look at the meal you've put in front of her and blurts out something insulting, it is understandable that you will be annoyed. Depending on her age and on how angry she already is about other things, your child might say, 'Yuk,' or 'I hate stew,' or 'I'm not eating that,' or 'This smells disgusting.' In most homes this counts as misbehaviour because an important rule about being polite and considerate has been ignored. But instead of reacting with annoyance, wait a few moments and then Descriptively Praise that she stopped being insulting or impolite. This takes self-control on the part of the parents!

Then do an *action replay*. In a calm, friendly voice ask, 'What should you do when you don't like the food?' She will be very aware of what the rule is because of the daily *think-throughs* you will have been doing. And she will usually be willing to say the rule because she has just been praised, rather than told off. When she tells you, find something in her answer to Descriptively Praise, maybe that she remembered the rule or that she answered politely or that she answered in a full sentence. Then say, 'Now we'll do an *action replay*. We'll pretend I just put the plate in front of you, and now you'll do the right thing.' This time your child is likely to do it right, having just told you the rule. When she does it right (which in this case is saying nothing if she doesn't like the look of what's on her plate) you will have something to Descriptively Praise. *Action replays* forge better habits.

As far as rewards are concerned, I strongly recommend that you <u>do not</u> make dessert a reward for eating a certain amount of food. That only makes dessert even more desirable, and it makes the food that has to be eaten to get the reward seem even more unappealing. Because food is so symbolic of love and nurturing, it is much better never to use food as a reward, a comfort, a bribe, a threat or a punishment. Descriptive Praise for good behaviour at mealtimes is the most effective reward you can give.

Summary

These strategies can transform mealtimes in your home, improving mealtime behaviour and getting your children into the habit of tasting, tolerating and actually liking a wider range of healthy foods. Mealtimes will stop being stressful and start being a relaxing, enjoyable time for the whole family.

CHAPTER 11

SIBLING RELATIONSHIPS: REDUCING SQUABBLES, HELPING CHILDREN GET ALONG

Now my children get along

I didn't realise how much I was blaming our older son whenever there was a blow-up between him and his sister. I can see now why that made him even more resentful and just added fuel to the fire. Now when my children fight, instead of blaming, I bite my tongue and use the Reflective Listening strategy, empathising with how he's feeling: 'It's so frustrating when your sister plays with your games without asking you.' This really helps him get over it faster. We also use Descriptive Praise a lot. We notice and mention whenever our kids are being kind to each other or are sharing their toys or being generous: 'You shared your sweets with your brother. That was a kind thing to do.' Using a combination of Noël's techniques – Descriptive Praise, Reflective Listening and think-throughs – has been very effective with our children, and I'd say they now get along about ninety-nine percent of the time. They've developed a really sweet relationship, which I think will carry on into adulthood.

Mother of two, aged 8 and 5

When I ask parents what they wish could be different at home, one of the first things they mention is that they wish their children didn't fight and argue and compete with each other so much. It is not surprising that parents often bring this up because it is very stressful being around siblings who are niggling each other, putting each other down, teasing or contradicting each other.

Negative sibling interactions feel awful for parents. The conflicts also feel awful for the children, but that may not be so apparent because it often looks like the children are engaging in this sport of sibling-baiting with relish and glee. It looks like they are enjoying tormenting the sibling. But in reality, in many families the negative interactions have become compulsive and automatic. Behind that mischievous grin is a real need that is not being met. In this chapter I'll be sharing strategies to help you meet each child's real needs, and that will remove the causes of most sibling problems.

The techniques described in this book will significantly reduce fighting and arguing and other unpleasant interactions between siblings. But it is not realistic to hope we can eliminate all sibling rivalry. Even when parents learn effective discipline strategies, and even after we take steps to meet each child's needs, a small amount of sibling squabbling will always remain. That's because a small amount of sibling competitiveness and jealousy is natural, normal, inevitable and healthy. Sibling interactions are an important arena in which children can learn about peer relationships and about their impact on others.

Even though we know that it is too much to expect siblings always to be wonderful with each other, we do want them to be nice to each other most of the time. What we can realistically aim for is siblings who learn to play together, to respect each other and each other's belongings, to share and be kind to one another, most of the time. The strategies I talk about in this book will achieve that, and will also help the small amount of sibling rivalry that remains to become milder over time.

The questionnaire

Identify your current issues, and mark the relevant columns. When you revisit this page after two to four weeks of using the strategies, you will see significant improvements.

Your children	Hardly ever	Sometimes	Too often
Argue and contradict each other			
Tease and wind each other up			
Complain about each other			
Grab from each other			
Use the other's belongings without permission			
Find it hard to share			
Boss each other about			

Thankfully there are many, many strategies that can help siblings to fight less and enjoy each other more. First I will show you how to apply the core strategies you have been learning to help you improve sibling relations. And then I'll share a few additional tips that are very effective when you're dealing with a lot of sibling rivalry.

Action Plan for Calmer, Easier, Happier sibling relationships

For the purpose of clarity, I'm going to approach the Action Plan slightly differently for this big issue of siblings. I'll break up the Action Plan into two stages:

1. Motivation and prevention

What you can do to prevent a lot of rivalry, jealousy and competitiveness so that there are far fewer instances of siblings annoying each other.

2. Early intervention and crisis management

What to do when things are starting to go wrong so that you can avert many crises, and what to do when you're dealing with a full-blown fight.

1 Preparing for Success

• Be a United Front

Decide with your partner which sibling issues concern you most. Write down a few things you'd like to improve, and together get clear on what you both want the rules or expectations to be. This may require compromise.

Here are three common sibling issues that you probably want to make rules about.

Not sharing

Each child needs to have a 'sacred space', a place where he or she can play in peace or leave his belongings and know they will not be disturbed. I recommend a rule that any toy that is not in a child's sacred space has to be shared. Whoever picks it up can play with it for as long as they want. This rule helps motivate children to put their belongings back in the right place. And children learn important impulse-control skills when they forget to put a toy back in the sacred space and have to wait, without grabbing or complaining, while a sibling plays with it. This rule cuts down on a huge amount of squabbling over toys.

It is especially important that the older child has a place where she can safely leave her construction or art project without worrying that it will be destroyed by a marauding toddler. This will reduce a lot of the older child's resentment of a younger child.

Telling tales on each other

This is going to be a rule for you, rather than for your children. Make a rule for yourself that when one child comes to you complaining about the other, you will stay out of it. It doesn't work to ask what happened because you will never really find out; each child will tell you a version of reality that makes him look good and the sibling look bad. If you are wondering what really happened, I can tell you: the second one was born!

The more we give advice and suggest solutions, the more our children will assume they need an adult to be judge and jury. So instead of trying to sort things out for them or with them, focus on Reflective Listening. As you empathise, each child will feel heard, and they will both get the clear message that you trust them to find a way to get along together. They can! The more attention we pay to their tales, the more they will tell on each other. For the same reason don't respond with threats or punishments.

Hitting

Now here's something that might surprise you. I actually recommend <u>not</u> having a 'No hitting' rule! There are several reasons why.

As much as we would like our kids to work things out peacefully, by using their words instead of their fists, we need to recognise that siblings (even those who usually get on) will on occasion be physically aggressive with each other. So a rule like 'No hitting' is unrealistic because children, being immature and impulsive, will hit (and shove and tease and grab).

A 'No hitting' rule ignores the fact that siblings can become masters of the subtle art of provoking each other! The child who often gets hit by a sibling may well have learned how to get his sibling into trouble: wind him up and then sit back and watch him lash out. This gives one child far too much power over the other.

Another problem with a 'No hitting' rule is that often you

won't be able to find out who really did what to whom and why, so you won't be able to *follow through* with a consequence. And without a consequence, a rule is not a rule. It's just a suggestion or a nag. And in any case, a consequence is not a magic wand. A consequence by itself doesn't motivate children to control their impulses or teach them how to. Consequences tend to breed resentment and revenge, which is the opposite of what we want!

It's important not to make one kind of aggression worse than the other. Verbal aggression can hurt just as much as physical aggression does. And sometimes the emotional scars from verbal aggression can last much longer, even decades, long after a physical bruise has disappeared.

So if you don't have a rule about 'No hitting', what can you do instead? Using *think-throughs*, we can teach children what they should do when they're angry at a sibling. Kids know what they shouldn't do because they hear about that a lot, but they often aren't clear about what they should do instead.

- Do daily think-throughs to clarify and establish your expectations, rules, routines, rewards and consequences

Examples of think-throughs

1. The first example is about reducing physical or verbal aggression. Here's how that *think-through* might go. Remember always to do *think-throughs* at a neutral time, not right after there has been an altercation. In this example the parent is not introducing a new rule, but rather expanding on an existing rule.

Think-through: At a neutral time

Parent: *Carter, when you're angry at Nigel, instead of hitting or kicking or insulting, what should you do?*

Child: *Not hit.*

Parent: *That's right. You shouldn't hit. So what should you do instead?*

Child: (Thinking) *Shout at him?*

Parent: *I can tell you're thinking about it. Yes, shouting is better than hitting or name-calling. That might get him to stop annoying you. If that doesn't work, what else could you do?*

Child: *I don't know.*

Parent: *It's not easy to think of new ideas. So take a sensible guess.*

Child: (A long pause) *Walk away?*

Parent: *That would be sensible. It might be really hard to walk away when you're so angry at your brother. But it would definitely keep you from hitting each other. If you can't make yourself walk away, what else could you do?*

Child: *Ummmm . . . hit the sofa cushions?*

Parent: *That's a great idea. You might have to hit the cushions really hard if you're feeling furious! You've come up with three things you can do instead of hitting. Very grown up.*

If the hitting or insulting problem is severe, you'll need to do lots of think-throughs about the possible alternatives. You'll also need to do lots of Reflective Listening. A child who is physically or verbally aggressive often feels hard done by. This child needs lots of Descriptive Praise and frequent Special Time.

2. Here is an example of a two-part *think-through* to introduce a new rule about sharing and respecting one another's belongings. The new rule is that each child will have one place in the home where their belongings are completely off-limits to their siblings. Any belongings not in that sacred place are available for the other children to play with. For children who have their own bedrooms, that will be their sacred place. The reason this *think-through* is in two parts is that there is more to the rule than can be conveyed in one minute. And one minute is the limit for each *think-through*.

First think-through: At a neutral time

Parent: *Daddy and I have come up with a new rule so there'll be less arguing about toys and less grabbing. There are two parts to this new rule. One part I think you'll like, but the other part you might not like. The first part of the rule is that each of you will have one place in the house where you can leave your things, and your brother and sister are not allowed to touch them. So that's the part of the rule I think you'll like.*

Child: *But where can I put them so Sophie and Ben can't touch them? They're always playing with my Lego when I'm at school and breaking my airplanes and rockets.*

Parent: *I know that really makes you angry. That's why we've come up with this new rule. You deserve to be able to leave your constructions and to know they'll be safe. So you can choose where your own safe place will be.*

Child: *They won't listen. They'll still take my things.*

Parent: *At first they might still take your things; that's quite possible. And it's so annoying. Since this will be a rule now, it won't be your job to stop them. Whose job will it be to teach them not to play with other people's things?*

Child: *Yours and Dad's?*

Parent: *That's right. So tell me, what's the first part of the new rule?*

Child: *What's the second part?*

Parent: *You'll see. First tell me, what's the first part of the new rule?*

Child: *We each get our own place to keep our stuff and nobody can touch it.*

Parent: *That's almost right. But Mummy and Daddy can touch it; we might need to. So who is it who can't touch your stuff if it's in your own place?*

Child: *My bratty little sister.*

Parent: (Waits silently with a smile)

Child: *Sophie and Ben.*

Parent: *That was a much friendlier way to say it. And our time is up so I'll tell you the second part of the rule later.*

(Remember that *think-throughs* should last one minute or less, so break them up into two or more bits if you need to)

Second think-through: At another neutral time

Parent: *You're probably wondering what the second part of the new rule is about each of you having your own place for your belongings. But first, tell me again, what's the first part of the new rule?*

Child: *Nobody can touch the stuff that's in my own place.*

Parent: (Waits silently, smiling)

Child: *You can.*

Parent: *That's right. You remembered. So tell me again the first part of the new rule.*

Child: *Everything that's in my own place, Sophie and Ben can't play with it. And the same with their stuff.*

Parent: *You remembered that part. Now here's the part you might not like. Anything that you leave somewhere else, they can pick it up and play with it for as long as they want.*

Child: *But that's not fair!*

Parent: *It won't be easy watching them play with your things. So if you don't want them to play with your things, what do you need to do?*

Child: *I need to keep my things in my place. But what if I'm playing with them somewhere else and I just have to go to the loo? Then when I come back they're playing with my toys all day long and they don't put them down so I can't play with them.*

Parent: *That would feel awful! So if that happened, what would you have to do instead of grabbing or arguing?*

Child: *Well, I could ask nicely.*

Parent: *You could. I'm glad you thought of a friendly strategy. And they might give it back to you. But they don't have to.*

Child: *Well, then I'm going to play with their things when they leave them out.*

Parent: *Yes, you could. And they won't be able to do a thing. So tell me the new rule, both parts.*

Child: *I can keep all my things in my own place, but if I forget and leave them out, somebody else can play with them.*

Parent: *That's the rule. You remembered both parts. And we're going to do that for one month, and we'll see if it helps.*

- Prepare the environment

Give your children, especially boys, many opportunities to play-fight.

Stay close so that you can Descriptively Praise when they are not hurting each other and Reflectively Listen to their feelings when someone does get hurt. Rough and tumble with a parent and supervised play-fighting teach children how to rein in their more aggressive impulses.

- **Plan your day realistically**

We know that it's much easier to stay calm when we're not over-scheduled. We need to give ourselves plenty of time. That will help us stay positive and purposeful in the face of the inevitable sibling flare-ups.

- **Plan Special Time with each child separately several times a week**

Aim for at least ten minutes, and if you can do it every day, even better! Special Time cuts down on sibling squabbles in an almost magical way. Children do not vie for their parents' attention nearly so much when they are getting the individual attention they need and crave and deserve.

2 Descriptive Praise

Siblings squabble primarily to get our attention. The more attention we give the squabbling, the more they'll do it. So we've got to turn this dynamic upside down and make sure siblings get a lot of Descriptive Praise whenever we hear them using a friendly tone of voice with each other, whenever we see them sharing, not interrupting, being patient, not grabbing, being gentle and not reacting physically. Descriptively Praise any time that you see them playing together or even just leaving each other alone. Here are a number of examples:

In the past ten minutes, you haven't said anything annoying to your brothers, even though they can be a nuisance. You've been keeping calm, and that takes self-control. Keeping calm isn't easy!

You're both sharing the coloured pencils and nobody's grabbing. Very friendly.

I can tell you're both angry, but no one's hitting. You're keeping your hands to yourselves. That's the right thing to do.

You each wanted to play a different game, but you didn't argue for long. You came up with a solution all by yourselves. And neither of you came to me for help.

You came home from the birthday party with three cars in your party bag, and you let your sister play with one. You didn't have to do that. No one told you to. You chose to do it and be generous all by yourself. That was very thoughtful and mature.

You didn't make fun of your brother when he didn't know his four times table. Maybe you remembered that he's not as good at maths as you are, even though you're younger. You didn't make him feel bad about it. He already feels bad that he's not that good at his tables.

It's so lovely when you're not fighting. It makes being with you much nicer.

Stemming sibling rivalry with Special Time

We had a unique situation when my sister and her family came to live with us after the death of her husband. We suddenly blended two families with six children between the ages of twelve and one! But thank goodness for Calmer, Easier, Happier Parenting. Before my sister and her two girls arrived, we Prepared for Success by talking through so many issues, letting everyone know what the house rules would be, who would be sleeping where, where they could keep their things in a sacred space that nobody else could touch and setting up schedules for sharing the bathrooms, etc.

All this preparing made for a much easier transition, but what really kept the peace was making sure each child had individual attention with Special Time. It helped ease so much tension. My husband was especially good at scheduling quality time with each child. He actually made appointments in his appointment diary, which he didn't break easily, and he gave them undivided attention. For example, he'd take our son to a café for something to eat or take our daughter for a hot chocolate. He did something for all the children, not just his own. Each child needed to feel they were as important as the others and as loved and as heard. Seeing their names in his appointment diary made the children feel important and privileged and really helped to stem sibling rivalry.

Mother of four, aged 12, 10, 7 and 1

Additional strategies for prolonging the harmony

Give your older child a few special privileges.
This could be a slightly later bedtime or a bit more pocket money. These perks go a long way towards minimising resentment of the younger sibling, helping the older one to feel proud of himself that he is more mature.

Have each of the children play alone for some time every day (not in front of a screen), even when a sibling is home.
Over time, this will teach self-reliance, which keeps children from bothering their siblings whenever they are at a loose end and don't know what else to do with themselves. And you will find that siblings who are required to play separately get along better afterwards. They appreciate and enjoy each other's company more.

Early intervention and crisis management – how to calm things down when your children are squabbling

Stay positive.
Do not blame, lecture, moralise, criticise or try to resolve their conflict.

If you are worried about a child's safety, move in close.
A parent's close presence usually reminds children of the family's rules and values. As you get closer, one or both of the children are likely to make a small move towards stopping, although probably not as quickly as you would like. As soon as they start to stop, Descriptively Praise that they stopped hitting or pushing or pulling hair.

If you are not worried about safety, stay out of their conflict, even if one of the children is crying or complaining.
Don't try to solve their problem. Siblings are capable of resolving their differences. When an older and younger child are squabbling, parents tend to get angry with the older child because, being older, he should know better, perhaps saying, 'What did you do to your sister? Why is she crying?' Parents want to protect the younger child from the older child.

This is unnecessary because your children are more evenly matched than you may think! Usually the older child is the stronger one, and will use his physical superiority, or the threat of it, to upset and annoy. Or he may be adept at verbal put-downs. The younger child soon learns to be wily; he becomes an expert at subtle winding up. The younger child annoys and provokes the older one. The older child retaliates, and the younger child cries or 'tells'. The older one tends to be blamed and scolded; the younger one is rescued and comforted.

But the older child is almost always more jealous than the younger one because he had the parents' undivided attention and cuddling until the second one came along. Being blamed only makes the older child resent the younger even more, and the younger child's victim role is further reinforced. A vicious circle develops, where no one wins. Over time, the younger child may adopt the unpleasant tactics of the older child.

Instead of intervening, find something to Descriptively Praise.
That will motivate your children to handle their conflicts more positively. For example, if the siblings are bickering:

I can see you're both angry, but no one's hitting. Arguing is better than hitting.

3 Do lots of Reflective Listening.

She messed up your game. That's so frustrating.

You really wanted that toy. I can see you're angry.

It must really hurt your feelings when he teases you.

Maybe you wish you could make detailed drawings like your brother.

Have a 'squabbling place'.
When children are squabbling in your presence, the sound of it can be very irritating. Let them know that it's fine if they bicker – but they are not allowed to do it near you. Designate

a room as the squabbling place, and if the children are squabbling near you, insist that they both go there. Once there they can squabble or chat or play; that's up to them. And you are the one who decides when they can come out of the squabbling place. Since most of their squabbling is for your benefit, when they don't have your attention, they usually stop quite soon!

The squabbling room

My son and daughter used to fight a lot. It used to make me so upset, and I would get angry with them and threaten to punish them with no telly or taking away privileges. Of course, this didn't work. It just made them feel resentful and want to retaliate.

So, we decided to try Noël's strategy of sending the children to a squabbling room. We told them about this ahead of time and explained that if they started fighting, they would have to go to this room, and they could sort out their squabble on their own. It worked absolutely brilliantly. After a few minutes in the squabbling room, they would stop fighting and start playing.

Mother of two, aged 7 and 4

4 Are you remembering to use the Six Steps of the Never Ask Twice method, rather than repeating and reminding?

When siblings are playing together and it's time for them to transition to the next activity or task, focus the six steps on whichever child is least likely to cooperate.

5 What about Rewards and Consequences?

Parents ask me what the consequences should be for siblings fighting or deliberately annoying each other.

Most consequences focus attention on the negative behaviours, giving children the impression that they've done something wrong. Fighting, name-calling, grabbing, teasing, etc. – let's not think of these behaviours as <u>bad</u>, but as immature responses. Our job is to teach and train more mature responses, rather than punish, which often makes the problem worse. Most consequences don't motivate our children to do it right the next time. And most consequences don't teach self-control.

As I mentioned in Chapter 8, 'Rewards and Consequences', the best consequence for most misbehaviour is an *action replay*. Both children will re-enact the scenario, and this time they'll do it the right way. This teaches children constructive ways to handle their problems and ends the incident, whether large or small, on a positive note.

Rewards are often very effective motivators. A well-chosen reward makes it easier for children to treat each other nicely. Over time, this becomes habitual, and the reward can then be transferred to some other behaviour you want to improve.

Summary

The more you continue to practise all these strategies and techniques, the more your children will enjoy each other, appreciate each other and play together peacefully. They will be learning how to resolve the inevitable conflicts that arise in all relationships. Sibling relationships will improve, and family life will become calmer, easier and happier.

CHAPTER 12

SCREEN TIME: GETTING BACK IN CHARGE OF THE ELECTRONICS IN YOUR HOME

Switching on to rewards

I'm the father of a boy and a girl, ages eight and eleven. We've always limited the amount of television and computer time they were allowed, but even so, it became a really unpleasant situation. It was hard to get them to turn off the telly, and even after they did they were cranky and uncooperative about everything else. It really seemed like they were addicted – they were desperate to get their 'fix,' and then acted sort of 'hung over' afterwards. I would threaten to take away the TV privilege, but frankly it was hard to follow through, and it just made them angry and less cooperative anyway.

After we went to one of Noël's seminars I realised the key was to turn it around and make screen time a reward they could earn – instead of a privilege for me to take away. My partner and I made sure we could be a United Front, then we sat the children down and explained that there was a new rule (we think 'new rules' are brilliant!) We explained that on Saturday and Sunday they could earn thirty minutes of telly after dinner if they had completed all their chores. We expect our kids to set the table for meals, so they have to do that and their piano practice. Saturday they have to tidy their rooms, and Sunday all their homework has to be finished before dinner.

It's amazing how the dynamic has changed now they see that it's up to them whether they get screen time. They usually remind each other to get their chores done – and I'm not the bad guy any more.

Father of two, aged 11 and 8

Many parents feel quite overwhelmed by the way screens have crept into every corner of children's lives. Getting back in charge of the screens in your home may feel impossible or not worth the hassle. It is possible, and it is worth the hassle.

Making children earn their screen time, as the father in this story did, is just one way that parents can get back in charge of the number of hours that children spend in front of a screen. You can also get back in charge of the quality and suitability of what your children are being exposed to.

If you worry that your child is spending too much time in front of a screen, and if you have tried unsuccessfully in the past to curb it, don't give up. You don't have to accept that this is just the way life is nowadays. The strategies in this book will help you get back in charge.

In case you need something to help strengthen your resolve, here are some of the many important benefits that parents have reported once their children were spending significantly less time in front of screens:

- Children learn to entertain themselves and are far more willing to. They play more and talk more, which improves their social skills as well as their vocabulary and sentence construction and their thinking skills.
- They are more willing to read, even those children who had previously never been seen with a book.
- They are able to focus for longer, and they develop the patience to enjoy activities that challenge them intellectually.
- Physically they usually become more active, which improves muscle tone, posture, even digestion, sleep habits and concentration. Physical exercise also burns off adrenaline so it is calming.
- They are more pleasant to be around. They are less

grumpy, irritable or inclined to say 'No', and they are more willing to do their homework and to help around the house.

In short, when screen time is reduced, life becomes calmer, easier and happier, and so do your children. We can achieve these delightful results if we stay determined and strong and brave.

The questionnaire

Fill this in before you start putting the screen time strategies into practice, and then again two weeks later to record how much progress you've made.

Your child	Hardly ever	Sometimes	Too often
Spends too much time in front of a screen			
Watches unsuitable programmes or plays unsuitable electronic games			
Resists switching off			
Turns on screens without permission			
Would prefer to be in front of a screen, rather than making his own entertainment			

How much screen time is too much?

Of course, it's up to the adults in your home to decide how much time your kids should be allowed to spend in front of a screen. But if you're not sure, the advice below, which is based on the most up-to-date brain research, may help you:

- Birth to three years old: Screens aren't recommended.
- Three to eight years old: Up to half an hour a day in front of a screen.
- From eight years old through to adulthood: One hour daily of leisure screen time (except on special occasions, eg. going to the cinema or watching a football match on television). And this means all screens combined, not an hour of DVDs, another hour on the computer and another hour playing a game on the mobile phone or other electronic device. And the daily hour of screen time cannot be saved up over several days for an all-day marathon at the weekend. The daily hour of leisure screen time does not include the legitimate use of the computer for homework and school projects.

Action Plan for Calmer, Easier, Happier screen time

1 Preparing for Success

- **Become a United Front**

Do you (and your partner if you have one) need to make new rules? Or firm up existing rules?

It's important that the rules governing screen time are clear, simple and easy to remember. Post the rules in several locations around the house, and don't be surprised if the rules keep mysteriously disappearing at first! Here are some suggestions for screen time rules that you may find helpful:

Allow leisure screen use only on certain days.
For many families it works very well to have Monday through Thursday as screen-free days so that children can concentrate in the evenings on their homework and on family time. Another solution that works for some families is 'one day on, one day off'.

Screen time has to be earned.
Require all the little daily tasks that your child might try to avoid or might rush through or forget about altogether to be completed to your satisfaction before any screens can be switched on. This might include homework, reading, walking the dog, feeding the pets, helping with housework, etc. This way you are making screen time a reward for small daily successes.

Have children ask first before switching on a screen.
And make a rule for yourself that you will answer positively. You can say, 'Yes, as soon as you show me your completed homework,' or 'Yes, once your list is all ticked,' or words to that effect.

Limit screen time during playdates at your house.
Not only is 'old-fashioned' playing better for children's and teens' bodies and brains, but it will improve their social skills in a way that spending time together in front of a screen will not.

Sometimes parents notice that a child keeps begging to go over to a friend's house, rather than to play at home, because he has more access to electronics over there. The solution is to alternate playdates at your house with playdates at the friend's house.

No screens on schoolday mornings.
This rule will help children stay more alert and focused while they are getting ready for school and also once they are at school.

Avoid screens on short car journeys.
It's important for children to be able to entertain themselves, rather than relying on screen stimulation.

No screens on during meals.
Let's keep the focus during mealtimes on enjoying the food and the companionship.

Turn off screens without a fuss today to earn tomorrow's screen time.
If getting your child to turn off screens is a problem, you can make a rule that in order to earn tomorrow's screen time, he has to turn it off as soon as he is told to today. Most kids are so drawn to screens that they are willing to do almost anything to earn their screen time, if they can see that there is no other way to have access to screens. It will probably take only a day or two for your child to realise that the only way to earn tomorrow's screen time is to cooperate without a fuss today.

Require children to get plenty of exercise.
Requiring children to get lots of exercise will naturally start to curb their appetite for screen time. Children need at least

thirty minutes of vigorous exercise daily. Vigorous means that they become hot and sweaty. It doesn't matter what type of exercise children do: ball games, running, martial arts, dancing and swimming are all good forms of exercise.

If your child doesn't like any sport, it is most probably because he feels he is not good at sport. When children are allowed to avoid exercising just because they feel they are not good at sports, they don't get a chance to improve, and the gap between them and other children who do exercise regularly grows even wider over time. They will feel less and less adequate in PE lessons at school. They will lose out, not only in terms of their health, but also their self-esteem.

The best way to get reluctant children to exercise is for parents to play active games with them. Also, walk rather than drive wherever possible. Not only will this automatically give your children more exercise, it will also help them to become familiar with their local area, and it will teach them how to behave in public.

It is recommended that children spend two hours per day outdoors or next to a window with very strong light. Natural light enables some of our body systems to function at their best. The more time you can spend with your child outdoors the better.

Ball games and other team games also give children an excellent opportunity to develop social skills. Children learn to cooperate, to take turns, to do their best, to win without gloating and to lose without sulking. If your children find it difficult to play with others, you can teach them these important social skills.

Be clear about exactly what will happen when the time
limit for screens is almost up

- Give him a *countdown* about five minutes before. This
  gives him time to save the level he's on, etc. During
  those five minutes, stay in the room with him so that
  he takes you seriously and so that you can Descriptively
  Praise and Reflectively Listen. Keep track of the five
  minutes with a timer. This is friendlier than if you
  keep checking your watch, which looks as if you are
  impatient. When the timer goes ding, say <u>once</u>, 'Now
  it's time to switch off' or similar words, and require
  him to respond to you in words (not just a grunt) as
  well as by action.

- Taking into account your child's natural reaction
  speed, give him a few seconds to comply. If he does,
  Descriptively Praise to show that you are very pleased.
  If he does not switch off, take immediate action and
  switch it off yourself, with no further warnings or
  reminders.

- Do think-throughs to introduce new rules and to
  make rules stick

When you change the rules about screen time, it's quite likely
your child will be upset at first, and he may test you to see if
the rules will stick. So it's important to Prepare for Success
with daily *think-throughs*.

Examples of think-throughs

Here's an example of a *think-through* that introduces the new
rule that there will be no screens in the morning on schooldays. The child in this example is so resistant to this new rule

that it takes two separate *think-throughs* before she is willing
to answer the parent's questions.

First think-through: At a neutral time

Parent: *The new rule is that starting next week, there will be no
screens on in the mornings on school days.*

Child: (Grimacing) *What?*

Parent: (Reflectively Listens) *I know that's not what we're used
to. It's not always easy to get used to new rules, especially
this one. I know you love texting your friends in the morning
to find out what they're going to wear.*

Child: (Shouting) *But it helps me wake up! It's not fair. What's
wrong with texting?*

Parent: (Reflectively Listening) *You sound angry!*

Child: *Duh! It's a stupid rule.*

Parent: (Smiling, waits for a pause) *Even though you're angry,
you're not shouting any more. I'll help you think of some other
ways to wake up, but they might not be as much fun as texting
or Facebook.*

Child: *I hate this house! You're always making up new rules!
Nobody else has this dumb rule.*

Parent: *You really don't like this new rule. As soon as you're
ready, please tell me what the new rule is.*

Child: *I'm not ready! I'll never be ready because it's the stupidest
idea I've ever heard.*

Parent: *I can hear how angry you are. I'll ask you to tell me
later.*

Second think-through: At a neutral time

Parent: *Are you feeling ready yet to tell me the new rule?*

Child: *Huh? What are you talking about?*

Parent: (Waits silently with a smile)

Child: *Oh, that. No, I'm not ready.*

Parent: (Waits silently with a smile)

Child: *No mobile in the mornings. But I can have it in the car.*

Parent: *Not on the days Dad or I drive you to school. Because the new rule is no screens before school. But when Jenny's mum drives you, she may have different rules.*

Child: *You'll probably tell Jenny's mum to make the same rule.*

Parent: *You're still angry, but you told me the rule. When does the new rule start?*

Child: *Monday?*

Parent: *You were listening, and you remembered.*

Child: *And that means Joe* (the brother) *can't play his DS in the car either.*

Parent: *You're right. I'm glad you're thinking about what this rule will be like.*

As always, you will need to do the *think-throughs* at a neutral time, <u>not</u> right before screen time, because by then your child's mind has already been hijacked by thoughts of being in front of a screen, and he will not be giving you his full attention. And the *think-throughs* must not be right after an argument or showdown because your child will not be in the mood for listening.

- Preparing the environment

Here are some steps you can take to make it easier for your child to spend less time in front of a screen:

- Get all electronics out of the children's bedrooms and into the public, often-frequented parts of the house. This includes having children put their mobile phones outside their bedrooms at night.
- If your kids are really fixated on screens, then at first, until they can see that you mean business and are determined to *follow through*, you may need to keep all hand-held electronic games, all remotes and all chargers in your possession (and possibly even the aerials or cords), except for when they have earned their screen time rewards.

- **Planning your day realistically**

Plan with your children what they will watch on television and when they will each have their turns on the computer, assuming they have earned it. The key to making this work is to give them plenty of time to choose carefully, and then do <u>not</u> let them change their choices. Have them make a chart so that nothing is left to imperfect memories.

- **Special Time**

The more frequent and predictable your Special Time with each child, the less fixated on screens they will become. You may not believe this! Try it and see.

2 What can you Descriptively Praise?

Once your children start cooperating with your new rules about screen time, you will find lots that you can Descriptively Praise. Here are some Descriptive Praise phrases you could use:

Thanks for turning off the TV the first time I asked, with hardly any arguing. That's cooperation.

I like how responsible you're being. You've already fed the dogs and finished your homework. So now you've earned playing your computer game for an hour.

You remembered the rule about only half an hour on the computer. When the timer buzzed, you turned it off immediately. That takes a lot of self-control, because I know you wish we didn't have this new rule.

3 Reflective Listening

If your children are upset about the new screen time rules, Reflective Listening will help them get over their upset more quickly and accept the rules more quickly.

You probably wish we didn't have the new rule about only an hour a day of screen time.

It's so annoying when you have to turn off the game right in the middle.

We used to let you watch TV for much longer, so maybe it feels like you've hardly had any screen time at all today.

It's upsetting when your friends get more computer and TV time than you do.

You probably wish there wasn't a limit on screen time.

And for maximum effectiveness, we can combine Descriptive Praise and Reflective Listening.

I'm glad you answered me in a friendly voice when I asked you something, even though it can be very annoying being interrupted while you're playing on the computer.

Today you had to miss your favourite programme because we got home so late. I thought you might complain about it, but you didn't! Even though you were disappointed, you understood that it wasn't anybody's fault. You were very flexible.

4 Never Ask Twice

Don't make the mistake of doing the Six Steps while your child is in front of a screen. He's likely to be too absorbed in what's in front of him to pay much attention to you. Get the screen off first. I explain how to do this in Chapter 6, 'Never Ask Twice'.

5 Rewards and Consequences

Look back at the rules I suggested under United Front (see page 342). You can use rewards and consequences to motivate your children to follow your screen time rules.

Summary

The firm approach to screen time that I am advocating may seem hopelessly old-fashioned. With all the different screens that are vying for your children's attention, you may not really believe that you can reclaim your home as a largely screen-free environment. Many Calmer, Easier, Happier families have done it, and so can you!

CHAPTER 13

HOMEWORK: MAKING IT HASSLE-FREE

Making homework more manageable

The school said my eight-year-old son's homework was supposed to take thirty minutes a night, but it was regularly taking him an hour or more. He whinged, complained that it was boring or too hard, and kept getting distracted. We redirected, nagged and shouted. Homework was a daily hassle that left everyone feeling upset. It didn't feel like his homework any more; it felt like our homework!

We realised that not only was all the repeating, reminding, redirecting and correcting making everyone miserable, but the school didn't have an accurate picture of what our son was managing to do within thirty minutes.

My wife and I decided to make a new rule that once he started his homework, we would set a timer for thirty minutes, and when the timer went ding, homework was over for the day. We also Prepared for Success by telling his teacher what we were doing. We did several think-throughs about this new rule, and it worked.

There was initially some resistance, but instead of negotiating as we had always done in the past, we Reflectively Listened, empathising about how he was feeling: 'Maybe you're worried that your teacher will be upset if you don't finish all your homework.' Descriptively Praising his effort also helped build his confidence. We've seen a complete turnaround in three weeks. It's amazing how much he can get done in half an hour!

Father of twins, aged 8

You might have a child, like the boy in this story, who makes a big fuss about homework, possibly due to a lack of confidence. Or your child may be very conscientious and desperate to do well, so ends up spending too long over her homework in a struggle to keep up or to be top of the class. Perhaps your child thinks the purpose of homework is to get it over with as quickly as possible; he rushes through it, barely reading the instructions and not doing his best. Whatever homework problem you're dealing with, the Calmer, Easier, Happier Parenting strategies will help improve your child's homework habits.

Sensible homework habits are very important. School is a child's 'job'. If we allow our children to dawdle through their job half-heartedly, or to rush through it with poor attention to detail, they will not get much satisfaction from it, they will not be proud of themselves, and they will not learn all that they are capable of learning from each task or activity. On the other hand, when we teach and train children to pay attention and do their best, they feel more and more successful, and they grow in confidence, motivation and self-reliance, as well as becoming more cooperative and less resistant. So for our sakes, as well as for our children's sakes, we need to help our children and teens to 'learn how to learn'.

The questionnaire

Fill in this questionnaire to help you identify the homework issues in your family. Then revisit the questionnaire in two to four weeks to see the progress you've all made.

Your child	Hardly ever	Sometimes	Too often
Rushes through homework			
Spends too much time on homework			
Leaves homework until the last minute			
Takes a long time to settle down to homework			
Gets easily distracted during homework time			
Complains and whinges about having to do homework			
Leaves homework at school			

Action Plan for Calmer, Easier, Happier homework

1 Preparing for Success

- **Have you established a United Front?**

Have you agreed with your partner what the problems are (filling in the questionnaire will help you with this) and what the rules and routines should be?

Here are some homework routines and rules that have consistently achieved success in many Calmer, Easier, Happier families. These are rules for you as much as they are rules for your child. You're the one who has to teach and train your child to stick to the routine!

Have a sacred homework time every day (except Sundays).
Start the habit of having your child sit down and do some homework every day except Sundays, even if no homework has been set by the school for the next day.

Having one day off a week gives your child the pleasure of one day each week when no thought of work need enter his mind. This is especially important for the pupil who is not feeling successful.

It might seem strange to suggest doing homework if none has been set, but there's a good reason. Two or more days in a row without homework can make re-establishing the routines on Monday much more difficult. A break of two days is a long time in the life of a child or teenager. Over the weekend he can mentally start sliding out of the productive habits that you have been putting so much effort into reinforcing during the week. These homework-free days are a perfect time for practising maths facts, spelling, handwriting, reading aloud with expression, revising, working ahead, etc.

During holidays your child can have a shorter homework, revision or memorising session, and of course there may need to be more flexibility, but it doesn't do him any favours in the long run to take the entire holiday off. On non-school days, set the homework time for <u>early</u> in the day to make sure it happens. The evening before, have a *think-through* about the homework plan for the next day so that your child is prepared. This always helps to reduce resistance. If you wait and talk about it right before you expect him to do it, it will feel like you're springing this on him, and you're likely to get complaints and resistance.

Only allow your child to spend the amount of time on homework that the school recommends.

Find out from your child's school what the guidelines are in each year for how long homework should take. However long the school says that the homework should take, do not let your child spend longer than the recommended amount of time on it. This rule is important for a number of reasons:

- The child who wastes time earlier in the evening by complaining or arguing may panic a few hours later and plead to be allowed to stay up past his bedtime to finish. This child may end up with no guilt-free leisure time and not enough sleep. He is left with the feeling that all he ever does is schoolwork and homework, even though we know that for a large chunk of the evening he was staring at, rather than actually doing, his homework.

- Some children, particularly those who are more sensitive or inflexible, become perfectionists and would choose, if allowed, to spend most of their evening working. This is no good for them; all children need to have free time every day.

- A child may be working diligently, but find the work so difficult that it takes him longer to finish than the school expects it to take. This child also needs guilt-free leisure time. And the school needs to know that he is not capable of completing the homework within the recommended time. Otherwise, his teachers will continue to set homework that is not appropriate for this child.

If your child is very anxious to finish his homework but hasn't managed to within the allotted time, you can allow him to get up early the next morning to finish it. Explain to the teacher how long the homework took him altogether.

Do homework when fresh.
Start the daily homework time early enough so that the work is finished while your child is still fresh and not tired; otherwise both behaviour and academic standards will slip.

After school, most children need to unwind and have something to eat before they plunge into their homework. A healthy snack and an <u>active break</u> will relax and refresh them: a short bike ride, playing catch, trampolining, etc. Sitting in front of a screen, however, does not refresh or motivate; in fact, it saps enthusiasm for any other activity.

Work before play.
One of the best ways to help children take homework seriously is to make a rule that homework and revision need to be

completed, to the parents' satisfaction, in order to earn coveted leisure activities such as:

- television, computer, video games, etc.
- telephoning or texting friends
- going out
- playing music, etc.

This rule helps ease children into the habit of <u>earning</u> the goodies in life, rather than expecting instant gratification.

Build in realistic breaks.
Homework and revision can feel frustrating and emotionally exhausting, especially for children and teens who are not yet successful learners. To prevent overload, make a rule that your child has an active break (not in front of a screen) every fifteen to thirty minutes, depending on his current ability to concentrate on academic work. Decide in advance when your child can have breaks. This will, over time, curb the child's tendency to complain or to invent ingenious excuses for getting up and doing something else.

Worst first.
Make sure your child tackles the most troublesome subjects or tasks while his brain is freshest. This will promote optimum learning. It will also remove the nagging dread that eats away at anyone's good humour when they are putting off something that they expect will be unpleasant.

Examples of think-throughs
Here is an example of a *think-through* to introduce a new rule. This rule limits the amount of time each evening that the child can spend on his homework.

Think-through: At a neutral time

Parent: *Daddy and I have made a new rule to help homework time be calmer. The new rule is: starting Monday you have an hour to do your homework. That hour is going to be from four o'clock to five, except on the days when you have football practice, and then it will be after dinner. If you're finished with your homework before the hour is up, we'll do some times tables and spelling practice. If the hour is up but you're not finished, that's still the end of homework for the night. And then you can have your playtime.*

Child: *But that's not fair! What if I don't finish? The teacher will kill me!*

Parent: *It sounds like you really want to finish your homework. And I want you to finish it too. Here's what you can do. If you don't finish it all in the hour, you can wake up early the next morning and finish it. And if you'd like me to keep you company in the morning, come and wake me up and I'll be glad to sit with you. I'll do my own work while you're doing your homework.*

Child: *But what if I don't wake up?*

Parent: *I'm glad you're thinking ahead.*

Child: *But sometimes I set my alarm wrong and it doesn't go off.*

Parent: *I can teach you to set your alarm the right way. Each evening, after you've set your alarm, bring it to me, and I'll check to see if you've set it right. Pretty soon you won't need me to check any more because you'll know how to do it right. Now tell me, what's the new rule?*

Child: *I just have an hour to do all my homework. But some days I have tons of homework! Why do we have to have this rule?*

Parent: *You remembered the new rule, even though you don't like it. And you asked an important question. Why do you think Dad and I are making this rule?*

Child: *Because I take too long?*

Parent: *Yes. Right now it's taking you longer than the school says homework should take. So we're going to keep track and only spend an hour on it because that's the amount of time your school says you should spend on it. And we want you to have some free time every afternoon.*

You can also use *think-throughs* to help children become more organised about their homework. Ask leading questions such as:

Where do you want to put your diagram so it won't get wrinkled?

Where should you put the highlighter so that you'll know where it is the next time you need it?

What do you need to do to make sure you bring home all your homework?

To help your child remember what she should do, make sure she answers your questions in words, and not just by putting the highlighter back in the pencil case or pointing at her homework diary.

Teaching and training children to do their best
To help children get the maximum benefit from their homework, divide each homework task into three distinct stages:

Stage One
You and your child begin with a *think-through*. In this vital
first stage, we help the child think about how to do the task
well so that he will learn whatever there is to be learned from
the activity. Even for simple pieces of work, ask your child to
tell you exactly what he needs to do and how and where and
why. Ask leading questions to guide him to think carefully
about any aspects of the task that he may be unaware of or
that he tends to overlook:

How many pages does this essay have to be?

What will you do if you think you can't spell a word?

Do you have to write full sentences?

Where do you put the carry number?

Your job is to ask the questions; your child's job is to think for
himself and to answer your questions. The only time that you
would switch from asking to telling him what to do and how
to do it is when one of his answers is incorrect, incomplete or
confused. Once the point has been clarified to your satisfaction, ask him the same question again, as many times as
necessary, until he can tell you exactly what he needs to do
and how he will do it.

Earlier I said that *think-throughs* should take a maximum of
one minute. But homework *think-throughs* are rather different
because in each piece of work there are likely to be several

issues you want your child to think about and remember. Therefore, a homework *think-through* will take a bit longer, but should not be more than five minutes. If you find that the *think-through* is taking much longer than that, it may be that the task is too difficult for your child. If you suspect this, talk to the teacher straight away. Together you may be able to pinpoint the problem and rectify it.

Stage Two
Your child does his homework, without any help. With very few exceptions, homework is not meant to be a collaborative effort! Homework should be ongoing training in self-reliance, so in the second stage the child works completely on his own, <u>with no help</u>. If you think he might need help with any aspect of his homework, include questions about that in the Stage One *think-through*.

Stage Three
The last stage is the improving stage. This is when we guide the child to improve his attention to detail, his thoroughness, his editing and his proofreading skills.

- First, you and your child each find three good things to Descriptively Praise about the piece of work. <u>You must not rush this.</u> Children learn a great deal from discussion of what they have done <u>right</u>.
- Don't let your child say vaguely, 'It's OK,' or even, 'My answers are right,' which would be a bit more descriptive. Instead, insist that your child be specific. He could say, 'I wrote four facts about photosynthesis,' or 'I looked up how to spell "Mediterranean", so I know it's right.'
- Then, you and your child each notice and mention two things about that piece of work that he will need to

improve. The more thoroughly you have done the *think-through*, the less there will be that needs correcting or improving. Even so, on most days you will probably notice more than two things that could be improved. But mention only two; otherwise you risk discouraging your child. Together, discuss the things that he needs to improve, and then have him make those four corrections.

Stage Three is very important, so give it plenty of time. And do not be surprised if your child resists noticing and talking about his good work as much as he resists noticing and talking about his mistakes. He may be in the habit of assuming that his homework is over as soon as he stops writing. Your insistence on Stage Three may come as a shock.

- **Preparing the environment**

What can you do to make it easier for your child to do the right thing?

Your child's brain needs high-quality fuel in order to do high-quality work.

Make sure you give your child healthy after-school snacks. This is an easy way to reduce hassles and improve your child's brain functioning, as well as his willingness and his attention to detail.

Eliminate distractions.

It will be much easier for your child to settle down and concentrate on homework if there are no distractions in the whole house during the sacred homework time:

- Make sure that no screens are on within the child's earshot.
- Together with your child, remove all toys, mobile phones and unnecessary equipment from the table.
- Put in another room any pets that might distract your child.
- If you have a toddler who cannot safely be left in another room, set him up with a highly absorbing activity (one that you bring out only at this time) so that he will not be interrupting the homework session.

Supervise the use of computers for homework and projects.
Unsupervised, children who should be working can easily be tempted to surreptitiously play computer games, 'chat' online, email their friends or surf the net, quickly switching the screen back to their work as soon as you enter the room. You can prevent this by keeping all screens in areas of the house that you can easily supervise. And make sure the screen is facing you as you walk by. In addition, use all the mechanical and electronic methods now available to put all leisure computer functions off limits during the sacred homework time. And take immediate action if you even suspect misuse.

- **Planning your day realistically**

Plan for homework to be done at the same time every day, whenever possible. That way it is predictable and therefore easier for everyone to remember and accept. Of course, this may not always be possible with after-school activities, parents' work schedules, household tasks, emergencies, etc. But making homework an absolutely clear priority by devoting some time to it six days out of seven is an important key to school success. Make a plan and post it in a prominent place so you can all refer to it frequently. This will greatly reduce confusion and resistance.

- **Special Time**

A lot of negative attention-seeking at homework time can be significantly reduced, or eliminated altogether, by making sure to have frequent, predictable and labelled Special Time.

2 Motivate with Descriptive Praise: What small steps in the right direction can you notice and mention?

Here are some Descriptive Praises that will help children become more willing to tackle their homework and be more willing to do their best:

You remembered to write your homework in your planner today. Very sensible. Now you know exactly what you have to do tonight.

You started with your trickiest homework first. It's sensible to do the hardest things when you're not so tired.

Even though you're frustrated, you're hardly complaining or arguing. You're sitting there trying to work out the answer. Very brave.

I noticed just now, when you were reading out loud, that whenever you made a mistake you went back and corrected it. And I didn't even have to tell you. It takes maturity to notice your own mistakes and be willing to correct them.

You're sitting in the right place at the right time. You're remembering the new rule.

You have six sentences in your story, and you remembered to start five of them with a capital letter. That's attention to detail.

I really appreciate how you're not rushing through your homework today. You're working carefully and slowly, and your writing looks much neater.

Today, when I asked about your homework, you didn't swear or shout, even though you don't like to talk about it. You told me in words how you feel about homework, and it's so nice that I didn't hear any swearing.

Twice this week you brought home all your homework and all your books. That's an improvement over last week.

3 Reflective Listening: How can you help your children deal with the emotions they may be feeling about their homework?

Here are some Reflective Listening examples you could use:

I can see you really don't feel like doing your homework.

You might be feeling ashamed that you didn't do so well on that exam. And maybe you're worried you've let Mum and me down.

Sometimes essays can be hard, especially getting started. Seems like you're confused about what to write first.

It can feel scary trying something new, especially if you think you might get it wrong.

4 Never Ask Twice

If you have a child who habitually resists settling down at homework time, you may not believe that the Six Steps of the Never Ask Twice method will get him started. You may need to do the Six Steps first for getting him to the table, then for getting him to open his exercise book, then for getting him to pick up his pencil, etc. Don't give up! It gets easier! But keep in mind that no amount of behaviour strategies will transform homework hassles if the work feels too difficult for your child. If this seems to be the case, it's important to talk to your child's teacher.

5 Rewards and Consequences

This can provide additional motivation for children to do their best, rather than simply rushing through their homework at breakneck speed to get it done so they can go play. Require your child to do his or her 'personal best' before earning the reward.

Summary

Homework does not have to be a battle. As you put into practice the strategies outlined in this chapter, your child's attitude to homework can be transformed. He may never grow to love it, but he can learn to find satisfaction in doing his best.

CHAPTER 14

TIDYING UP AND LOOKING AFTER BELONGINGS: FOSTERING RESPONSIBILITY, REDUCING RESISTANCE

How we got Sam to tidy his bedroom

I guess our son, Sam, was like lots of other ten-year-old boys. He hated tidying his room. He'd promise to do it, and then he'd either 'forget' or he'd do a bit and then get distracted. We'd remind him some more; eventually he stopped even listening.

Talking it over, my wife and I decided that Sam's room should be tidy every morning in order to earn his screen time. We chose a weekend to start the new plan because we thought he might not take the new rule seriously to begin with, so it might take him quite a while the first day. On the Friday evening we did a one-minute think-through about what should happen the next day. Sam had to explain, in his own words, where he would put his dirty clothes, his clean clothes, his Lego, his books, his homework papers, his Pokémon cards, his sports equipment and his used tissues.

Knowing how keen Sam was on his screen time, we took the precaution of removing all the remotes and the hand-held electronic games until after he had earned his screen time. On Saturday morning I went to find Sam, who was in the sitting room looking at a comic, and stood in front of him until he looked up. I Descriptively Praised him for looking up and said in what I hoped was a strong but calm and friendly voice, 'Now it's time to tidy your room.' Sam groaned and went straight back to reading his comic. But pretty soon he looked up again, maybe to check to see if I looked angry. I Descriptively Praised him for stopping reading and looking up and then I asked him what he should do next. He replied, 'But it's too hard!' I kept standing there and Reflectively Listened about how he probably didn't feel like cleaning his room. And within a couple of minutes Sam stood up and stormed off in the direction of his bedroom, still complaining that the job was too hard. He yelled, 'Dad, you have to help me!' so I said, 'No, because you didn't ask politely. After you've put a few things away and your room is looking better, you can ask me politely, and then I'll help you.' I followed Sam into his room and praised him as he picked up some socks from the floor and put them in the laundry basket. Then he asked for help in a friendly, polite voice so I did help him. But I made sure I did much less than Sam so he knew it was his job.

We ended up both enjoying the clean-up time, and the best thing was that instead of asking for his screen time afterwards, he wanted his reward to be kicking a ball around the garden with me.

Father of a 10-year-old

Tidying up and looking after belongings do not come naturally to a lot of children – and this story about Sam's reluctance to keep his bedroom tidy is probably familiar to lots of parents, especially the parents of boys! As far as many kids are concerned, tidying up is 'boring' and 'stupid', and it's much easier to ignore the nagging and wait until Mum does it – which she usually does. This vicious circle can be so frustrating, feeling that we have to nag to get children to tidy their things away. And we know we can do it more quickly ourselves and avoid a fuss, so it's easy to give in and do it for them.

But of course, our children need to be taught and trained to look after their belongings and to tidy up after themselves. This means we must not do it for them, however much we might be tempted to at times. The good news is that the more focus we put on teaching and training our children to take care

of their belongings, the more self-reliant, confident, motivated and cooperative they will become. And the more
consistently we teach and train our children to be helpful, the
more respectful, appreciative and responsible they will
become. This maturity and self-reliance starts at home and
will soon spread to school and to other social situations.

So how do we teach and train our children to be tidy and to
look after their toys, equipment, books and clothes? The keys
are Preparing for Success, the Never Ask Twice method,
Descriptive Praise and Reflective Listening. By investing some
time, thought and action in these useful strategies, in just a
few weeks you can teach your children how to keep their
belongings tidier and more organised. Once you have taught
them how, then you can train them so that neatness and
organisation gradually become a habit. Quite soon your children will be proud of their clean, tidy room!

The questionnaire

Fill this in before you start practising the strategies I talk about in this chapter, and then fill it in again two to four weeks later. You should see quite a difference in your answers.

Your child	Hardly ever	Sometimes	Too often
Leaves his belongings strewn about the house or flat			
Argues or complains about having to tidy up			
Doesn't put things away after using them			
Is disorganised or forgetful so he can't find what he's looking for			
Has a messy bedroom because he doesn't routinely put things away			
Starts tidying, but gets easily distracted			

Action Plan for Calmer, Easier, Happier tidying up and looking after belongings

1 Preparing for Success

• **Become a United Front.**
Take the time to sit down with your partner and decide what you would like your child to be responsible for tidying, when it should happen, and what standard you're both aiming for.

The following rules have helped many families to get on top of the clutter that can accumulate so quickly:

Have five minutes of tidying-up time before dinner.
Daily tidying up prevents clutter from building up in your child's bedroom. Soon he will begin to register neatness and organisation as the norm. And not having so much to tidy up each time makes the task less daunting. If your child is very good at making messes, it may be helpful to have more than one tidying-up session each day.

Any toy or game, art project, etc. that has been taken out needs to be put away before the next activity begins.
Similarly, with messy projects, such as baking or making collages, the equipment for each stage needs to be put away before the next stage can begin. Because activities like these are so absorbing, in their enthusiasm children can easily forget this rule. So you might start the first *think-through* by saying, 'The new rule is that from now on, when you put something back in the right place, straightaway, without a fuss, you can play with it the next time.' The flipside of this new rule is, obviously, that if she makes a fuss or ignores your

instruction, she won't be allowed to play with it the next time. But that consequence rarely needs to be stated; children generally understand it immediately. This rule is very different from threatening to confiscate or throw out toys that have not been put away; that feels very negative, whether you *follow through* with it or not.

Any toys or clothes left lying around the house will be removed by the parent and need to be earned back.

- Do think-throughs to establish new rules for keeping things tidy and to help children remember what they need to do

With *think-throughs* it won't be long before these rules become routines that your children remember with very little prompting.

Examples of think-throughs
Here's an example of a *think-through* that explains a new rule in detail. The rule is: Once a day the parents will remove any of the children's belongings that are not in their rooms. The children will then need to earn back their belongings.

Think-through: At a neutral time

Parent: *Mummy and I have come up with a plan so we can stop nagging you about leaving your things all over the house. Here's the new plan. You might not like it, but we're going to do it for a month and see what happens. Starting this Saturday, every day before dinner Mummy or I are going to walk around the house, and if we see anything of yours that's not in your room, we'll pick it up for you without any nagging.*

Child: *Huh?*

Parent: *Yes, we'll pick it up for you, and we'll hold it for you until you earn it back.*

Child: *That's not fair! It's my stuff.*

Parent: *Yes, it's your stuff, and we'll make sure to take very good care of it.*

Child: *How do I get it back?*

Parent: *That is such a sensible question. You're already thinking about strategies. There are a lot of ways to earn your belongings back. What do you think they might be?*

Child: *Feeding the guinea pig?*

Parent: *Yes. You're thinking.*

Child: *Finishing my homework?*

Parent: *Yes. And there will be lots of other things as well.*

Child: *But that's bribing. It's my stuff anyway.*

Parent: *You might be wishing we didn't have this new rule . . . I have a feeling you're mostly going to remember to keep things in your room. Why do you think Mummy and I are making this new rule?*

Child: (Groaning) *To annoy me.*

Parent: *You've got a good sense of humour. Now answer me sensibly.*

Child: *Because you don't like the house to be messy.*

Parent: *Exactly right. And nobody enjoys doing big clean-up projects. This way we can stay on top of tidying up. So what's the new rule?*

Child: *Before dinner, you'll take any of my stuff that hasn't been put away. I can earn it back.*

Parent: *You remembered.*

Think-throughs are a really useful tool for helping your child remember what she needs to do to keep her things tidy and

to prevent mess from building up. Ask leading questions, such as:

Before you go out in the garden, where do the paper aeroplanes go?

What will you do if your drawer is too full and you can't close it properly?

What should be on your desk?

What do you need to do before I'll say yes to screen time?

What time do your toys have to be in your room by every day?

Who decides if your bedroom is tidy enough?

Requiring your child to answer the *think-through* questions in full sentences will help transfer the rule into her long-term memory. And make sure your child answers in a polite, friendly tone of voice to help her to respect you and to take the new rule seriously. Descriptively Praise something about each answer, even if it is only partially correct. This will help motivate your child.

• Prepare the environment

Here are some ideas to make it easier for your child to be willing to tidy up.

Many children find tidying away their belongings and cleaning their rooms difficult – and so avoid doing it – because they have too much stuff and there isn't a designated and accessible place for each item. By addressing these problems and doing a few other things to prepare the environment, we can make the job of tidying and looking after their belongings more pleasant for our children.

With your child, sort through his belongings, and weed out all the unnecessary duplicates, as well as all the outgrown or broken equipment, books, games and toys.

This will make it much easier for your child to know what he has and to value and take care of it. Take your child with you when you drop off the unwanted items at a charity shop, and he will be learning important lessons about compassion, sharing and recycling.

Remove from your child's room all the toys and equipment that can't easily be put away.

After the initial weeding, your child may still have more sports equipment, electronic gadgets, clothes, toys, games, stuffed animals, CDs and DVDs than there is adequate space for. Box up the overspill and put it out of sight. When you bring one of these boxes out again after a few weeks or months, the contents will be 'new' again, fresh and exciting. This way your child's natural craving for stimulation and novelty can be satisfied without your feeling that you have to keep buying new things.

Having fewer items available makes tidying up much easier and quicker. Here is another benefit: with fewer possessions scattered about to distract her, your child will probably concentrate on each toy or game for longer. This improves attention span, imagination and the ability to tolerate frustration, as well as problem-solving skills and perseverance.

Designate a specific, easily accessible place for all your child's belongings.

Labelling shelves and containers clearly (with added pictures for children who are not reading yet) makes the child's job much easier.

For a child who seems to be disorganised and distractible by temperament, it helps to take a photograph of each part of her room after it has been tidied to your satisfaction.
This way she will know what standard she needs to aim for, and she will know when the job is done.

Keep very enticing or potentially messy games up high.
This means that your children will only have access to them after you have checked that the toys they last played with have been put away.

How I made it easier for my children to have tidier rooms

When I heard about how to prepare the environment to make it easier for children to do the right thing, my mind leapt to my kids' messy rooms. What we needed to do was make sure they had places to put everything. So I got some new bins to make toys easier to put away, and we put in some lower hooks for jackets and a small rack for shoes.

I involved my kids in the project. They helped decide which toys would go where, which jackets would go on the hooks based on the season, etc. I also did think-throughs about what they should do with their toys after they finished playing with them, so it was clear that they understood the new routine.

The key to our success was remembering Noël's advice about teaching and training. I was prepared for the fact that just them knowing how to do something wasn't enough. They had to get into the habit, so I made sure to be in the room the next time they finished playing with the Lego. I Descriptively Praised them for not leaving the room while there were still toys on the floor. As soon as I said that, they started putting the Lego away in the right bin! Then I praised them for remembering the new routine. Pretty soon, with a few more think-throughs and Descriptive Praise, they got into the habit. It's a lot nicer going into their room now with most things put away. Their rooms aren't one hundred percent tidy, but it's a big improvement.

Mother of two, aged 9 and 5

- **Plan your day realistically**

If we're rushing from one activity to another, it's easy to let clutter accumulate. The solution is to build in a little extra time in between each task. Use that time to require children to clear up a few things.

- **Special Time**

The thought of tidying up will not be at all appealing if it is followed immediately by having to go to bed. Arrange the bedtime routine so that Special Time with a parent comes right after tidying up.

Children are less resistant to putting things away when a parent is sharing the job or even just keeping them company. You can make tidying and organising an enjoyable activity for you and your child. Think of it as Special Time – relax, smile, Descriptively Praise, chat and laugh. This can transform your child's attitude towards tidying up.

You may be surprised that I suggest offering to share some of the tidying away with your child.

Yes, it is his job, and we want him to learn to take responsibility for putting things back where they belong. But the parent's willingness to pitch in often softens the child's initial resistance, which may be coming from a feeling that the task is too complicated or will take too long. Sometimes children have come to feel that having to put things away is a punishment, especially if we often tell them to do it in an annoyed tone.

Notice that I did not suggest that you <u>help</u> your child put his things away. That's because your child is completely capable of doing it by himself – he doesn't need 'help'. Instead, I suggest we use the word 'share'. Usually children hear the word 'share' when they are not sharing and when they do not feel like sharing. So the whole concept of sharing is often tainted with unpleasant associations for a child. That starts to change when we say things like, 'I want to share this job with you.'

And in case your child thinks that this means he can start playing again while you end up doing the tidying away, a fool-proof solution is to demonstrate that you will put one Lego, stuffed animal or coloured pencil back in the right place for each one your child puts away.

2 What can you find to Descriptively Praise?

Descriptive Praise is an important motivation strategy. It will help your child get into the habit of putting things away consistently, whether it is putting toys and equipment back in the right boxes, putting dirty clothes in the laundry basket, clean clothes in their drawers, homework in the backpack or their cup in the sink.

Your job will be to notice and mention, several times every day, whenever your child puts something back in the right place, or even just <u>near</u> the right place.

You didn't leave your jacket on the floor.
(Even though he threw it on a chair instead of hanging it on the hook.)

You were careful not to walk on that book. You stepped over it. (Even though you wish he had picked it up off the floor and put it on the table.)

Thanks for picking up that spoon.

All the shoes are now in the shoe basket!

When parents Descriptively Praise these tiny steps in the right direction, children start to see themselves in a new light. They start to see themselves as someone who puts things away, someone who is organised. And the more they see themselves that way, the more they will be willing to put things away the first time you tell them to. This will eventually lead to their remembering to put things back in the right place without having to be told. This won't happen every time, because no one is perfect, but you'll notice it happening more and more.

Here are some more Descriptive Praises you can say to help motivate your children to take good care of their belongings and to put things away when they have finished using them:

You're putting all those toys away, with no complaining, even though the baby dumped out some of them. You're setting a good example.

You remembered to put your dirty clothes in the basket. You didn't leave anything on the floor. That helps keep our house neat.

I see you've put some toys back on the shelf. This room already looks better, and we've only been clearing up for two minutes.

You picked the towel up off the floor as soon as I asked you to. And you hung it up smoothly, not all bunched up, so now it can dry out more quickly.

3 Be willing to Reflectively Listen – a lot!

Maybe you don't feel like tidying up now. You'd rather keep playing.

It's so annoying to be interrupted. You just want to finish your game.

Wouldn't it be great if you had a robot that put your toys away!

It feels horrible to dismantle your Lego village. It took such a long time to set it all up.

4 Use the Never Ask Twice strategy to reduce the likelihood of your child resisting the transition from playing to tidying up.

At first, when you are teaching and training this habit, build some extra time into your schedule so that you can wait for cooperation without becoming stressed.

As long as you're putting into practice the Calmer, Easier, Happier Parenting strategies you've been learning so far, rather than repeating yourself or sounding annoyed, the time you need to wait will become shorter and shorter.

Give your child a five-minute countdown.
Rather than expecting your child to be able to instantly tear himself away from an absorbing game or activity, say 'In five minutes it will be time to stop playing and start putting things away.' The trick is to stay with your child for those five minutes, instead of leaving the room, which would make your words immediately ignorable. Set a timer, and during those five

minutes you could talk about the next activity to help your child's mind start to visualise what he will soon be doing. You could say, 'I wonder if you want to have your horses in the bath tonight?' or 'Which of your dolls are you bringing to Grandma's with you tonight?' or 'I'm really looking forward to the next chapter of Harry Potter once we are all cosy on the bed.'

Because you are staying with your child for those last five minutes of playtime and engaging with him, he will not feel hurried or bossed about. By the time the timer rings, he will usually be quite ready to put his toys away, especially if you offer to share the job of tidying with him. In fact, many parents tell me that this version of a *countdown* works so well that their child often starts to put his things away even before the timer rings. Now that is a result!

5. Rewards and Consequences

When your child comes to you asking for something, and you want to say 'Yes,' instead say, 'Yes, after you put your shoes in the basket (or the furniture back in the doll's house or the books back on the shelf, etc.)' Children are often asking us for something, so with this strategy your house will soon be spotless!

Summary

The strategies I talk about in this chapter can transform your children's resistance to tidying up and looking after their belongings. Quite soon you will see the resistance melt away.

CHAPTER 15

HOUSEHOLD CHORES: IMPROVING WILLINGNESS, TEACHING TEAMWORK

Now it's just a routine

Our boys, who are eight and ten, were in the routine of clearing their dishes after meals, but my wife and I knew they were capable of more clean-up. We didn't want them to grow up feeling like we were their 'unpaid staff', cooking and cleaning up after them. One of our values is that our kids grow up to be self-reliant, so we knew it was time to add some chores. Truthfully, though, we worried about the complaints we would get if we asked them to do more!

My wife and I started by deciding what we wanted them to do, and we committed ourselves to the idea that there would be some upfront training time in teaching them how to wash the dishes carefully. Then we had a meeting with our boys and told them the new rules – at a neutral time, not at dinner. We did a think-through about the new rules, where they told us what chores they would be responsible for. Funny thing was that all the resistance we expected didn't happen! It's been a few months since we started having them do the table-setting and washing the dishes, and now it's just a routine. Now we need to look for other jobs for them to do!

Father of two, aged 10 and 8

Getting children into the regular habit of sharing in household chores is an issue that many parents tell me they need help with. In some families, children help a bit with clearing the table after meals, like the boys in the family above, but the parents feel they could and should be helping even more. In other families, children have got so used to their parents doing all the household chores that they resent being asked to contribute beyond the bare minimum. This is exhausting for those parents.

You may have heard the old saying, 'Sweep the floor and wipe the table, children love to 'til they're able.' We can probably all remember how delighted a toddler is to put dirty clothes in the laundry basket, bring cutlery to the table, put books back on the shelf, put away the shopping. But because their 'help' slows us down and we can do things more easily without their help, we tell them to go and play. So it's not surprising that a few years later, all our children want to do is play, and they groan and make a fuss when we ask them to give us a hand!

You'll be pleased to hear that it is not that difficult to change children's attitudes so that they willingly pitch in with <u>all</u> the household jobs, not just setting and clearing the table. Children can grow to enjoy the satisfaction that comes from doing a job well: cleaning and hoovering, putting a load of laundry in the washing machine, raking leaves, emptying the rubbish and any other task that needs doing.

By putting in place the Calmer, Easier, Happier Parenting strategies, you will be teaching and training your children to be more thoughtful and considerate as well as more self-reliant and mature. And you will enjoy the confidence that comes from knowing that your children are learning very useful life skills.

The questionnaire

Fill this in to focus your mind on what changes you want to see. Then revisit it in two to four weeks. You should see quite a difference in your answers.

Your child	Hardly ever	Sometimes	Too often
Complains when asked to contribute			
Forgets what he has to do or is easily distracted			
Rushes through her chores; doesn't take the time to do her best			
Helps when asked, but rarely volunteers or notices what needs to be done			

Action Plan for Calmer, Easier, Happier household chores

1 Preparing for Success

• **Establish a United Front**

Have you sat down with your partner and agreed on what chores you would like your children to do? If you're not sure what you can reasonably expect your child to do at what age, my advice is that it is almost never too early to start teaching and training. If you look at documentaries of children in less affluent parts of the world, you will see even very young children collecting firewood, helping to prepare meals, washing clothes, sweeping the house, weeding the garden and even taking care of younger siblings – and all with a great big smile!

Start experimenting. Ask your child to do one small part of unloading the dishwasher or sorting the laundry or making his bed or putting the towel back properly on the rack. If he resists doing even a small, easy part of the task, then the problem is not that he can't do it, but that he thinks he doesn't have to. It is time to insist that he does what he's capable of doing. It is time to make some new rules.

You may be wondering what new rules you can make that will help your children to contribute willingly, to remember their responsibilities and to do their best, without rushing or dawdling or complaining. Here are some rules that many families have used to become Calmer, Easier and Happier:

Set aside the same time every day (straight after dinner works best for most families) when <u>all</u> family members spend ten or fifteen minutes together doing some household task.
One person might be scrubbing the pots and pans, another might be sweeping or hoovering, another might be wiping splatters off the hob, another might be collecting cups or rubbish from other rooms or putting in a load of laundry or making a shopping list. Teamwork and support can transform a tedious, dreaded chore into an enjoyable activity. This plan is far preferable to interrupting what your child considers to be his free time with a reminder to do his chores. And daily chores soon become a habit, whereas weekly or twice-weekly chores seem to come as a shock each time.

So that your child doesn't feel bossed about, you can offer her two choices.

This could be a choice between two tasks or a choice between two times to do it, eg. before dinner or before screen time. Your tone of voice and your words, while staying friendly, need to make it clear that contributing to the household is not optional. Avoid saying things like, 'How about emptying the bins?' or 'Would you like to take Rover for a walk?'

For particularly unpopular tasks, at first require only five or ten minutes.

That will feel much less daunting.

Another good rule is that children take it in turns to do certain tasks.

That way no one is stuck for very long doing a task that they don't like.

- Do think-throughs to set new rules and clarify existing rules

If your children are in the habit of being waited on, you may need to invest in quite a few *think-throughs* on the topic of what contributing to the family means and why you now expect your children to be more involved. You might need to do five or even ten *think-throughs* a day at first. This may sound a lot, but as each *think-through* takes a maximum of one minute, even if you were to do ten *think-throughs* a day, that would only be an extra ten minutes a day.

And you won't need to do this many *think-throughs* for long. Parents consistently report that the initial resistance to helping around the house can melt away in less than a week with *think-throughs*, as long as you are combining them with Descriptive Praise, Reflective Listening and Special Time.

Examples of think-throughs

Here is an example of a *think-through* in which the parent is firming up an existing but neglected rule that the children alternate setting the table before the meal and clearing the table after the meal.

Think-through: At a neutral time

Parent: *I have a few questions to ask you. And I can see you're looking at me with a friendly face. You're smiling. A while ago we made a rule that you and your brother would each set the table or clear the table. But we've all been forgetting so it's time to start remembering again. I'm going to remember not to set the table and not to clear the table because it's not my job. Whose job is it to set the table and clear the table?*

Child: *It's ours. But I forget sometimes.*

Parent: *Me too. That's why we're doing this think-through right now, to help us all remember. So tell me, which days will you set the table and which days will you clear the table?*

Child: *We're supposed to take turns, but sometimes Harry isn't home, and then I have to do everything!*

Parent: *Of course you don't want to do double the work. So Daddy and I have come up with a solution for that. On the even-numbered days of the month you'll set, and Harry will clear. What's going to happen on the even-numbered days of the month?*

Child: *Ummmm . . . I'll set the table?*

Parent: *That's right. You remembered.*

Child: *But what if it's an even-numbered day and Harry isn't there? Do I have to clear for him?*

Parent: *I can see you're thinking carefully about this new plan. You won't have to do his job, even if he's not there.*

Child: *Who's going to do it?*

Parent: *Take a guess. Who do you think is going to do it?*

Child: *You or Daddy?*

Parent: *That's right; we'll do it. But if you want to earn a little extra pocket money, then you can do it.*

Child: *That's not fair. Harry gets you to do his job, just because he's at swimming.*

Parent: (Waits, smiling) *So what will happen on the odd-numbered days of the month?*

Child: *I'll clear. But if I'm not here, you and Daddy have to do it.*

Parent: *Of course, unless Harry wants to earn a little extra pocket money.*

• **Preparing the environment**

Visual reminders, in the form of charts and checklists, work very well to remind and motivate.

What happened when I Prepared for Success

With my six-year-old daughter, who is quite spirited, getting her over her resistance to setting the table in a reasonable time frame took a bit of time. What I did was to start really early. As soon as she came back from school, which was hours before dinner time, I'd ask her to set the table. This meant that I had plenty of time to deal with her running off, which she always did at the beginning. Each time she'd eventually come and ask me for something, and then I'd say, 'I'd be happy to do this for you, after you've set the table.'

I remember one time when I forgot to build in enough time and left it until just before dinner time. She didn't set the table, so her brother put out the knives and forks and plates without setting a place for her, and we sat down and started to eat the meal. She came in and said, 'Where's my dinner?' I knew I had to follow through, so I said, 'I'd be happy to give you your dinner when you do what I asked and set the table.' She got out more knives and forks – so now we all had two of each! But it did the trick, and now setting the table has become a firmly entrenched habit for her.

Mother of two, aged 9 and 6

- **Plan your day realistically**

Teaching and training new habits takes time; there's no getting around that. To begin with, you will need to make the time to teach your children new skills. You'll also need to make the time for training good habits by insisting and waiting, as this mother discovered with her daughter. Allowing yourself plenty of time, particularly if your child is initially resistant to your new rules, will help you feel calmer.

Here are ways that you can build teaching and training time into your already busy day:

- All day long, whatever household task you are involved in, think about which parts of the task you could start teaching your child to do. Children can even start learning how to do parts of grown-up tasks such as DIY or ringing to schedule a doctor's appointment.
- Take advantage of the times when your child wants you to play with her. Develop a routine where first she helps you with a part of what you're doing; then you play with her.

- **Special Time**

Include one child in each task you do around the house, such as folding laundry, sorting the recycling, changing the sheets or scrubbing the bath. At first set the timer for five minutes, or even for two minutes if your child is extremely resistant. Remember to Descriptively Praise! If you do this every day, quite soon your child will want to keep going beyond the five minutes. That is because it naturally feels good to be helpful. It also feels good to be appreciated. In fact, doing household chores together can become delightful Special Time.

2 Descriptive Praise

Notice and Descriptively Praise every tiny little thing your child does that could possibly be construed as helpful to the rest of the family. This will motivate your child to want to think of even more ways to be helpful.

Thanks for helping your brother set the table. You shared the job. And when he put the forks on the wrong side, you corrected him gently, without making him feel embarrassed. That was kind.

Your sheets are pulled so tight, and there are no lumps in your blanket. I can tell you took your time making your bed.

You've remembered to put all the cutlery on the top plate before you stacked them. That helps keep the plates from tipping and breaking.

I noticed there wasn't any food left in the sink after you did the washing up. You pushed it all down the drain, and the sink is clean.

I saw that after you fed Spot, you didn't leave the spoon in the sink. You washed it off very carefully. You took care of the whole job yourself, from beginning to end. That was very responsible.

I want to tell you some good news. I noticed how helpful you were today, bringing in the shopping, and putting some of it away. And you made the baby laugh when he was crying. So your reward is that you can stay out an extra half-hour. You've earned it by being so mature.

You've done all your chores. Now you've earned the sleepover. Have a lovely time.

You're helping your sister sort the recycling. You're both sharing the job.

3 Reflective Listening

These examples of Reflective Listening can reduce upset and defuse resistance. Reflective Listening shows that you understand how your child is feeling and that you care about his feelings:

You wanted to be helpful, and it was so frustrating when you couldn't find the right attachments for the hoover.

This used to be something I always did, so you might feel resentful about having to do it now. You probably wish you didn't have to set the table every day.

It might seem silly to you that you have to make your bed even when we don't have company coming over.

Having to stop what you're doing to get your chores done can feel awful sometimes, especially when you'd rather be playing.

Wouldn't it be fun if we could rub a magic lamp and a genie would pop out and grant us three wishes? We could get all the windows washed in a few seconds!

I bet you wish that I would still do this for you.

4 Never Ask Twice

The Six Steps will save you lots of nagging!

5 Rewards and Consequences

The right rewards can make almost any job more palatable. Rewards can help ease your child or teen over the hump of her resistance. You won't need to keep rewarding the same behaviour for very long because with Descriptive Praise, Reflective Listening and *think-throughs*, children soon internalise the habit of being more helpful.

Summary

If you are currently meeting a wall of resistance about household chores, or if your child is willing in theory but 'forgets' time and time again, it may be hard to believe that any strategies could make much of a difference. Challenge yourself to put the Calmer, Easier, Happier Parenting strategies into practice, and see for yourself! You'll find that even very immature, stubborn or self-absorbed children will feel better about themselves, and will behave better, when they are required to contribute to the household in meaningful ways.

CHAPTER 16

PLAYING INDEPENDENTLY: TRAINING SELF-RELIANCE AND PROBLEM-SOLVING

How we stopped being entertainers

Teaching our four children, aged from sixteen down to eight, how to play on their own, not in front of a screen, and making it a rule that they did this every day, has been a real life-saver for us. Until we did this we were spending a lot of our time thinking up things the kids could do so that they wouldn't get bored, especially at weekends and in the holidays. We had become our kids' entertainers. And when we didn't provide them with things to do, they'd start fighting. So then we'd let them have more TV and computer than we knew was good for them because at least that kept them entertained and allowed us to get on with what we had to do. But of course we felt guilty.

I have to admit that the kids weren't at all keen on the new rules. The first week was pretty rough. We had tears, outbursts and complaints of 'I'm bored' and 'This is so unfair'. But we kept going with think-throughs, Descriptive Praise and Reflective Listening.

By day ten the complaining had completely stopped, and the children admitted that they were actually enjoying the new rules. They were proud that they were doing things they'd never thought of doing before. And when the independent playtime was over, they got on together much better. There was much less fighting, and we could get on with doing our stuff without feeling guilty.

Father of four, aged 16, 13, 10 and 8

Does this sound familiar? This family is typical of many I have worked with; the parents have, without quite realising how it happened, taken on the role of 'entertainment directors'. They find themselves spending more and more time and money providing activities out of fear that their children will get bored. And the more parents take on this job description, the less skilled children become at making their own entertainment. When activities aren't laid on, the only entertainment many children can think of is spending hours in front of a screen. Parents know this is not good for their children, but they may not know what they can do about it.

There are a host of reasons why I recommend that parents resign from their role as entertainment directors. When children are in the habit of playing alone for a good chunk of time every day, they become significantly more self-reliant and also more cooperative. They are less demanding, less clingy and less irritable. They fight with their siblings less and they enjoy playing and hanging out with their siblings more. They become more confident, more creative and more skilled at problem-solving. One of the most important school skills and life skills that a child needs to learn is how to occupy himself for longer and longer stretches of time, without needing much adult input to keep him focused. Most children will not be able to do this very well at school unless they are regularly practising this skill at home. And parenting becomes less stressful when parents are spending less time chauffeuring and arranging playdates, after-school lessons and weekend activities.

Many children are very capable of playing by themselves, but they are only willing to do it when they choose to or when no siblings or playmates are available. It's important to guide these children into the habit of occupying themselves not only when they feel like it, but also when parents or the sitter are too busy or stressed to interact with them positively.

You may wonder whether your kids would ever willingly spend much time doing activities on their own not in front of a screen. I promise that when you start practising the Calmer, Easier, Happier Parenting techniques, you will be amazed at how resourceful your children really are.

The questionnaire

Fill in this questionnaire to help you identify which issues you want to improve. Fill in the questionnarire again after two to four weeks. You will be pleased with your progress.

Your child	Hardly ever	Sometimes	Too often
Complains that he is 'bored' and that there is 'nothing to do'			
Expects the parent to organise activities			
Spends more time in front of a screen than you would like			
Squabbles with siblings if he is not occupied			
Is dependent on screens for entertainment			
Becomes upset when he has to occupy himself			
Wants you to play with him			

Action Plan for Calmer, Easier, Happier independent playtimes

1 Preparing for Success

- **Be united**

Agree with your partner on a new rule to help your children develop the habit of playing on their own. This rule will soon become a familiar and enjoyable routine. This rule might be: Every single day, at a certain time, each child has to play quietly in a room by himself.

Remember, time spent in front of a screen does not count as playing alone!

- **Use think-throughs to establish your new rules about playing independently**

At first you may need to do several *think-throughs* each day until the resistance has melted. But you'll be glad to hear that this will not take long because playing by oneself is quite natural. All babies are born knowing how to occupy themselves! When we resign from our role as entertainment directors, children soon demonstrate that they are capable of enjoying their own company.

Examples of think-throughs

Here is an example of a *think-through* you could do about the new rule.

Think-through: At a neutral time

Parent: *Mummy and I have decided on a new rule. Every day after dinner you and your sister will each have to play by yourselves in a separate room, not playing together.*

Child: *Why?*

Parent: *I'm glad you're thinking about why we make rules. Take a guess. Why do you think we're making this new rule?*

Child: *So we won't fight?*

Parent: *Yes, that's a sensible answer. It will help you to fight less. And playing by yourself is a good habit to get into.*

Child: *It won't work! We'll always fight because you always take her side. You think it's all my fault. You don't see how mean she is to me when you're not looking. You think she's perfect.*

Parent: (Reflectively Listens) *It sounds like you think I don't understand what's happening.*

Child: *You don't.*

Parent: *We have made mistakes in the past. Mummy and I used to blame you a lot, because you're older. That must have felt horrible!*

Child: (Silent, looking sad)

Parent: *Now we're practising not getting angry and not telling you off when there's a fight. So what's the new rule about playing alone every day?*

Child: *Every day. All alone. But where?*

Parent: (Descriptively Praising) *You remembered the new rule: every day, all alone. One day, you'll have your alone time in your room, and your sister will be in the sitting room. Then the next day you'll switch rooms.*

Child: *What if she comes and bothers me?*

Parent: *She has to stay where she is told, just like you have to.*

Child: *Yeah! You'll make her follow the rule too.*

Parent: *I certainly will. She's not a baby any more.*

- Preparing the environment

Here are some steps to make it easier for your children to play on their own:

How much time should your child spend playing alone?

If you expect resistance, start with a very short playing-alone time every day, maybe only five or ten minutes. Use a timer that your child will be able to see (but cannot get at). That way you will not be tempted to answer when he calls out piteously, 'Is playing-alone time nearly over?'

As your child sees that he can survive this experience and even enjoy it, you can increase the time by a few minutes every few days. Eventually your children will feel quite comfortable occupying themselves for half an hour or even an hour, not only when they feel like it, but also when you say they have to.

Designate a place where your child will play on her own.

This might be her bedroom. If you have more than one child and they share a bedroom, they can alternate between their bedroom and the sitting room.

Help your children make a list of activities they might enjoy doing independently.

Children often dismiss our suggestions as 'so boring'. And even when they do follow our suggestions, they are not learning to think for themselves. Instead, at a neutral time, not right before playing-alone time, together with your children draw up a list of all the activities they enjoy that they could do by themselves. Challenge them to add activities that they have not yet tried but that they might find appealing. If all of you keep expanding this list over several days, your children will see that it is a much longer and more varied list than they at first imagined.

Here are some activities that parents have found, sometimes to their surprise, that their children enjoy doing on their own:

reading
drawing
model-making
messing about in the garden
writing in a journal
playing their instrument
adding to and organising their collections
rearranging the furniture in their bedrooms
trying out a recipe from a magazine
playing cards
playing chess against themselves
playing with dolls and action figures
doing crosswords or jigsaw puzzles
writing a family newspaper
doing art projects
practising their karate, gymnastics or football

Lead by example – enjoy your own pursuits.
If our children see us enjoying our own interests, not in front of a screen, whether it's gardening, baking, stamp collecting or reading, playing independently will start to seem normal.

- **Plan your day realistically**

Schedule independent playtime into your day to make sure it happens.

- **Special Time**

Children are more willing to play by themselves when they know that they have frequent, predictable Special Time with a parent.

How to teach and train your young child to play independently

Some children have never got into the habit of playing by themselves. They may not really know how. You may need to teach this skill before you can train the habit. Here is how to begin:

1   Every day or two, put out a game that one person can play alone, or a puzzle, paper and coloured pencils, several books, toy cars, blocks, Lego, etc. Start playing with the toys or equipment yourself, without inviting the child over. Talk to yourself out loud with interest and enthusiasm in your voice about whatever you are doing, for example:

I've drawn a great big yellow bus.

This car needs some petrol. I'm going to pretend that this shoe is the petrol station.

I wonder where this piece goes.

2   Wait patiently for your child to wander over when he becomes curious or wants your attention.

3   Talk with great enthusiasm about whatever your child does in relation to the activity or equipment, no matter how minimal:

You've chosen the whale book.

That looks like a castle you're building. Those guys might be the knights.

Maybe your car needs petrol as well.

The purpose here is <u>not</u> to play with your child, which you can do during Special Time. Our aim here is to:

- demonstrate <u>how</u> to play alone
- show by our enthusiasm that playing alone is fun.

If your child asks you to draw or make something for him, don't, as that would shift the focus back onto you as the entertainer. It could also reinforce his belief that he cannot do these things well enough.

If you are willing to sit and play like this for ten or fifteen minutes most days, within a few weeks you can teach your child how to entertain himself, an invaluable skill for the child and a sanity-saver for you as the parent. After a few days or a few weeks of teaching your child how to play by himself, start requiring a short playing-alone time every day, and add on a few minutes every few days.

Some children are initially anxious when the parent is out of sight. If necessary, you can start by having the child's playing-alone time in the same room where you are, but make sure to be involved in your own activity and not talking to your child. Then you can graduate to being in the next room but still visible from the doorway. And eventually you can be in one part of the house or flat and your child will be playing happily several rooms away or on a different floor.

If you have a child who is transitioning out of a daytime sleep, this is a perfect opportunity for independent playtime. Here's how one family made this transition:

From napping to quiet time

When our son was four, he started to give up his nap. We weren't really ready at all because we still needed the break ourselves! We also knew that he still needed the quiet down time and that there was a chance he might sleep. So we kept the routine the same, taking him to his room at two o'clock, reading him a few stories and then snuggling for a few minutes before leaving. We just called it his 'quiet time'. We told him that we'd come and get him when quiet time was over. Sometimes he napped, but a lot of times he didn't and would just sing and hum and play with something in his room. It was pretty surprising how long he could play by himself. He was getting what he needed, and so were we!

Mother of two, aged 7 and 5

2 Descriptive Praise

If you keep Descriptively Praising your child's efforts, after the initial grumbling or tears he will become more and more self-reliant and self-confident, and soon he will start to find enjoyment and satisfaction in solitary play.

For the past fifteen minutes, you've been playing by yourself so patiently and not interrupting me. I feel so peaceful because I can really concentrate on what I'm doing.

When I said it was time for quiet time in your room, you didn't complain. You went to your room straightaway. That's real cooperation.

You found something to do by yourself when you saw I was busy. Thanks for waiting patiently.

I can see you're having fun making lots of little people out of those pipe cleaners. In a little while, when I'm ready, will you show them all to me?

I know you were disappointed that you couldn't have a playdate today. But now you're having a good time drawing. That shows flexibility.

You've been looking at books for ten minutes. That's a long time. You're being very independent.

You've been playing so quietly in your room.

3 Reflective Listening

To begin with, your child may feel quite upset about the new plan. As always, Reflective Listening will help her get over her upset and melt the resistance.

You really want me to play with you right now. I can see you're upset that you have to play by yourself.

I heard you shouting when the tail kept falling off your new giraffe! So infuriating when that happens. But you didn't come to me. You sorted it out all by yourself.
(This is another example of combining Reflective Listening with Descriptive Praise.)

You look so angry! You probably wish you could play with your brother, but it's still playing-alone time.

It sounds like you still don't like the new rule about playing by yourself. You're angry that all the electronics are off-limits. That's probably what you'd rather be doing.

4 Never Ask Twice

Even for a child who is resisting playing by herself, the Never Ask Twice method will make it happen.

5 Rewards and Consequences

Once again, rewards can get your child over the hump, helping him to tolerate, and eventually enjoy, playing by himself.

Summary

The more your children are in the habit of entertaining themselves for a good chunk of time each day, the more self-reliant, confident, creative and skilled at problem-solving they will become. This is a valuable life skill for every child to possess, and with these strategies, you have the tools to help your child achieve it.

CHAPTER 17

BEDTIMES AND SLEEP: ENDING THE DAY PEACEFULLY

How an earlier bedtime transformed our son's behaviour

When our son was four years old, we asked Noël to visit his school and observe him because the teachers suspected he might have attention deficit disorder. The school said he couldn't sit still, fidgeted most of the time, couldn't focus in class and was defiant and aggressive. Things weren't easy at home either.

Before she observed him, Noël asked us what time our son went to bed, and we told her his bedtime was nine-thirty. She recommended that we put him to bed by seven-thirty p.m. and said that this could make a real difference. We started this new plan that very same day, and within forty-eight hours we noticed dramatic improvements in his behaviour and mood. It was incredible.

By the time she observed him in school a few days later, many of the previous problems were no longer evident. He sat still, paid attention and was cooperative with the teachers. We could hardly believe that such a simple thing as moving his bedtime earlier could make such a transformation.

Mother of two, aged 8 and 5

This parent's story shows what a difference getting enough sleep can make to a child's behaviour. It also shows how quickly we can start to see positive results when we make changes to our children's bedtimes. A well-rested child is a happier child and a better-behaved child. When children and teenagers are regularly getting enough sleep, they smile more, they argue and complain less, they accept limits more readily, they focus better at school and on their homework, and they even squabble less with their siblings. Children may be able to manage on not quite enough sleep, but they will <u>thrive</u> on more sleep.

We know what the benefits of a good night's sleep are for our children, but making sure our children get the sleep they need can feel hard to achieve. Many parents find that bedtime, far from being the relaxing, calm time we want it to be, turns into a battle, with complaining and crying, stalling, getting out of bed or endless calling after lights out for just one more drink or hug. In some cases, children do not actually fall asleep until more than an hour after their bedtime. This is exhausting, both for the children who are not getting enough sleep and for the parents who, at the end of a busy day, find their whole evening is spent trying to get their children to sleep.

The Calmer, Easier, Happier Parenting strategies can help you overcome these problems and transform bedtime battles into bedtime bliss. The more of these strategies you are willing to put into practice, the sooner your children and teens will get into the healthy habit of going to bed at the right time with a minimum of fuss, falling asleep quickly and sleeping soundly until morning.

The questionnaire

Fill in this questionnaire before you begin the bedtime strategies. This will help you focus on the changes you want to make. Come back to the questionnaire after two weeks to see all the progress you've made.

Your child	Hardly ever	Sometimes	Too often
Complains about going to bed, cries or whinges or argues			
Dawdles during the bedtime routine			
Is finally in bed later than you would like			
Has difficulty falling asleep			
Wants you to stay in the room until he falls asleep			
Cries or calls out for you after lights out			
Complains that she is afraid of the dark, monsters, burglars, etc.			
Gets out of bed after lights out			

Your child	Hardly ever	Sometimes	Too often
Has difficulty waking up in the morning			
Is irritable or uncooperative in the morning			

How much sleep is the right amount?

More than you think. And more than your kids may want! Below are the Calmer, Easier, Happier Parenting guidelines (but you can do an internet search on this topic, and you will find experts who recommend fewer hours of sleep per night, as well as other experts who recommend more hours).

Three-five years	11½-13 hours a night, plus a daytime nap or rest
Five-seven years	11½-13 hours a night
Seven-ten years	10½-12 hours a night
Eleven-thirteen years	9½-11 hours a night

Action Plan for Calmer, Easier, Happier bedtimes

1 Preparing for Success

• **Be United**

You'll need to agree on what the rules and routines will be. Here are some guidelines and rules that help make bedtimes Calmer, Easier and Happier:

Decide with your partner what the right bedtime should be for your children, and make this the rule.
Remember, you're in charge, so it is up to you – not the children – when they should go to bed. If you don't support each other, your children will learn to divide and conquer, and it will be far more difficult to achieve an effective bedtime routine.

Bring the bedtime forward by fifteen minutes each week until you reach your goal. Be prepared for an older child to complain bitterly that you are the strictest parents in the world and that all his friends are allowed to stay up as late as they want. But hold your ground; don't compromise to avoid a fuss. Do lots of Reflective Listening instead.

The first few weeks that your children are going to bed earlier, two annoying things may happen, both temporary. Your children may take longer than usual to fall asleep, or they may wake in the morning much earlier than usual. Persevere because it sometimes takes the child's brain a few weeks to adjust to a new pattern, just as it does with adults.

Older children and teenagers may be allowed to read or draw in bed if they are not yet tired, but they must be in bed at the time you have set.

On non-school nights you may want some flexibility.
I recommend that you allow older children and teenagers to stay up a maximum of one hour later than their usual bedtime, and for younger children a maximum of half an hour later. When bedtimes are erratic, the brain reacts just as if it were experiencing jet lag. You do not want to risk disrupting the healthy rhythms you have established during the week, which are so important for school success and for general cheerfulness.

Stagger bedtimes so that younger children are getting to bed earlier so they get the rest they need.

It's easy to drift into the habit of putting all children to bed at the same time, but the younger ones will suffer and be more irritable from lack of sleep.

Allow no snacks after dinner is over, not even milk.

It is much easier to get to sleep and to stay asleep if the last food of the day is mostly digested.

If your child is attached to a special blanket or cuddly toy, make sure that it always stays on the bed and that he is not allowed to carry it around.

That will make his bed more inviting. This rule will also help your child learn to self-soothe during the day, when his comfort object is not accessible. He will become more emotionally self-reliant.

- Do plenty of think-throughs to make sure that your child understands and remembers both the new rules and the existing rules.

Examples of think-throughs

Here is an example of a *think-through* that re-establishes the time for lights out for a family that has let bedtimes get too late.

Think-through: At a neutral time

Parent: *Mummy and I realise that we've made a big mistake. We've been getting annoyed with you when you don't want to get out of bed in the morning, but we've realised it's our fault. We've been letting you stay up past your bedtime. So of course you're tired in the morning.*

Child: *I'm not going to bed earlier. I'm not tired!*

Parent: *So we're going to stick to the right bedtime. You might not like it.*

Child: (Groans and makes a face and mutters something inaudible)

Parent: *You need eleven hours' sleep, and you should be out of bed by seven so that you have plenty of time to get ready for school without rushing. So that means lights out at eight the night before.*

Child: *Eight! I'm not a baby. But I'm still doing my homework at eight o'clock.*

Parent: *And that's another mistake Mummy and I have been making: letting you do your homework when your mind isn't fresh.*

Child: *But I can't do it earlier because of football practice.*

Parent: *That's a problem we have to solve. But for now we're going to stick to what your bedtime is supposed to be. So tell me, what time is lights out going to be from now on?*

Child: *Eight o'clock, but that's stupid.*

Parent: *You told me the right time. That was brave of you to tell me because I know you don't want an eight o'clock bedtime. Now tell me again without the insult.*

Child: (Groans) *Eight o'clock.*

Parent: *That's right, and I can hear that you're feeling worried about when you'll do your homework, so Mummy and I will help you sort that out so you can get to bed at eight o'clock.*

- **Preparing the environment**

Keep the lights very dim during the bedtime routine; this helps children's brains to begin switching off.

Keep all screens and loud music off during the bedtime routine; this helps children gradually unwind.

During the hour before the bedtime routine begins, avoid all screens or noisy or exciting games. Substitute more relaxing activities to help your child wind down.

- **Planning your day realistically**

Start the bedtime routine earlier than you think necessary so that you are not tempted to hurry the children. Everything with children takes longer than we think it should take, and the more we hurry our children, the longer they seem to take. Slow down and enjoy being with your children. Find something to Descriptively Praise every few minutes. This will help all of you to stay focused on the positive.

Being consistent and following the same routine every evening reduces resistance, making it easier for children to accept bedtime rules.

- **Special Time**

When children are getting regular Special Time, they become more willing to cooperate at bedtime.

2 Remember to Descriptively Praise everything that is going right at each stage of the bedtime routine

Here are some Descriptive Praises that will help bedtimes go more smoothly and will foster healthy sleep habits:

You're cleaning your teeth now, even though you said you wanted to stay up and watch that programme. You stopped arguing and did what I said.

Thanks for not asking for any food after supper. You're starting to remember the new rule.

Last night you stopped reading at eight o'clock and turned out your light, and I didn't have to remind you.

You're in your pyjamas five minutes early!

You remembered to go to the bathroom before you got into bed. Good for you for remembering.

You're getting used to our new bedtime rules. You hardly complained last night.

You didn't ask for a third story tonight. You remembered our new rule about only two stories at bedtime. You remember a lot of things.

Last night you stayed in your own bed all night.

3 Reflective Listening

Reflectively Listening to how your child feels about bedtime will help him get over his upset more quickly and so make it easier for him to go to sleep. For example, your child may feel upset about having to go to bed earlier or having to miss a favourite television programme.

If your child wants to talk about his fears or worries, it is best to listen to these during the day only, not at bedtime or in the night. We want to make bedtimes as calm as possible.

Here are some Reflective Listening examples:

I think you're showing me how sad you are right now. You thought Daddy would be home in time to kiss you goodnight, but he'll be home too late.

Wouldn't it be fun if we could read stories until midnight?

It probably feels especially frustrating that I'm telling you to hang up your uniform when you're so tired. You're probably thinking about curling up in bed and reading stories.

Maybe you wish you were older and could stay up as late as your big brother.

4 Never Ask Twice

You will find this strategy invaluable at bedtime. To reduce resistance, at first be willing to do the Six Steps for each stage of the bedtime routine separately: first for getting into the bath, then for putting on pyjamas, then for cleaning teeth, then for getting into bed, etc.

5 Rewards and Consequences

Rewards help children get into better bedtime habits. You can use a chart to show cooperation at each stage. Never underestimate the motivating power of a tick or star. And, as I've said, the best consequence is a reward that doesn't happen. Remember to do *action replays* after each bit of misbehaviour.

Strategies to deal with specific bedtime problems

It may feel hard enough getting your children into bed with the lights out at a sensible hour, but for many parents, the problems don't end there. The next problem is often getting children to stay in bed and go to sleep.

The first thing I recommend is that you don't tell a restless child to try to go to sleep. The act of trying to go to sleep is likely to make her tense, which will just keep her thoughts spinning. Instead, tell her that she does not have to sleep; she just has to rest by lying still under the covers with her eyes closed, and she can think about anything she wants. (Don't suggest what she could think about; her brain can come up with something.) Resting is relaxing, and she is likely to drift off quite quickly.

Here are some other strategies to help with sleep problems. Before I address these, I want to make it clear that if you choose to sleep with your child in the 'family bed', that's fine with me. Families have very different lifestyles, including different values about where their children should sleep.

Many parents come to me for help because they have drifted into the habit of staying with their child until she falls asleep, and now they want to know how to teach her to fall asleep on her own. Or they have let their child sleep in their bed for a period of time but are now ready to make a change and want to reclaim their bed for themselves.

How to help your child fall asleep on her own.
If you stay in your child's bedroom after lights out until your child falls asleep, she will become dependent on your presence. A child who is strong-willed or anxious or who has an inflexible temperament may need to be weaned off this dependence in a series of small steps. If necessary, start by sitting on a chair near the bed (but not on the bed) until she is

almost asleep. Every day move your chair a little bit further away from the bed and closer to the door. By the time you are sitting outside her room and she can no longer see you or hear you, she will have learned how to get to sleep without you. Remember to Descriptively Praise every step in the right direction because learning the habit of going to sleep on her own can be a scary proposition at first for a child who is more sensitive, intense or anxious.

What to do if your child calls for you after lights out.
If your child often cries or calls for you after lights out, the solution is to have many *think-throughs* during the day about what will happen. You could make a rule that you will check on him frequently, but from the doorway, without going in to his room. After saying good night and leaving the room, wait about five minutes, then go back to the doorway for just a moment, and give some brief Descriptive Praise, nothing more. Do not chat or get him a drink or sit on the bed or lie down with him or give him a hug or answer any questions! Then leave the room again. Next, wait about ten minutes and do the same thing again. Carry on with this technique, gradually lengthening the time between your appearances in the doorway. If you are willing to invest the time to do this, your child's experience of bedtime will be transformed within a week or two. He will not be feeling abandoned or left out, and he will become more and more skilled at drifting off to sleep on his own. He will get the sleep he needs, and you will soon get back your evenings.

What to do if your child gets out of bed after lights out.
If your child gets out of bed after lights out on a regular basis, again you will need to do *think-throughs* with her at neutral times during the day – not at bedtime – about bedtime rules. For example you could say, 'There's a new rule about bedtime

and where you sleep. Starting on Friday, when Dad and I say good night to you after your story, you have to stay in your own bed all night long. So where should you stay after Dad and I say good night?' Your child will probably reply, 'In my bed.' And you could say, 'That's right, you know the new rule. Maybe you wish you could come into our room if you wake up in the night because you've been used to doing that. You might even feel sad that you can't do it any more. But what will you do if you wake up?' And your child might say, 'Stay in my bed.'

Because you are having these *think-throughs* at a neutral time and not at bedtime, your child is much less likely to be upset about the new rule. But if he does get upset and cry or whinge or complain, the best way to defuse his upset feelings is by Reflective Listening. Imagine how he might be feeling. 'You like sleeping in our bed, and you probably wish you could keep on doing it.' Let him have his feelings – it's natural for kids to be upset whenever we change a rule or routine.

What to do if your child still gets out of bed during the night.
Following through is essential. Once you make this rule, it's a rule for you and your partner as much as it is a rule for your child. When you do what you've said, your child will respect you more and resist less.

It is highly likely that he will test this new rule. First, do lots of *think-throughs* so your child will know what's going to happen if he gets out of bed. My recommendation is not to pick him up. Just take his hand and walk him back to his room, with absolutely no talking or eye contact. Picking him up and talking to him will seem like a reward and will actually reinforce the behaviour you don't want. The first few nights you may have to walk him back to bed numerous times, depending on how entrenched this habit is. If your goal is an uninterrupted night's sleep, invest the time and *follow through*, and you'll soon reap the rewards!

How we got our evenings back

Our three-year-old, Cathy, is very strong-willed and was resistant to everything we asked – or at least it felt that way. And no surprise, she was also resistant to going to bed and would plead for us to lie down with her. We were putting her down at nine o'clock until we went to a Calmer, Easier, Happier Parenting seminar and Noël explained how the amount of sleep kids get affects their behaviour. Over a week's time, we inched her bedtime forward to seven p.m., and we were shocked at how much easier she was to be around.

But we still had the 'lying down with her' issue to deal with. My wife and I were hardly spending any time together in the evenings because one of us was always lying in her bed with her. We made a new rule about Cathy's bedtime routine, clarifying that we would no longer lie down next to her. We would read two stories, give her a big hug and two kisses, and then we would say goodnight and shut the door. In our think-throughs about the new routine, we also covered what we would do if she got up after she went to bed – that we wouldn't talk to her or snuggle – we'd just walk her back to her bed. The first night, Cathy got out of bed a dozen times, but we gave her zero attention and walked her straight back to bed. The second night she didn't even try! There was a little more testing over the next two days, but then it stopped. Cathy is so much better behaved now, and my wife and I actually have a life together in the evenings again.

                                                    Father of a 3-year-old

Summary

Just like the parents in this story, you <u>can</u> have problem-free bedtimes and night-times. As long as you are consistent with your rules and routines, it will happen much faster than you may believe. When sleep problems are overcome, parents experience a huge sense of relief and a reawakening of confidence in their ability to be the parents they want to be. And life becomes calmer, easier and happier.

CONCLUSION

What I would like to leave you with is this. You do not need to believe that these strategies will work in order for them to work. All you have to do is start practising them, and you will see the results for yourself.

These strategies do not require parents to be super-organised or super-patient or exceptional in any way. You just need to be dedicated to trying new ways of doing things and saying things because the old ways haven't been getting you what you want.

You have nothing to lose except the stress of continuing to deal with the same misbehaviour again and again - and the exasperation and guilt that comes from repeating, nagging, threatening and shouting.

What you have to gain is a Calmer, Easier, Happier family life. Isn't the possibility of that result worth practising some new strategies for a month? Week by week you'll notice that it all gets easier and easier, and the results are a delightful reward for your efforts.

You may experience big successes initially and then find yourself slipping back into the old habits of repeating and reminding, forgetting to Descriptively Praise or do *think-throughs*. Problems that had faded away may start popping up again. This is absolutely natural. Often when we're learning something new, we take two steps forward and one step back. If we give up on the new strategies and drift back into the old, ineffective ways of trying to achieve cooperation, our children will go back to their old ways of resisting or ignoring our instructions.

The good news is that every day with our children is a new day. We get a chance to start afresh every day! As soon as you restart Preparing for Success with *think-throughs* and restart Descriptively Praising all the good (or the just-OK) behaviour, you will see better and better behaviour. As you remember to Reflectively Listen when your children are frustrated or angry or disappointed, they will get over their upsets much faster and will act out less. If, instead of calling up the stairs when it's dinner time, you go to where your children are and use the Never Ask Twice steps, you'll see more and more cooperation the first time and without a fuss.

All the strategies can be summed up in three words: positive, firm and consistent. In this context, positive means friendly, firm means being true to your values, and consistent means continuing to practise being positive and firm.

To remind you what this book can offer you, here are the experiences of some parents who have chosen to make the Calmer, Easier, Happier Parenting strategies a way of life:

I used to feel so tense. I never knew what kind of mood my son would be in. He could be charming, or he could be grumpy and defiant. It's no exaggeration when I say that Descriptive Praise and think-throughs have changed our lives. He's so much calmer now and more confident. And so am I.

It's been a hard year for us: major illness in the family, being made redundant, having to re-train. At first my wife and I found we were taking it out on the children, snapping at them and getting very irritated. Through the Calmer, Easier, Happier Parenting methods we've learned how to be less stressed and more positive. We made a promise to ourselves to Descriptively Praise each family member ten times a day for a month. The results were even better than we could have hoped for. The children are happier and more cooperative. They're even doing better at school. Descriptive Praise is a way of life for us now.

At first I was sceptical about Descriptive Praise and all the other strategies because I thought I'd never be able to keep it up. But the children responded so quickly that I was very motivated to do it more and more. My son is less anxious and more self-reliant; my daughter isn't so bossy any more, so now the other girls want to play with her. And the children do what they're told, first time! Bliss! I still have to pinch myself sometimes.

Would you like to experience a similar transformation? The only difference between these families and yours is that these parents started practising some new skills and didn't give up when things got difficult (as they are bound to, from time to time). With the same determination, you and your children can experience a Calmer, Easier, Happier family life.

RESOURCES

Noël Janis-Norton is the director of the Calmer, Easier, Happier Parenting Centre, a not-for-profit consultancy that works worldwide with families and with professionals who work with families.

The staff of certified parenting practitioners includes parent coaches, family coaches and group facilitators.

The Centre offers the following services:
Introductory talks for parents (at the Centre, in schools and in the workplace)
Parenting skills courses
Seminars and webinars
Private consultations (at the Centre, by telephone or in the home)
School visits to observe a child and guide teachers
Mediation between parents
Teacher-training

In addition, the Centre offers a wide range of products: books, audio-CDs and DVDs on many different aspects of parenting and teaching.

<u>CDs about the five core strategies of Calmer, Easier, Happier Parenting:</u>

- Descriptive Praise
- Preparing for Success
- Reflective Listening
- Never Ask Twice
- Rewards and Consequences

<u>Topic CD sets:</u>

Siblings with Less Rivalry (3 discs)
Calmer, Easier, Happier Mealtimes (2 discs)
Calmer, Easier, Happier Music Practice (2 discs)
Bringing Out the Best in Children and Teens with Special Needs (5 discs)

<u>DVDs:</u>

Bringing Out the Best in Boys
Transforming Homework Hassles

<u>Books for parents:</u>

Could Do Better by Noël Janis-Norton
How to Calm a Challenging Child by Miriam Chachamu
How to Be a Better Parent by Cassandra Jardine
Positive Not Pushy by Cassandra Jardine
Where Has My Little Girl Gone? by Tanith Carey

<u>Books for teachers:</u>
In Step with Your Class by Noël Janis-Norton
Learning to Listen, Listening to Learn by Noël Janis-Norton

For more information about the Calmer, Easier, Happier Parenting resources, please visit the following websites:

www.calmerparenting.co.uk (UK)

www.calmerparenting.com (North America)

INDEX

Other books by Noël Janis-Norton are available in paperback, ebook and audiobook

www.calmerparenting.com

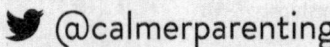 @calmerparenting